HOW THE WORLD IS MADE

THE STORY OF CREATION ACCORDING TO

SACRED GEOMETRY

John Michell

HOW THE WORLD IS MADE

THE STORY OF CREATION ACCORDING TO

SACRED GEOMETRY

with Allan Brown

Thames & Hudson

First published in the United Kingdom in 2009 by
Thames & Hudson Ltd, 181A High Holborn,
London WC1V 7QX

First paperback edition 2012

British Library Cataloguing-in-Publication Data
A catalogue record for this book is available from the British Library
ISBN 978-0-500-29037-8

Printed and bound in China by Toppan Leefung

Dedication

And Acknowledgements

Great minds and noble spirits have gone before us in the field of geometry. Still living is one whose influence in the modern renaissance of philosophical geometry in the ancient tradition is primary. He is our Pythagoras, a revealer of neglected truths and a teacher who has inspired and transformed generations of students from all parts of the world. His pupils and followers include practically everyone listed below. This book is dedicated to our master geometer:

KEITH CRITCHLOW

With hearty thanks to the following for the various ways they have all assisted with this work:

Richard Adams, Sam Adams, Alex Brown, Christopher Gibbs, Michael Glickman, Jason Godwin, Merrily Harpur, Frances Howard-Gordon, John James, Robert Lawlor, Roland Marti ('amicable' paper cutting on page 236), John Martineau, Joan Moore, Alex Munslow, John Neal, Scott Olsen, Christine Rhone, Michael Schneider, Malcolm Stewart, Rosemary Taylor, and Stephen Wilmoth.

Contents

Publisher's Preface xi

The Hand and the Computer
A Note on the Illustrations xiii

Part I
THE GEOMETER'S CREATION

1. How the World Began
And Why, and Why Worry? 2
- *The Geometer's Creator* 6
- *Creative Geometry: Introducing the Ratios* 10
- *Genesis and the Great Geometer* 13
- *The Number of the Universe* 16

2. The Number 5040
Key to the World Plan 20
- *Earth, Moon, and the Circle Squared* 22

3. The Circle, the Square
And the Meaning of Pi 36
- *π in Practice* 37
- *π in the Pyramid* 39
- *π Equals 3? An Antiquarian Fantasy* 44
- *The π Patterns* 46
- *Cosmological Revelations in Crop Circles* 57
- *The Revelation at Crooked Soley* 59

4. Initiation

And the Vision of Heavenly Order 62

- *An Initiate's Vision: St John and the Heavenly Jerusalem* 64
- *Heaven on Earth: The Pattern of the Sanctuary* 69
- *The Numbers of the Holy City and Their Meanings* 72
- *3168, the Number of Our Lord Jesus Christ* 73
- *1080, the Lunar Number, the Solar 666, and Their Sum, 1746* 74
- *864, the Foundation Number* 81

Part 2

THE PHYSICAL CREATION

5. The Dodecad

A Summary of the Numbers One to Twelve 86

6. The One and Only

Symbol of the Universe 87

7. The Geometry of Two

Duality and the World of Paradox 88

8. The Geometry of Three

The Vesica Piscis and Material Creation 90

- *The Vesica Piscis and the Marriage Made in Heaven* 90
- *The Net with 153 Fishes, a Geometer's Parable* 97
- *The Triangles That Fill Up Space* 102
- *Pythagorean Triangles* 105
- *The Second Pythagorean Triangle 5–12–13* 106

9. Four and the Square
Reason, Stability, Order 109
- *The Rational Square and the Root-2 Proportion* 109
- *Doubling the Area of a Square: An Exercise in Recollection* 110

10. Six and the Hexagon
The Perfect Number 119

11. Eight and the Octagon
For Peace and Justice 124

12. The Majestic Twelve
The Number of Universal Order and Harmony 150
- *Twelve Tribes and the Revelation of the Heavenly Order* 152

Part 3
THE CREATION OF LIFE

13. Five and Ten
Numbers of Life and Growth 166
- *Life and the Pentagon* 166
- *Five and the Golden Section* 168
- *Humanity and the Pentagram* 178
- *Pentagonal Dances* 182
- *Sex and the Pentagram: Meeting, Mating, and Breeding* 186
- *Pentagonal Marriages with Other Shapes* 202
- *Five and Seven* 208

Part 4
THE WORLD SOUL

14. The Holy Seven

Symbol of the World Soul 212

- *Seven and the Mysteries* 212
- *Seven, Nine, and the Septenary Number* 216
- *Twelve and Seven: The Supreme Numerical Marriage* 219

15. Geometry and Love

Approaching the Climax 232

Part 5
ATLANTIS

16. A Geometer's Nightmare

Plato's Pentagonal Allegory 240

- *Atlantis: The Historical Record* 240
- *Atlantis: Its Foundation and Growth* 243
- *Squaring the Circle, Atlantis Style* 247
- *Atlantis: The Pentagonal Edifice* 251
- *Atlantis: The Basic Geometry* 252
- *Atlantis and the Golden Section* 258
- *The Meaning of Atlantis* 260

About the Author 264

Index 269

Publisher's Preface

You have in your hands the final chapter in John Michell's written life. It is not entirely surprising—given his passionate interest in sacred proportion—that John would leave this world just as his final work was entering it. This inverse relationship is only deepened by the ideas put forth in the book—that everything is woven together in an all-inclusive world image—that "pattern in the heavens," as Socrates called it, "which anyone can find and establish within themselves."

John understood that in order to live happily—and anyone who knew him can attest that he did—people must incorporate sacred proportion into their lives. A champion of traditional units of measure, such as feet and pounds, which are based on celestial proportions, he knew that when we use these cosmic systems we help create harmony in society and the world as a whole.

John's rejection of the church of progress and its systems was not simply because "old is always better" but because he saw that the current alienation of modern humanity, the source of so much unhappiness, is aided and abetted by our abandonment of proportion. He knew that our loss of connection with the sacred had resulted in our inability to construct meaningful lives. As he said in *Confessions of a Radical Traditionalist:* "You do not have to be a New Ager to conclude that the only world order in which human nature can happily exist is the sacred order, the cosmological expression of ideal harmony and proportion which constituted the esoteric base behind every ancient lasting civilization."

Known for the twinkle in his eye, John was a living example that being attuned to the sacredness of the cosmos brings a happiness to your world not found elsewhere. Through his many works, both written and drawn, and his love of conversation, he shared this wisdom in vivid detail. The fascinating beauty of his drawings—stunningly showcased in this volume—attests to the profound power and importance of sacred proportion that he wished to convey.

Thank you, John, for sharing your harmonious world. May your pattern in the heavens be found within each of us.

The Hand and the Computer

A Note on the Illustrations

The watercolours and some of the coloured diagrams in this book were done over a stretch of years beginning in the 1960s. In 2003 many of them were exhibited in London at Christopher Gibbs's gallery in Pimlico. Others were added later and the process continues. Despite their embellishment and occasional whimsicalities, these drawings are not regarded as 'art' (a term somewhat degraded at present). Nor are they meant simply as decorations. Their purpose is to illustrate, as simply and attractively as possible, the basic types and characters in the world of geometry, their marriages and reproductions, and how the different types fit together within a comprehensive scheme of geometry that symbolizes the structure of the universe.

The drawings and paintings were mostly done before computers got the upper hand and mechanized draughtsmanship. This development has been much lamented—for example, in a new book, which happened to arrive just as this was being written, *Drawing Geometry* by the architect and geometer Jon Allen. Here is what he says.

> There is great value in drawing by hand, and good reason to resist the temptation to resort to a computer. We lose something when we use computers to draw geometry. However beguiling their mechanical precision, they lack "heart": in some subtle way we become observers rather than participants. . . . To surrender the experience of drawing by hand for the convenience of digital storage, revision, and transmission seems a great shame—and essentially misses the point, that drawing geometry is as powerful a meditation, or as inspiring a creative activity, as it is possible to find.

That is well said, but it is not the last word on the subject. Geometrical drawing, especially with colour, and above all in the spirit of research, is a delightful and satisfying occupation. It is like learning an instrument and playing music. Yet even before the computer took over, geometers had the use of mechanical aids, such as photocopying for the repetition of patterns. Many of the cursive designs here were augmented in this way. Since computers can override cutting and pasting by hand and achieve the required result more efficiently, it is reasonable to take advantage of this convenience. In the hands of an artist the computer is an artistic medium. That is shown here by Allan Brown, who designed this book, brought it to order, and composed many of its diagrams. With their clarity and precision and the sensitivity in their lines and tones, they are ideal in this context—and, with all respect to Jon Allen, they are certainly not lacking in 'heart'.

To illustrate the point, here is Allan Brown's computer-drawn version of the Heavenly City or New Jerusalem diagram (opposite, below), the central image of traditional cosmology. There are several views of it in this book, showing its various aspects and meanings. In this figure it is perfectly delineated while retaining its beauty and spirit.

Creation is not finished—the world occurs anew every moment.

Hans-Peter Durr, professor of quantum physics
at the Max Planck Institute

The grand book of the universe . . . was written in the language of mathematics, and its characters are triangles, circles, and other geometrical figures, without which it is impossible to understand a single word of it.

GALILEO GALILEI, 1623

Fig. 1 (opposite). The Heavenly City is a geometer's name for the traditional diagram that represents the order of the universe and the numerical code that underlies it. An illuminated version of it is shown opposite. There are many allusions to this diagram in ancient relics and writings, but it was not until 1971 that it came into the open to provide the key to the long-lost science and philosophy that has, at various times and places, created the conditions for a golden age.

The Heavenly City (depicted here in one of its many forms as a tree bearing "twelve manner of fruits") contains the numbers, measures, shapes, proportions, and musical harmonies that are constant in nature. It presents a universe which reconciles all the opposite and disparate elements that comprise it. It is an image of paradise, of the immanent perfection that can be found in every order of existence, from the cosmos to the individual. This perfection is by no means obvious, but many people in all ages have glimpsed it, with the effect of changing their lives. In the Heavenly City diagram visionary experience is combined with numerical and scientific reason to produce an active symbol of divine wisdom restored to earth.

Part I

THE GEOMETER'S CREATION

1 • How the World Began

And Why, and Why Worry?

How did the world begin? There is no certain answer to that or to any other of the big questions on the origins of life, consciousness, culture, and language. The very nature of our existence is a mystery. In the centre of human knowledge is a large gap which, for the sake of decency, we cover over with a veil of myths, faiths, and theories. Ignorance should not be seen naked, but the problem is, how should we cloak it?

This sounds like a problem for fashion experts, and in a way it is. There are fashions in cosmology, as in philosophy, religion, archaeology, anthropology, and every other field. Myths come and go, and so do scientific theories. It may not seem to matter very much which particular formula or fairy story is used to explain the universe, but in reality it is crucial, because the way we understand the world and our own origins largely determines our attitude towards life and how we experience it.

One thing we do know, not just from the ancient philosophers but from common observation, is that the world is reflexive and responds to however we choose or are taught to imagine it. There are two extremes to how our existence can be visualized. At one extreme this world is a reflection of the heavenly paradise, at the other it is hell on earth. You can choose whichever model you like, and the consequences will follow.

A simple illustration of the reflexive universe is the everyday phenomenon of coincidences. A word newly learnt is immediately heard again, a friend who has just been mentioned unexpectedly calls. There seems to be no meaning in these odd incidents, and we normally laugh them off. Speak of the devil, we say, or, it's a small world. But there are certain coincidences which we can hardly help seeing as significant. Sometimes they are so appropriate that they seem to be answers to prayer, need, or intense desire. It is as if we had actually willed them to happen. Almost every writer is familiar with the 'library angel' that causes you to pick up the one book or item in the whole of literature that you need at the time. Some of the recorded instances of this effect seem literally miraculous. Then there is the opposite effect, also well known to writers but less likely to be mentioned, of a needed book that vanishes from its usual place, cannot be found anywhere, but later reappears, just where it always should have been.

There are times when luck seems to be with you, when fortune smiles and everything seems to keep going right, and there are other times when it is just one problem after another. This brings up the interesting question, can one attract good luck and happiness—and, if so, how? Happiness, of course, is a state of mind, and the mind can only be happy when you feel at ease in your surroundings, not troubled by doubts, fears, and uncertainties. In normal, peaceful conditions, causes of unhappiness are mostly minor and localized. But there is a larger, more lasting cause which can overshadow the whole of life, depriving the mind of its natural state of contentment. A common and deep-rooted source of worry is doubt and fear about the nature of the universe, its creator (if any), what it is supposed to mean, and how we are supposed to relate to it. To deal with these anxieties, preparing the mind for receiving light, luck, and happiness, is the real purpose of cosmology.

Cosmology naturally has to do with the cosmos, the philosopher's term for the entire, self-contained universe, including ourselves and our own observations of it. Modern, scientific cosmology is artificially limited. It tries to exclude the human viewpoint, has no concern for human psychology, and fails to acknowledge the powerful influence that cosmography—the way the universe is described—exerts upon the minds of people exposed to it. Not just individuals but whole societies, nations, and cultures are conditioned by the prevailing view of the world. There is no such thing as an objective, value-free cosmology. Every type of world image has its corresponding effect on minds, perceptions, moral values, forms of government, and every other human system. However hard they may try, cosmologists cannot avoid being influential far beyond their

Fig. 2. The scientific creation myth in a nutshell, by cartoonist Merrily Harpur

own specialized field. Modern society and the modern mind are both to a considerable extent products of modern cosmology.

An example of the cross-influence between a cosmological image and human affairs generally is the expanding-universe theory. Briefly outlined, it states that the universe began suddenly, explosively, by some unique accident, with a big bang whose debris is still receding outwards into space. On this one small fragment of matter, this Earth, conditions happened to be suitable for the appearance of life, which came about through another accident, also perhaps unique, involving a highly improbable or outrageously coincidental chain of chemical reactions. Creatures arose of different orders and species, endowed with various levels of intelligence, and one species somehow acquired the art of abstract thinking, causing it to worry about such questions as how the world began, to invent all sorts of explanatory myths, and then to fight over them.

The big bang cosmogony (creation myth) reflects modern thinking with its belief in expansion and progress and is also used to justify it. It is a story that suits the big corporations, the monopolists, the ever larger and more elaborate institutions of politics, economics, science, and education. It goes well with the theory that corresponds to it in the world of biology, the theory of evolution, which also tells a story of chance origins from nothing, followed by growth and elaboration. Both these theories reject the notion of a creative intelligence at work. The qualities they tend to encourage are innovation and inventiveness at the expense of custom and tradition. You need not be a feminist thinker to identify these theories as products of the solar, imperial, masculine type of mind. A telling criticism of modern cosmology is that it is a creation of self-centred reasoning and tends to produce that unhappy being, the self-centred individual.

There is no compelling reason to believe absolutely in any particular theory of origins. The experts themselves cannot agree on what picture of the universe is the most true or likely. Against the big bang theory are others, a prominent rival being the steady-state cosmology. One version of this states that the universe has no beginning and no end, either in time or space. Conservative-minded people are attracted to that belief by its steady-state social implications, but it is unacceptable to philosophy because the universe is a material structure and neither immortality nor infinity are properties of matter. Another school of thought, an old one now in resurgence, sees Intelligent Design as the ultimate cause of things. Its followers are unconvinced by the notion of chance coincidences as the creative agency behind the finely tuned conditions in which life is possible. The odds, as they see it, are against chance and in favour of conscious thought and purpose—implying thereby a Creator.

These contrasting and contradictory beliefs are all drawn from the same scientific data, and each of them has its adherents among scientists of the same age and education, equally qualified to pronounce on the subject of cosmology. The existence of so many equal but opposite experts, each with his or her own idea about the origin and nature of the universe, demonstrates that on these essential questions nothing at all is known—for certain. Nor will it ever be. The scientific quest for a mechanistic blueprint of the universal system is ill-conceived—an example of 'misplaced concretism'—and can only lead to disappointment, confusion, and cynicism. For the world creature, as it is traditionally regarded, cannot be known simply by its chemistry and dynamics. Like all creatures it has its moods, whims, and irrationalities, and it reveals itself subtly, in its own time and manner, to anyone who becomes interested in and grows to love any aspect of it.

The aspect of nature illustrated in this book is its geometrical and numerical structure. This again is the traditional approach to cosmology, practised in the schools of antiquity and justified by Galileo in the seventeenth century. The "grand book" of the universe, he proclaimed, "was written in the language of mathematics, and its characters are triangles, circles, and other geometrical figures, without which it is impossible to understand a single word of it."

At the root of these geometrical studies, and developed through them, is a worldview that is very different from the scientific version. It fulfils all that is required of a cosmology, being in accord with our physical knowledge of the universe, but describing it as an organic whole—as the macrocosm or large-scale counterpart of its microcosm, the human mind. It is that constant, ever-recurring picture of the world which has many names and symbols—the perennial philosophy, the cosmic canon, divine law, the heavenly city, the garden of paradise, the philosopher's stone, the holy grail. Behind all these images is a central core of knowledge which is true at all times. It sanctifies the individual in whom it is established, and its periods of social influence are times of justice and the rebirth of culture.

The present age is a time of uncertainty, of actual or impending chaos, and it is also a time of revelation. As a natural response to the inadequacies of the present worldview, another mode of perception is spontaneously reappearing. It is the ancient and traditional outlook, never refuted but set aside by the modern 'enlightenment' in favour of a more literalistic assault upon the mysteries of existence. Returning with it are the long-lost secrets of the esoteric code of science that sustained all ancient civilizations throughout their legendary golden ages.

The Geometer's Creator

Traditional cosmology and the schemes of geometry that illustrate it develop from a central point. In practical geometry this centre is marked by the indentation made by the point of a compass in drawing a circle; in cosmology it symbolizes the pole of the universe. By geometric convention, the centre point has no dimensions, and neither has the universal pole. The existence of the pole is acknowledged through necessity, because the circle of the universe, like any

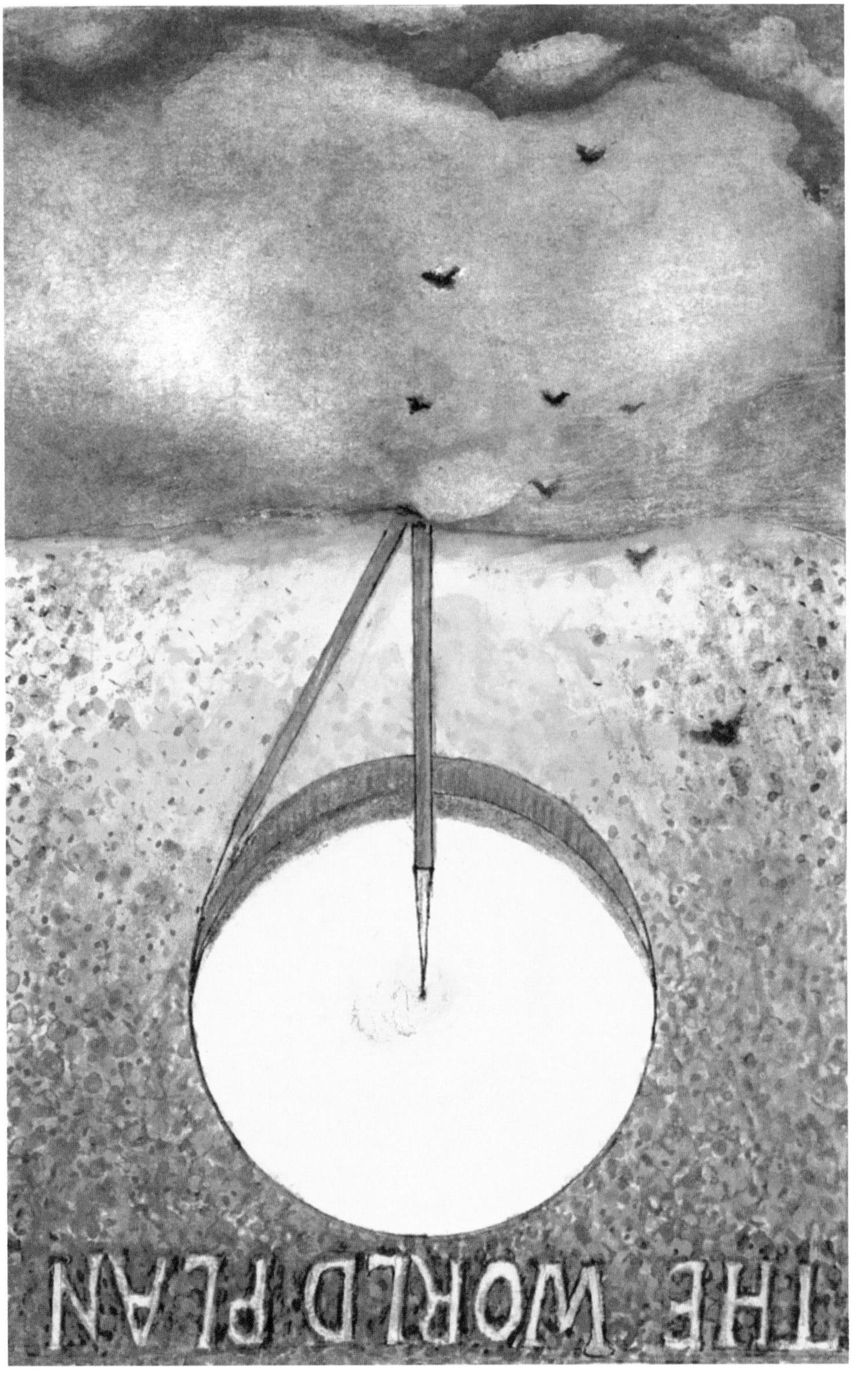

Fig. 3. From behind the cloud or veil of mystery that conceals his nature, the Creator protrudes his compass and having, like any author, written the title of his work, outlines it by his spinning axis. That, more or less, is the geometer's story.

revolving disc or sphere, must have a fixed centre or axis on which it spins. The nature of this constant but dimensionless fixed element is a mystery beyond rational resolution, and the same mystery arises with the question of who or what is the source of Creation. The answer of course is the Creator, the Great Geometer of our creation myth, otherwise God, Allah, the Great Spirit, the Higher Power, the Unlimited, the First Cause . . . an archetype with many names but no definitions. By convention and without further implications, the Creator is called 'he', and his central position in the universe is symbolized by the universal pole. The pole itself is taken to represent divine law—the unchanging, everlasting code of harmonies and proportions on which the universe revolves.

The Creator in this story dreamt up the world as an imitation of his own ideal state. He made it as a spherically shaped living creature, complete with body, soul, and spirit. It is the only independent creature that exists, for all other creatures are merely parts of it, dependent upon it and upon each other. Other dimensions and existences there may well be, but all are embraced by the unique Whole. This universal creature is therefore the natural symbol of the number One. It is an autonomous entity and outside it there is nothing.

Traditional cosmogonies (stories of how the world began) are centred upon the Creator simply because there is no better alternative. One option is to centre the universe upon oneself and one's own transitory existence. That is called solipsism, and its sad effects can be seen in anyone who suffers from being self-centred. Also solipsistic are the images of modern cosmology, whose source and centre are in the inventive minds of mathematicians. The least controversial attribute of the cosmic centre is Mystery. You cannot depict a mystery; it has no image and nothing definite can be said about it. The same is true of the philosopher's God. This is the God known to Jewish cabalists as En Soph, meaning an existence to which nothing positive can be attributed because it combines and reconciles all the opposite elements to which it gave birth. In certain mystical religions the Creator is so transcendent that he is not even allowed existence. This is not the sort of God upon which cults and faiths can flourish, for there is nothing there to grasp hold of.

Fig. 4. The geometer's breakfast. On a blue-rimmed china plate sits a poached egg on toast—a humble image of the geometer's universe. The hexagon, drawn on the diameter of the egg yolk, is contained by the ring of white which is held within the square of toast. Through the corners of the toast passes the blue circle which, in the geometer's creation diagram, contains the whole universe. The chequered mat is a double square and the rest of the figure is developed from it.

In this book the traditional creation myth is developed and illustrated by means of geometry, the principles of which are not human inventions but are discovered ready-made in nature. Geometry, it can be said, is more deeply rooted in nature than any of nature's physical products. It is the same and as true everywhere, at all times. It is even older than the world itself, for it is the art by which God framed and measured out his creation. "He made all things in number and measure and weight", says the apocryphal Book of Wisdom.

Creative Geometry: Introducing the Ratios

The Creator, according to our myth, did everything in the simplest, most economical way, showing his benevolence by making his work easy for anyone to follow. The material part of his creation was accomplished in three stages, using the first three proportions in geometry. These are π, $\sqrt{2}$ (the square root of 2),

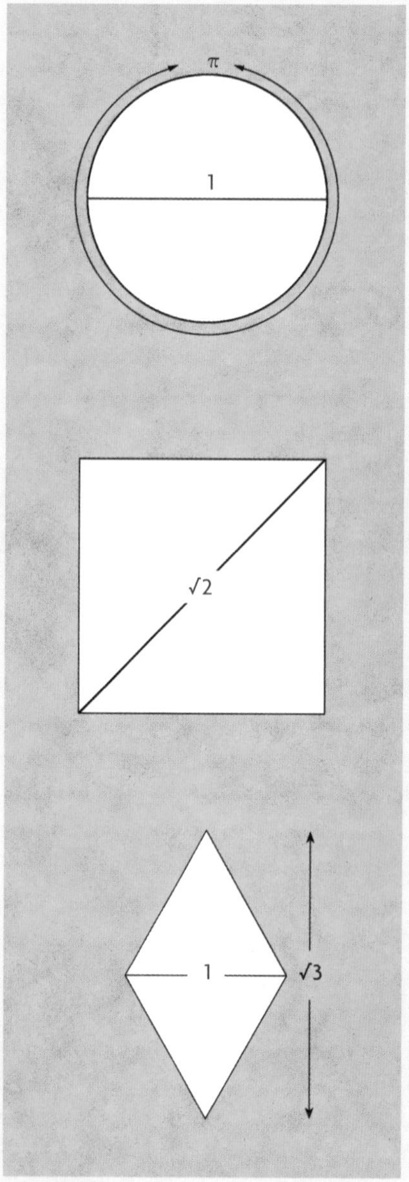

Fig. 5. The first three ratios

1. The first ratio in geometry is 1 to π, the ratio between the diameter of a circle and its circumference.

2. The second ratio is 1 to the square root of 2, or 1 : 1.4142 . . . the ratio between the side of a square and its diagonal.

3. The third ratio is 1 to the square root of 3, or 1 : 1.732 . . . the ratio between the length and breadth of a rhombus (two equilateral triangles back to back).

and √3 (the square root of 3). The figures that correspond to these are the circle, the square, and the triangle.

There is a fourth basic ratio, √5 (the square root of 5) and its derivative, the 'golden section'. These pertain to the creation of life and occur at a later stage with the geometry of 5 and 10.

Fig. 6. Combining the ratios to construct the universal diagram

1 (a). The circle representing the sublunary world is enclosed by two arcs struck from each end of its diameter. This provides the cross-axis which is then used to generate two similar arcs.

1 (b). The whole figure is then enclosed in a circle.

2. A square is added and a circle drawn through its corners. The result is a central circle surrounded by two rings.

3. Taking the area of the inner circle as 1, the area of the first ring is 2 and the outer ring 3.

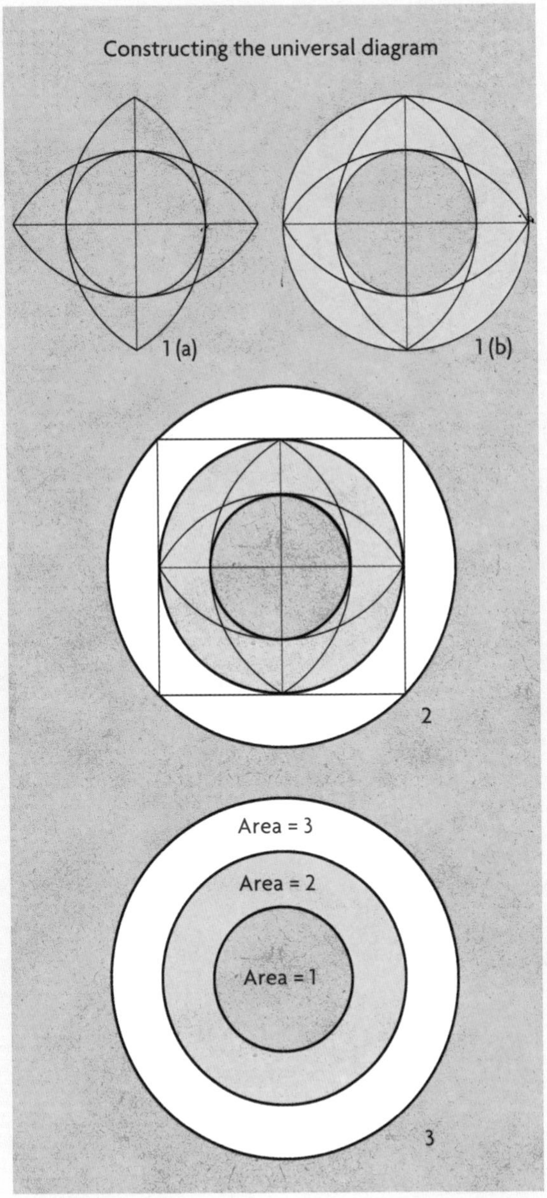

Fig. 7 (right). The universal diagram appears at the centre of the poached egg on toast (page 9). The total area of the plate is six times that of the yolk, and the area of the yolk is half that of its white.

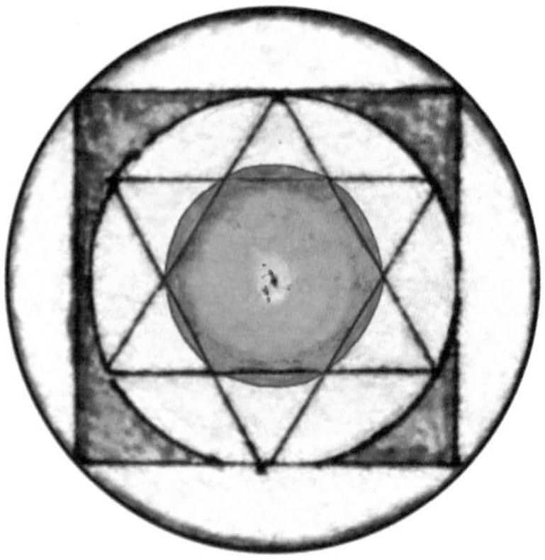

Fig. 8 (below). The successive root ratios are combined in one diagram. The square 1 by 1 has a diagonal of √2 which is swung down to the base line, making a rectangle with sides 1 and √2. The diagonal of this figure is √3. The series continues through √4 and √5 onward.

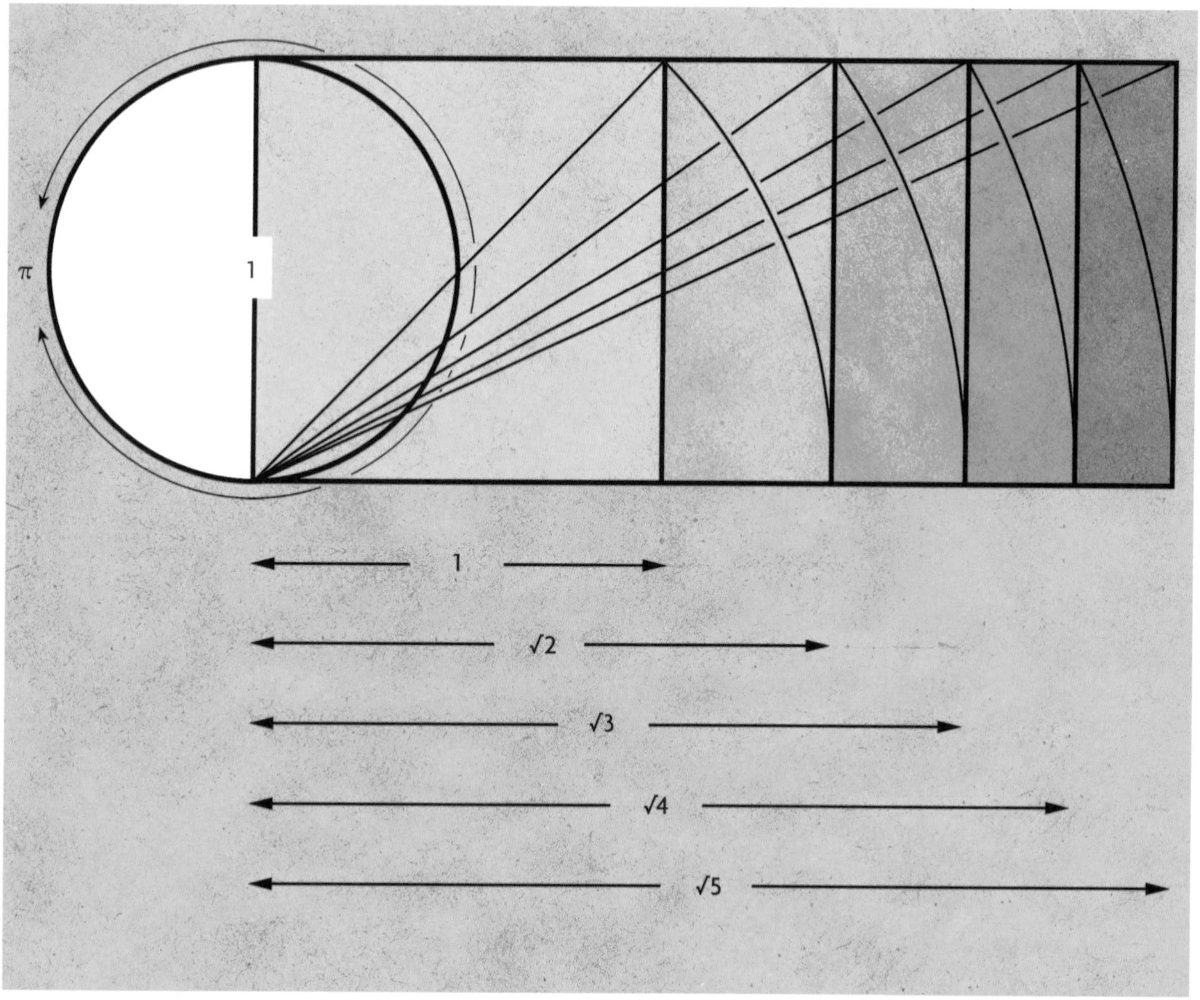

Genesis and the Great Geometer

Developing naturally along with the first stages in geometry is a cosmogony or story of how the world was made. It starts with a Creator, the Great Geometer, whose benevolence caused him to undertake the work. He was equipped with a ruler and compass by which can be constructed the primary figures of plane geometry, those that correspond to the first twelve numbers (with the exceptions of the mysterious Seven and Nine and the unsubstantial Eleven). The world was designed by reason so that geometers can discover and reproduce its essential structure. Since everything about it is as good as it can possibly be, the universe was formed in the most perfect of all shapes, the sphere, represented in two dimensions by the circle. The story is that the Creator, from his position at the centre, revolved the shaft of his compass, corresponding to the world pole, and swung a circle which includes everything.

A simple version of the geometer's creation myth is in Genesis, chapter 1, where the Creator's work is described in six stages—or seven including his Sabbath day of rest. A parallel account is given in Plato's *Timaeus,* written in the fourth century BC, which has been called a commentary on Genesis with added geometrical details. There are, however, doubts about the prior antiquity of Genesis, and it may be the other way round: that the *Timaeus* was the original version and the biblical account followed. In any case, both were derived from the same source, from the scientifically grounded, numerically structured description of the universe that was adopted by successive religions and cultures throughout the ancient world. The story that goes with it is a geometric allegory. It was never meant to be taken too literally; but since we evidently need a creation myth, it might as well be the best one. That was Plato's reasoning in *Timaeus* where he accepted the traditional account as "the most likely story".

In the Genesis cosmogony the first three stages follow the classical development of geometry, beginning with the point, line, and circle and continuing with the square and triangle, as shown on page 14.

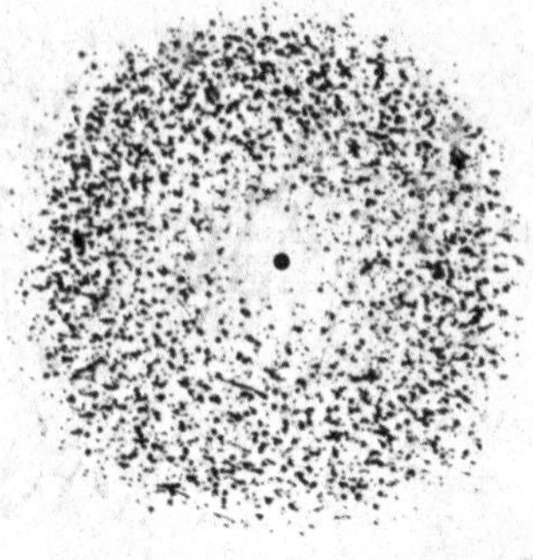

1. Primordial chaos

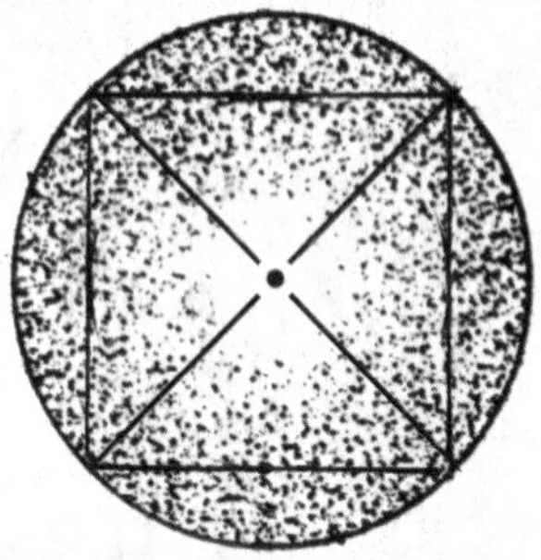

2. The world brought to order

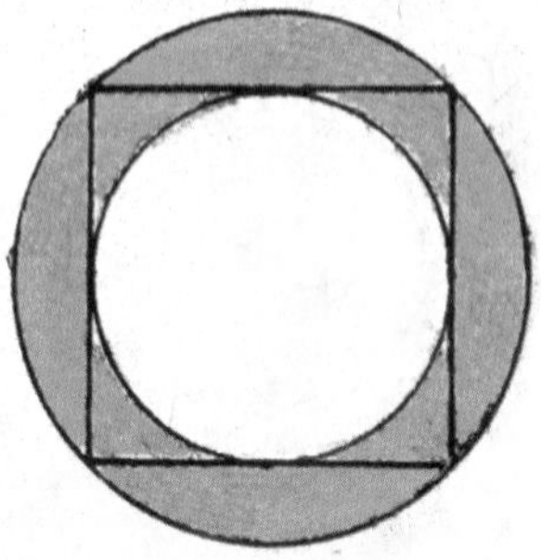

3. The heavens divided from the earth; equal areas of dark and light

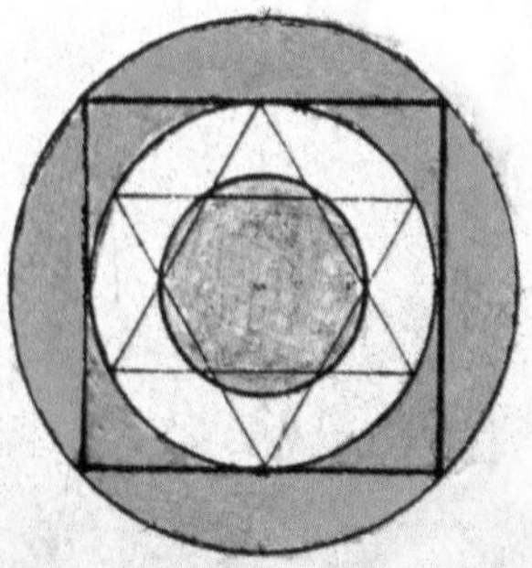

4. The land (centre) separated from the ocean

Fig. 9. The Creator's geometry

1 and **2.** The Creator conceives of the universe, draws the cosmic circle to define its limits, and brings it to order by adding its two axes. He is then able to draw a square within the circle. This introduces the first two ratios in geometry. The first is π, the ratio between the circle's diameter and its circumference, and the second is $\sqrt{2}$, by which the side of the square is related to its diagonal.

3. He then draws a circle within the square. The area of this circle is half that of the original circle, so in this way he has divided the universe into two equal halves, upper and lower, representing light and darkness and all the apparent dualities in nature. The circumference of the inner circle provides the Firmament by which the Creator separates the 'waters above' from the 'waters below'.

4. Within the lower circle, the Firmament, the Creator constructs two triangles overlapping to form a hexagon. Thereby he introduces the third, $1:\sqrt{3}$ ratio in geometry. He draws a circle through the six corners of the hexagon. This central circle represents the sublunary world of our existence. The ring outside it is the heavens and the outer ring is the Zodiac, the realm of the twelve gods.

The inner circle and the two rings around it have relative areas of 1, 2, and 3. The completed diagram depicts the created universe, perfectly structured but devoid of animals and human intelligence. These are provided at the next stage in creation (see part 3).

Fig. 10. Stages in the creation story: Genesis and Plato

1. In the beginning God created the heaven and the earth. And the earth was without form and void. —Genesis 1

He wanted everything to be as near to his own perfection as possible. —Plato, *Timaeus* 29

He made the universe as one whole, made up of all whole entities, perfect and undecaying. He gave it the shape that befitted its nature. The proper shape for the creature which was designed to comprehend all creatures within itself is a figure which contains every (geometric) figure. Thus he made it in the shape of a sphere, the figure which is most similar to himself. —*Timaeus*

2. Seeing the universe in a restless state of inharmonious and disorderly motion, God brought it into order because he considered that order was in every way better than disorder. —*Timaeus*

3. God divided the light from the darkness. . . . He made the firmament and divided the waters which were under the firmament from the waters above. —Genesis

4. And God said, Let the waters under the heaven be gathered together unto one place, and let the dry land appear. —Genesis

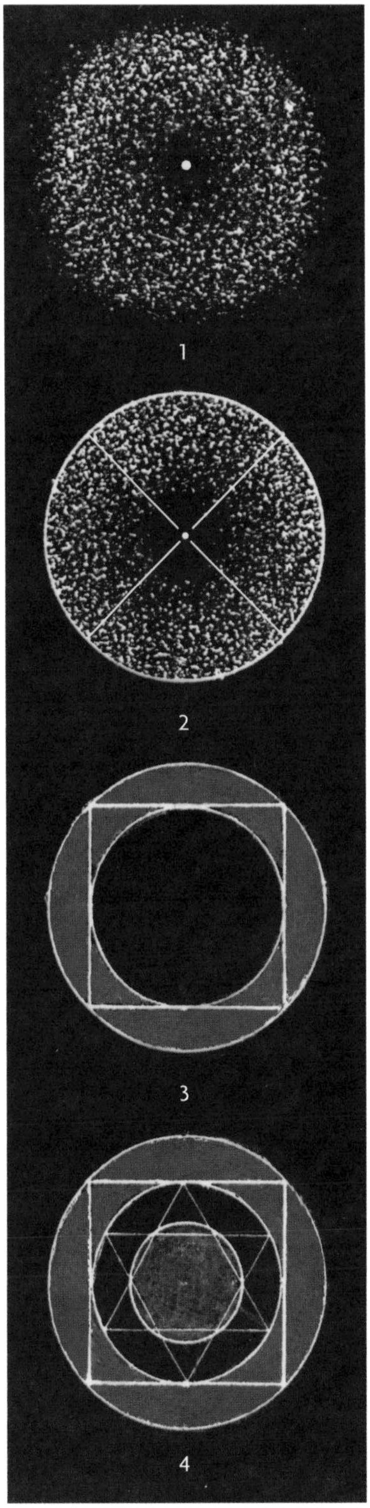

The Number of the Universe

The universe was made spherical because that is the most perfect shape, and it was also given the perfect number. As the only created entity that is totally self-sufficient, it is the natural symbol of One. But it also has another number, that of the sacred power or principle to which it is dedicated. The practice in religious architecture was to express the dedication of a temple through the area of its ground plan. The universe was dedicated to the traditional twelve gods of the cosmos, each represented by one of the first twelve numbers. Its area as a circle, the two-dimensional form of a sphere, is therefore the number 479,001,600, or $1 \times 2 \times 3 \times 4 \times 5 \times 6 \times 7 \times 8 \times 10 \times 11 \times 12$, known to mathematicians as 'factorial 12' and denoted by the symbol 12!.

In the geometer's cosmogony, illustrated on the previous pages, the universe is divided into two equal areas by inscribing within it a square containing a circle. The diameter of the universal circle (area 12!), divided by $\sqrt{2}$, gives the diameter of the inner circle as 17460. The reference is to 1746 which is called the 'number of fusion' because it unites by addition the two numbers which symbolize the two opposite principles in nature, positive and negative. The first of these is the number 666, a solar number applied to the rational, decisive part of the mind. On the opposite pole is 1080, standing for the imagination and all that is influenced by the moon. Their sum, 1746, has many important associations on the esoteric number code, introduced on page 72.

Within this circle of diameter 17460 (the circle representing the firmament between the upper and lower worlds) a six-pointed star or hexagram is drawn, together with the circle that passes through its inner angles. The area of this inner circle is precisely a sixth part of the original 12! circle, and its calculated radius is 5040 or 7!. It represents the sublunary world, the sphere of the earth within the orbit of her influential companion, the moon. This circle with radius equal to 5040 or $1 \times 2 \times 3 \times 4 \times 5 \times 6 \times 7$ is the 'cosmological circle' of the 'Heavenly City' diagram, the central symbol in the geometer's creation myth.

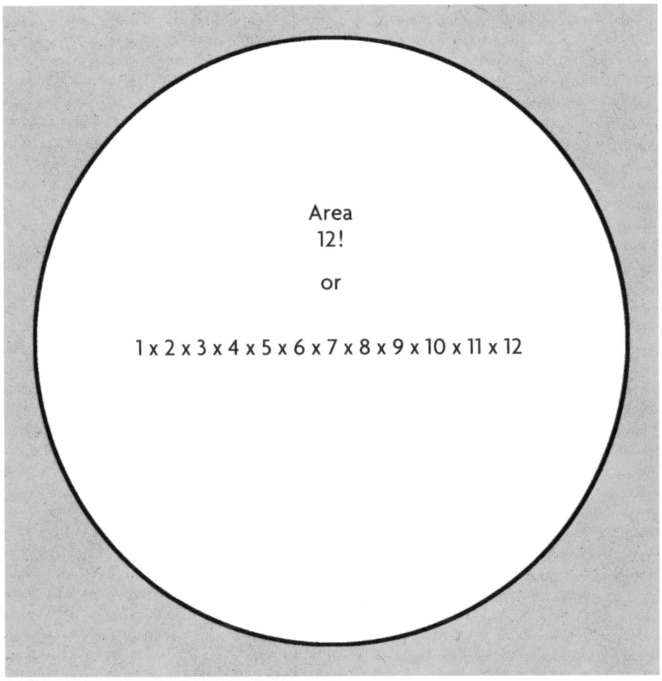

Fig. 11. The geometer's universe is traditionally dedicated to the twelve gods, symbolized by the numbers 1 to 12.

Multiplied together they produce 12! or 'factorial 12' or 1 x 2 x 3 x 4 x 5 x 6 x 7 x 8 x 9 x 10 x 11 x 12. This is the area of the whole universal circle.

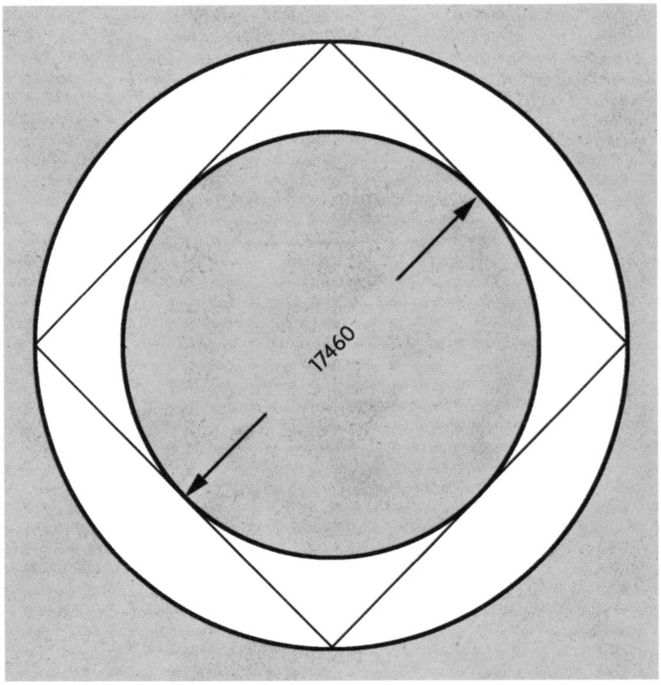

Fig. 12. The square drawn within the universal circle, and the circle within that square, both have a width of 17460. 1746, the 'number of fusion', unites by addition the numbers 666 and 1080, symbols of the solar and lunar aspects of nature.

The area of the cosmological circle, being a sixth part of the 12! circle of the universe, can be expressed as 2 × 11!. Around it is the ring bounded by the firmament, whose area is 4 × 11!, and the area of the outer ring within the universal circumference is 6 × 11!. The areas of the inner circle and its two concentric rings are therefore in the proportion 1, 2, 3. This cosmological figure includes the first three ratios, the twelve gods, types, or tones, and the numerical harmony of the universal system. It is an image of a living being, perfect in all its parts, "one whole of wholes" as Plato called it, satisfying its own needs and dependent on nothing but the will of its creator.

Fig. 13. Within the circle of diameter 17460 is a six-pointed star or hexagram with a circle drawn through its intersection points. This circle has a radius of 5040 or 7!. Its area is a sixth part of the area of the universal circle. It represents the sublunary world and is elaborated in the Heavenly City diagram.

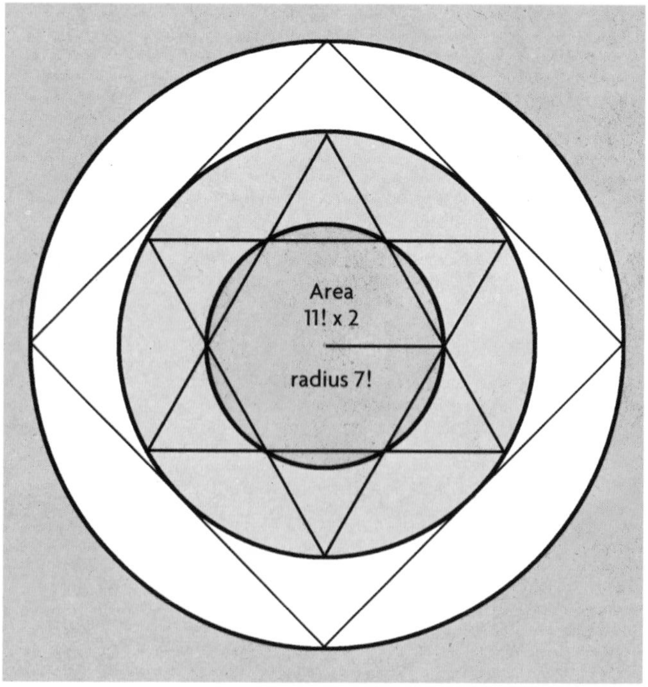

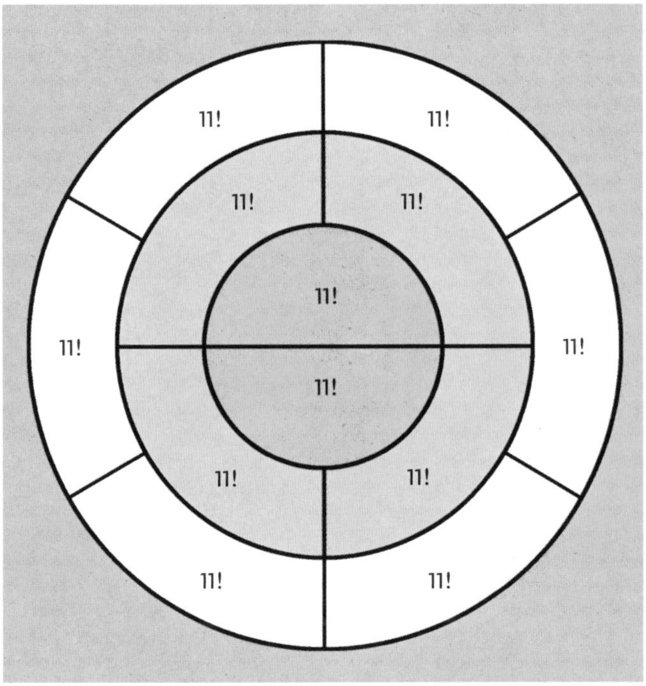

Fig. 14. The area of the inner circle is 2 x 11!. The area of the middle ring is 4 x 11!. The area of the outer ring is 6 x 11!. Total area = 12!. By this construction the area of the universal circle is divided into 12 equal parts corresponding to its twelve ruling gods.

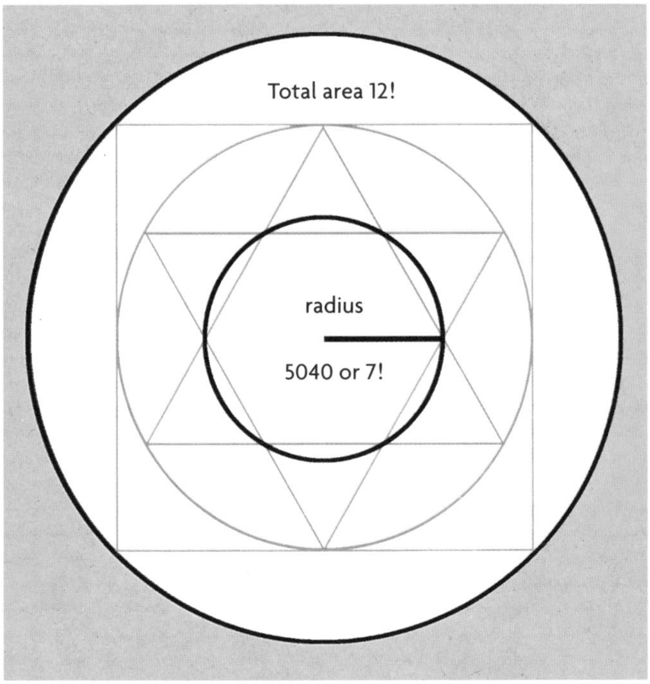

Fig. 15. Area of universal circle = 12!
Radius of 'sublunary world' circle = 7!
At this early stage in cosmography the numbers 12 and 7 appear together in their expanded forms 12! and 7! (meaning the first 12 numbers multiplied together and the numbers up to 7 multiplied together, respectively).

2 • The Number 5040

Key to the World Plan

The most interesting part of the universal diagram—and the main subject of this book—is its central part, the circle of radius 5040. The number 5040 stands above all others as the characteristic symbol of the traditional canon of number and proportion. This numerical code was the source and basic standard of all the arts, sciences, and institutions of ancient civilizations that were founded upon cosmological principles to reflect the order of the heavens. Plato throughout all his writings refers to the canon of number. It was upheld, he says, by the ruling priests of Egypt and was responsible for the long endurance of their civilization. In *Laws* he insists that the ideal state constitution, as a whole and in all its departments and divisions, should be based on the number 5040. This is the number of citizens in his ideal city-state, and the land is divided between them into 5040 equal portions.

In explaining his choice of this number, Plato gives the simple arithmetical reasons that 5040 is divisible by every one of the first twelve numbers, apart from 11, and is also the product of the first seven, i.e., $1 \times 2 \times 3 \times 4 \times 5 \times 6 \times 7 = 5040$. It therefore allows the greatest possible variety of subdivisions within the state pattern. He left it at that and said nothing about the cosmological significance of 5040. The importance of that number, as Plato was well aware, is that 5040 is the radius of the inner circle in the world-plan diagram on which his constitution was modelled. The circle with radius 5040 represents the 'sublunary world', the sphere of the earth beneath the one face of the moon that is shown to us. It is made up of the moon's radius, 1080 miles, plus 3960 miles, the mean radius of the earth.

The world plan and the code of number that comprises it are essentially duodecimal, based on the numbers 1 to 12. Our sublunary world, however, is dominated by a lesser range, the numbers 1 to 10. In these first ten numbers, called by geometers the Decad, 7 is the pivotal number, the pole of the system, producing, by multiplication in each direction, the number 5040.

$$1 \times 2 \times 3 \times 4 \times 5 \times 6 \times 7 = 5040, \text{ and}$$
$$7 \times 8 \times 9 \times 10 = 5040$$

Among the many other properties of 5040 is that it forms the radius of the circle which, in the geometer's picture of creation, represents the sublunary world. That radius is the distance from the centre of the earth to the centre of the moon when the two bodies are placed tangent to each other. They are, of course, far apart, but the mean distance between them, 237,600 miles, like all the dimensions and ratios of the solar system, is commensurable with them both, for 237,600 miles is equal to the earth's mean radius times 60 or the moon's radius times 220.

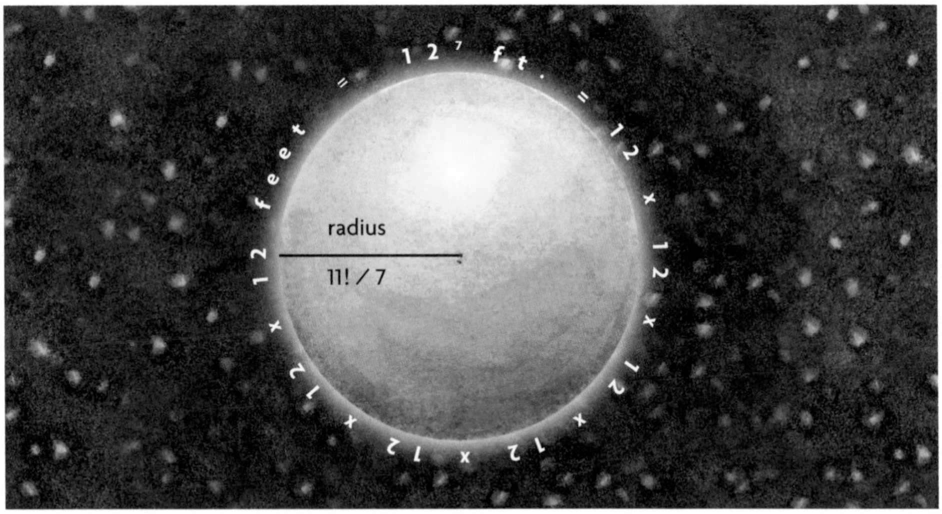

Fig. 16. Seven and Twelve in the measure round the moon. The moon is traditionally the source of measure and time-keeping. In its dimensions are encoded all the numbers of the Dodecad, the numbers 1–12. Measured in feet its radius (1080 miles) is 5,702,400, a number equal to 1 x 2 x 3 x 4 x 5 x 6 x 8 x 9 x 10 x 11. The only numbers missing from this sequence are 7 and 12. They are reserved for the lunar circumference whose length is simply 12 to the power of 7 (i.e., 12^7) ft. In this calculation the Fibonacci π, 864/275, is used (see pages 36–38).

Earth, Moon, and the Circle Squared

A primary and essential operation in creative geometry is the squaring of the circle. This work can be approached in two ways; either it means constructing a square of the same area as that of a given circle, or the circle and square are drawn with equal perimeters. Either way the squared circle represents the first marriage of opposites. The circle, with its perimeter measured by the irrational number π, and with no point where it begins or ends, is the natural symbol of the divine, eternal element in creation, preceding matter. In contrast, the square is a rational figure, the measure round its perimeter being precisely four times its width. It is the symbol of earth and solid matter, and of human works rather than products of nature. In sacred architecture the circle of the dome refers to the heavens and the square base to earth. The combination of circle and square, heaven and earth, spirit and matter, provides the foundation pattern of temples universally, going back to very early times. It is the basic plan of historical cities, laid out on cosmological principles by the priestly geomancers with their ritualised science of land-surveying. These in ancient Rome were the augurs, whose duties included the design of towns and landscapes. The first augur, according to legend, was Romulus, the founder of Rome. He marked out its ground plan as a circle and a square combined.

The largest and most obvious squared circle in nature is provided by the earth and the moon, whose combined radii amount to 5040 miles.

Earth's mean radius	=	3960
Moon's radius	=	1080
		5040 miles

With radius of 5040 the circumference of the sublunary circle is 31680, the same as the measure round the square containing the earth.

Radius of circle	=	5040; circumference	=	31680
Side of square	=	7920; perimeter	=	31680

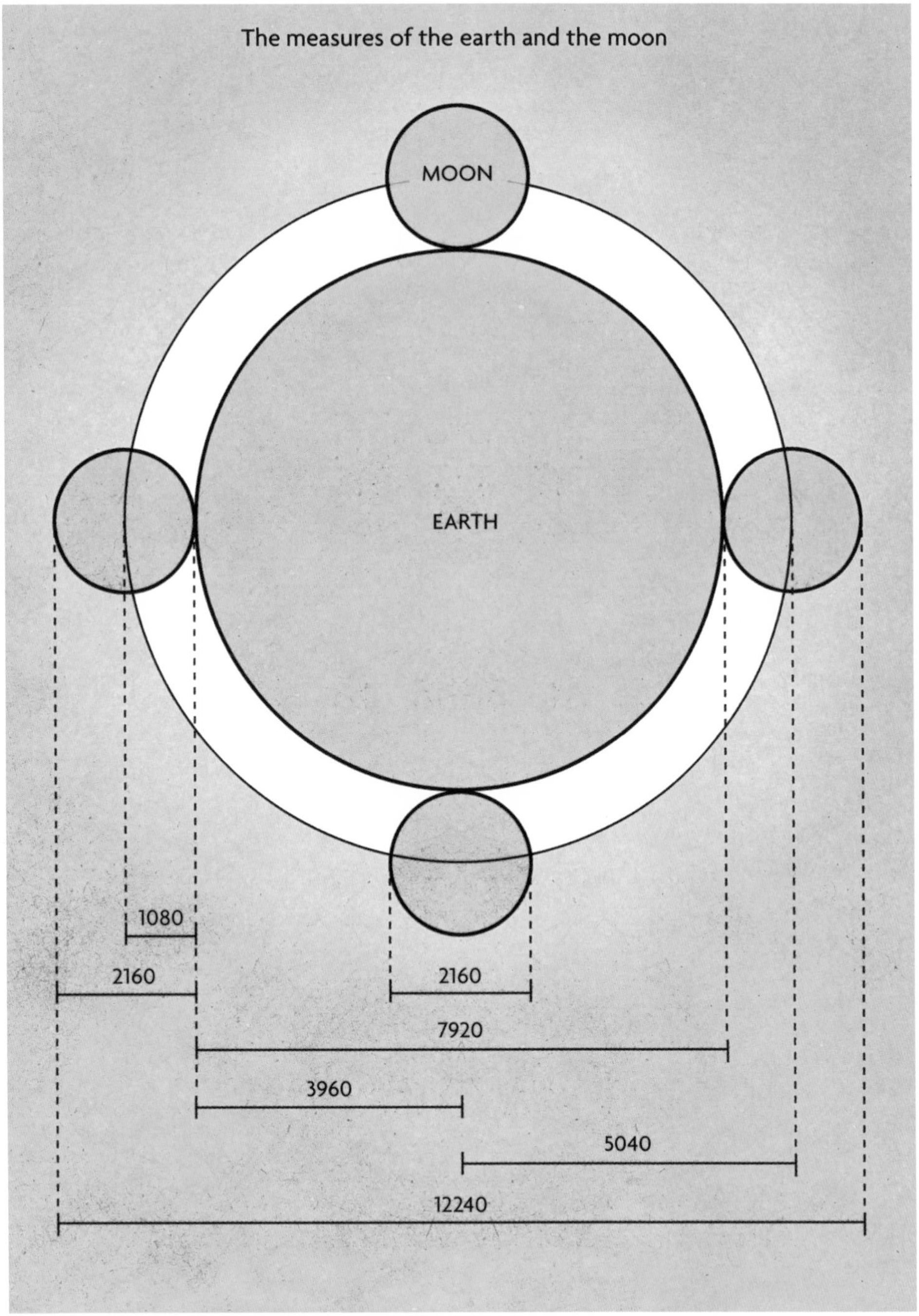

Fig. 17. The circle of the sublunary world, radius 5040 miles, passes through the centres of the moon circles (radius 1080 miles) that touch the central circle of earth (radius 3960). The sum of 1080 and 3960 is 5040, the key number in the traditional cosmology.

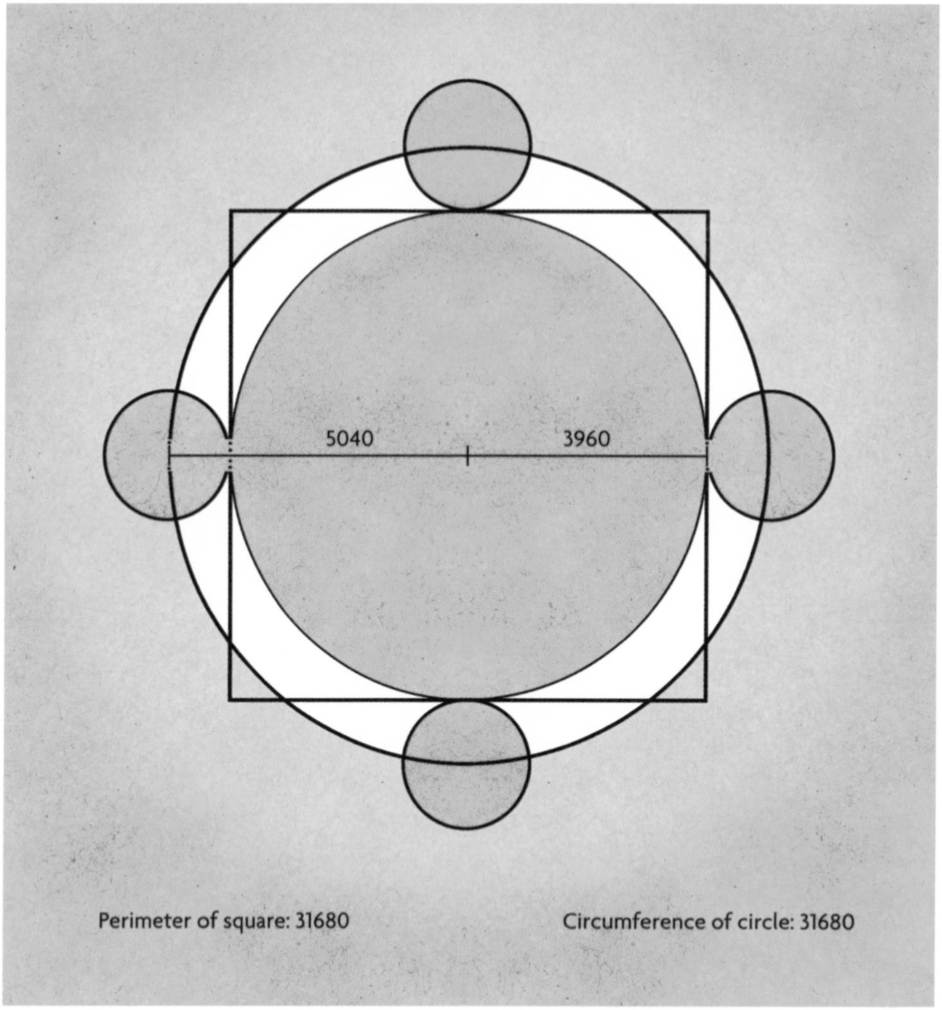

Fig. 18. The diagram of the earth and moon in mutual contact produces the squared circle (square and circle with equal perimeters). The square containing the earth has the same measure round its four sides (4 x 7920 = 31680) as the circle through the centres of the moons (5040 x 44/7 = 31680).

This striking fact of nature is not, as might at first be supposed, the origin of the ancient numerical cosmology, but merely one of its manifestations and only apparent when the dimensions are given correctly in miles. More basic is the code of number in which 5040 (= 1 x 2 x 3 x 4 x 5 x 6 x 7), the radius of the circle, and 7920 (= 8 x 9 x 10 x 11), the circle's quadrant, are the core components. Multiplied together, these two numbers produce 39,916,800 or 11!. Twice 11! gives the area of the circle with radius 5040 and, as already shown, the geometric expansion of that circle produces 12!—the symbolic, two-dimensional area of the universe.

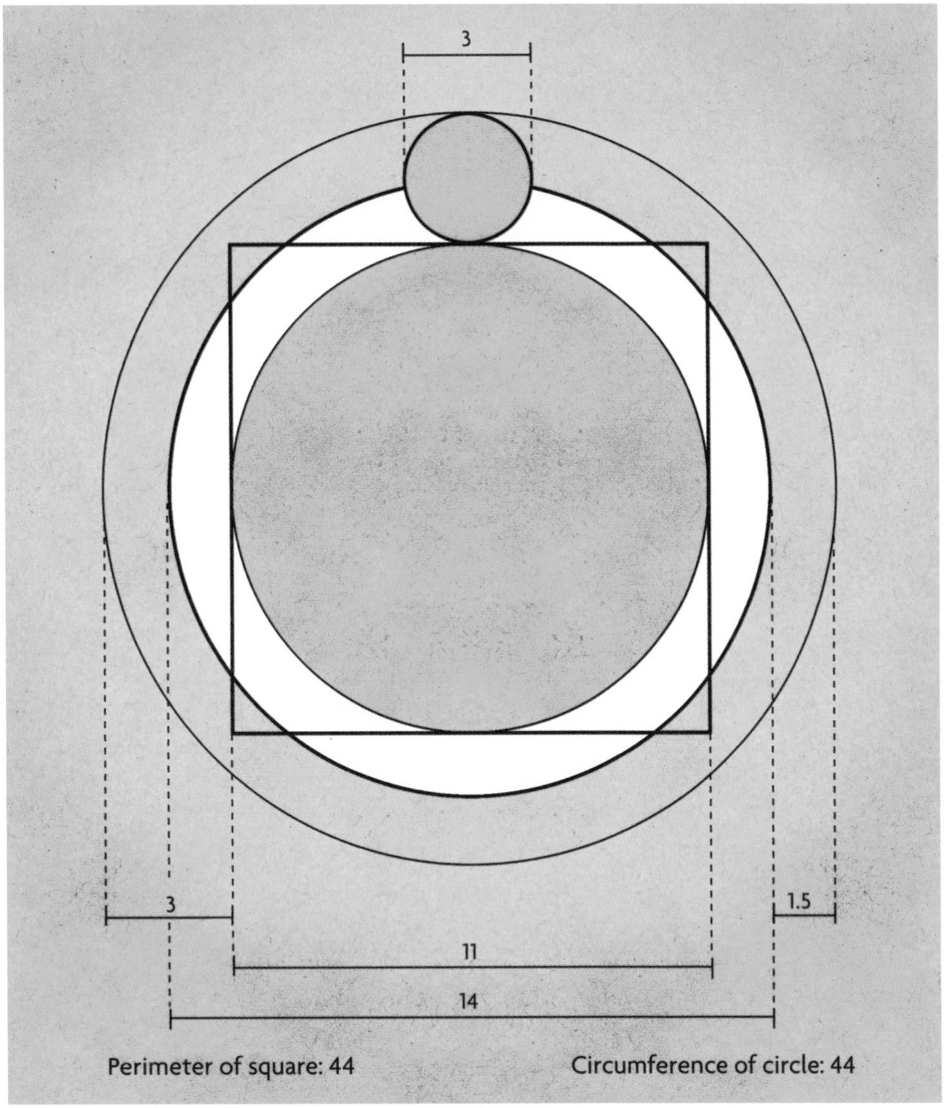

Fig. 19. To procure the actual dimensions of the earth, moon, and other features of this plan, multiply the basic measures by 720 (= 1 x 2 x 3 x 4 x 5 x 6 = 8 x 9 x 10)

All these numbers are multiples of 720 (= $1 \times 2 \times 3 \times 4 \times 5 \times 6$), and when divided by that number they give the dimensions of the squared circle diagram in its simplest terms: the radius of the circle is reduced from 5040 to 7, the moon's diameter becomes 3, the earth's 11, and 44 is the perimeter of both the circle and the square.

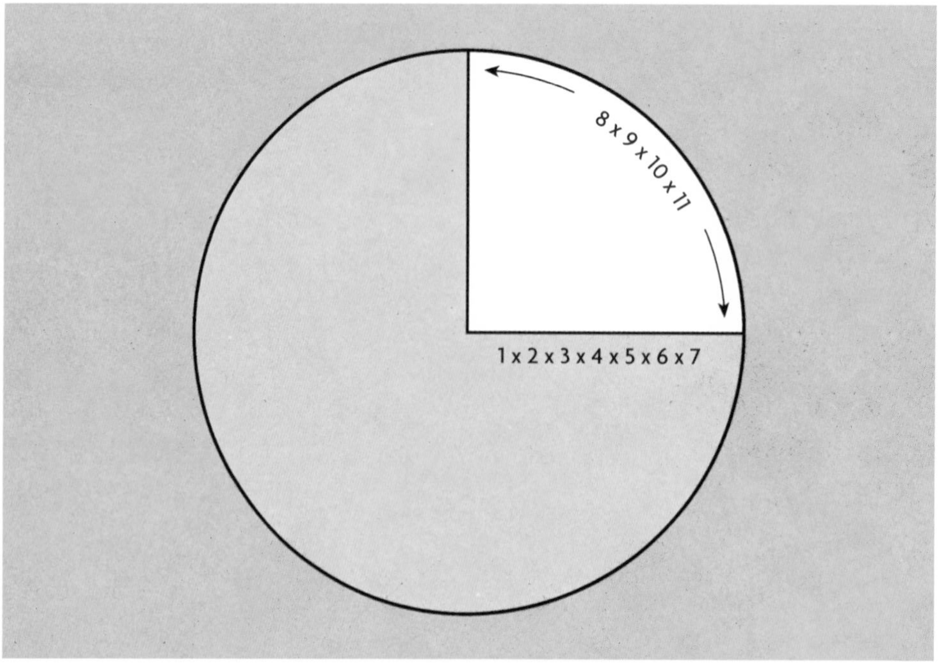

Fig. 20. Area of cosmological circle (radius x ½ circumference) = 2 x 11!

It so happens—by a barely credible coincidence or by an inexplicable action of conscious design—that the actual dimensions of earth and moon codify the numbers 1 to 11 in the most economical manner through the circle with radius 5040. The quadrant or quarter part of its circumference is 7920. The dimensions of that circle consist of the first eleven numbers, for:

$$\begin{array}{llcl} \text{radius,} & 5040 & = & 1 \times 2 \times 3 \times 4 \times 5 \times 6 \times 7 \\ \text{quadrant,} & 7920 & = & 8 \times 9 \times 10 \times 11 \end{array}$$

The product of these two numbers, 5040×7920, is 11! and twice that number is the area of the sublunary circle with radius 5040.

$$\overbrace{1 \times 2 \times 3 \times 4 \times 5 \times 6}^{720} \times 7 \times \overbrace{8 \times 9 \times 10}^{5040}$$
$$\underbrace{1 \times 2 \times 3 \times 4 \times 5 \times 6 \times 7}_{5040} \times \underbrace{8 \times 9 \times 10}_{720}$$

$$\overbrace{\underbrace{1 \times 2 \times 3 \times 4 \times 5 \times 6 \times 7}_{5040} \times \underbrace{8 \times 9 \times 10 \times 11}_{7920}}^{39916800 = 11!}$$

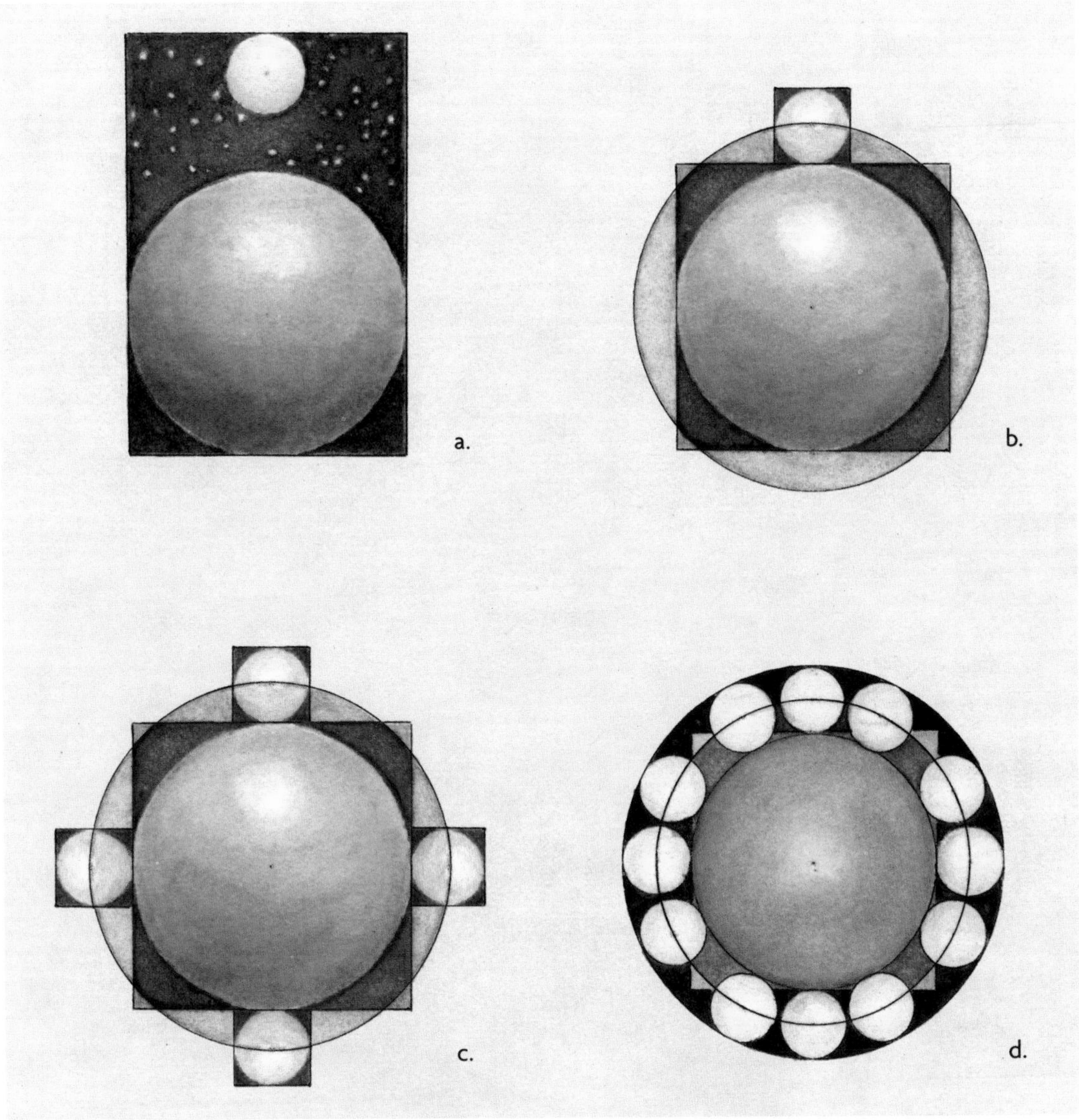

Fig. 21. The squared circle formed by the earth and moon

a. Earth and moon with their relative dimensions of 11 to 3.

b. Earth and moon forming the squared circle.

c. Four moons occupy the quarters of the squared circle.

d. Eight further moons complete the cosmological circle. Their circumferences pass through the eight points where the equal square and circle meet.

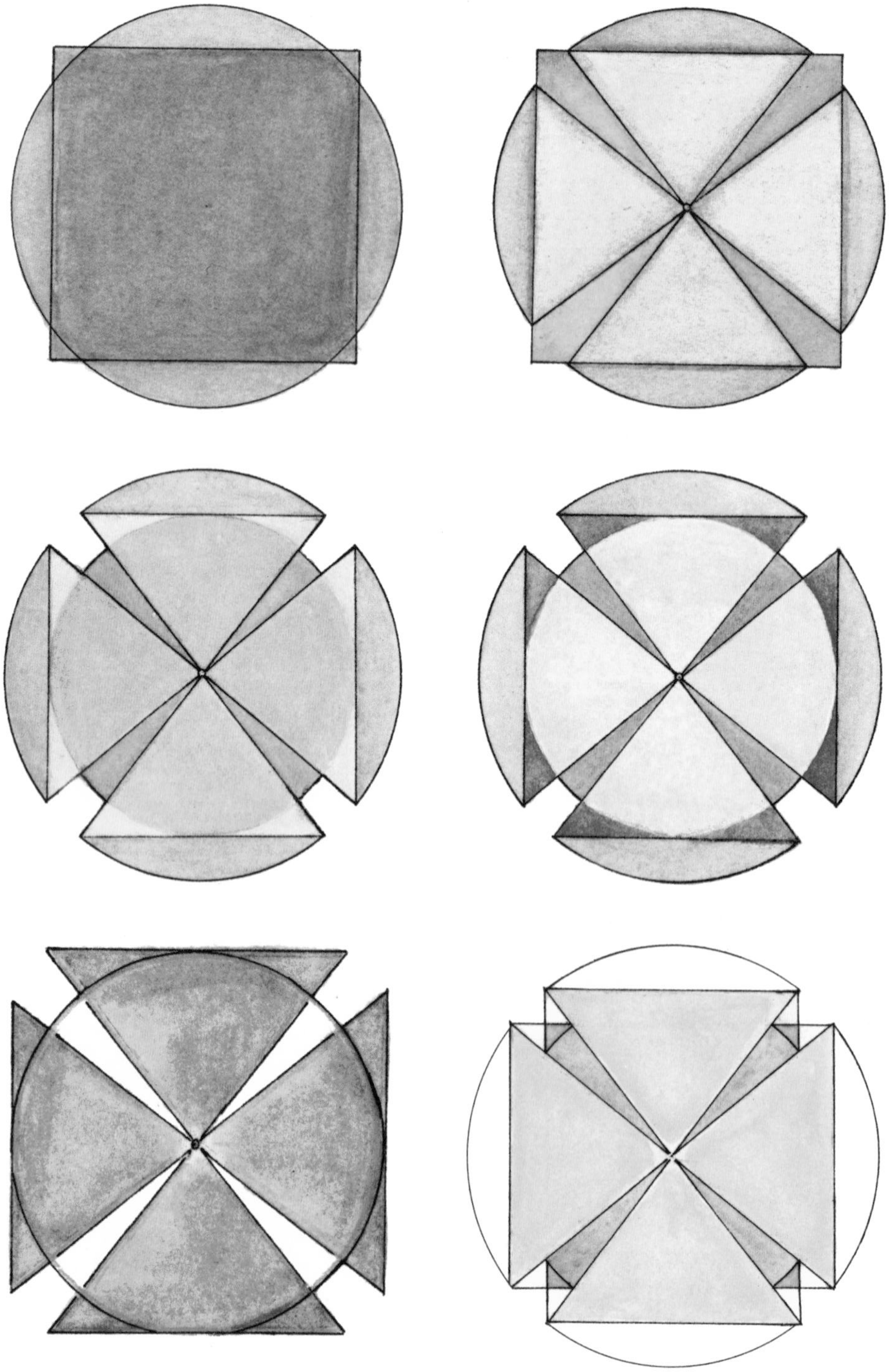

Fig. 22. Symbols and images of the squared circle

Fig. 23. Beneath the circle (dark) of the Firmament, the ring of twelve lunar circles is divided into quarters at the points where the circle through the moons cuts the corners of the square. In cosmographic imagery, through these gaps the four rivers of paradise flow outwards and heavenly influences enter the sublunary world.

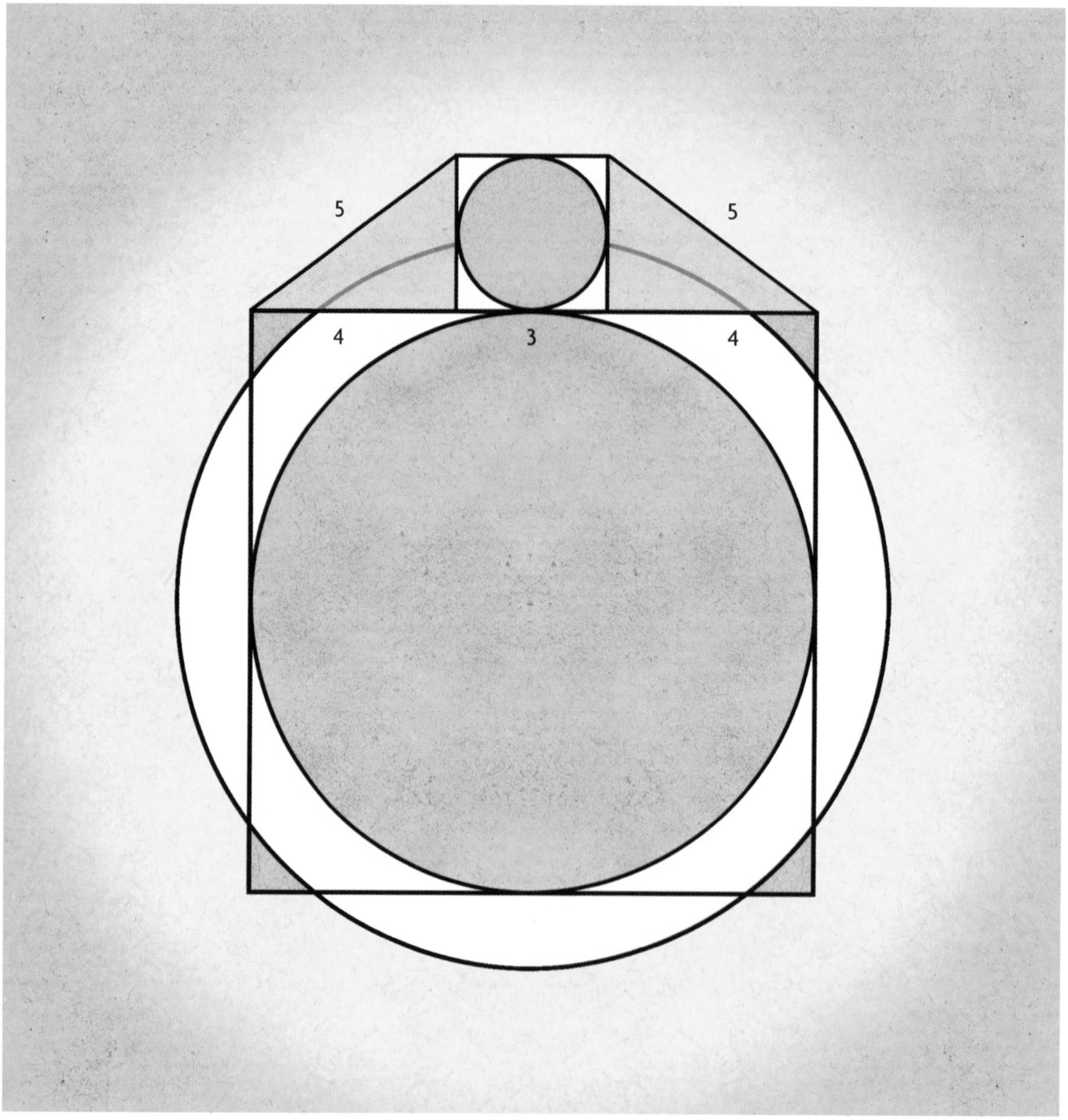

Fig. 24. A simple way of constructing the traditional plan of the Heavenly City is to begin with the first Pythagorean triangle (see pages 105–8) with sides of 3, 4, and 5. On the 3 side draw a square and on the far side of the square place another, reciprocal 3–4–5 triangle. This produces a baseline of 4 + 3 + 4 = 11. Draw a square on the baseline, inscribing a circle within it and another circle within the square 3 by 3. These two circles are same-scale images of the earth and moon. From the centre of the earth circle draw a circle through the centre of the moon. Its circumference, with π as 22/7, is 44, the same measure round the four sides of the square containing the earth.

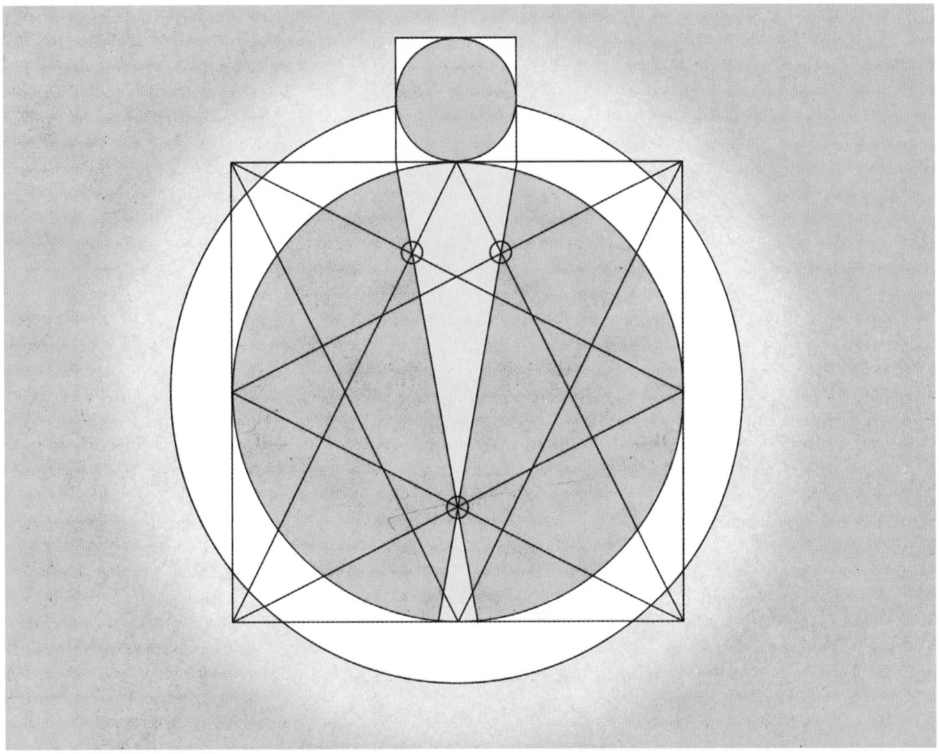

Fig. 25. Division into 11 parts and development of squared-circle figure (after M. Stewart)

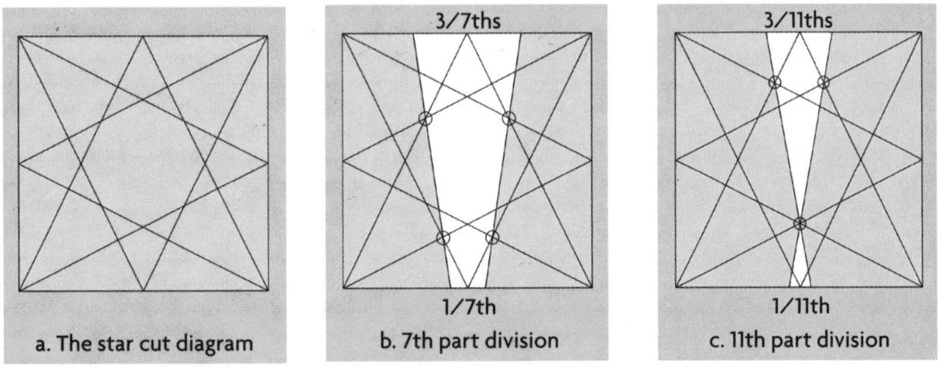

Fig. 26 a–c. The key to constructing the Heavenly City plan is to divide a given line into 11 parts. This can be achieved precisely by means of an ancient and ever-useful geometric device named after Archimedes, the 'sand-reckoner's diagram' or the 'star cut'. Through the intersections of the lines with the square containing this diagram, the geometer can divide the sides of the square into 11 and 7 parts as well as into the musical ratios, 1:2, 2:3, 3:4, 8:9. This diagram has been closely analysed by geometer Malcolm Stewart and is the subject of his monograph (yet unpublished).

Fig. 27. A third way of constructing the Heavenly City plan is through the most sacred of numerical marriages, the union of Twelve and Seven. The construction begins with the division of a circle into 4 x 7 or 28 parts. For this see fig. 194. These 28 points are the framework for positioning the twelve lunar circles of the Heavenly City plan. As seen in the diagram above, 12 of the 28 points indicate the centres of the lunar circles, which are each drawn to touch the two adjacent arms of the 28-pointed figure. Another 8 points fit between and touch the pairs of circles on either side of them, and the remaining 8 touch the 8 circles that mark the spots where the square and circle meet. These last 8 points do not themselves mark the intersections of square and circle but position the circles that pass through the intersection.

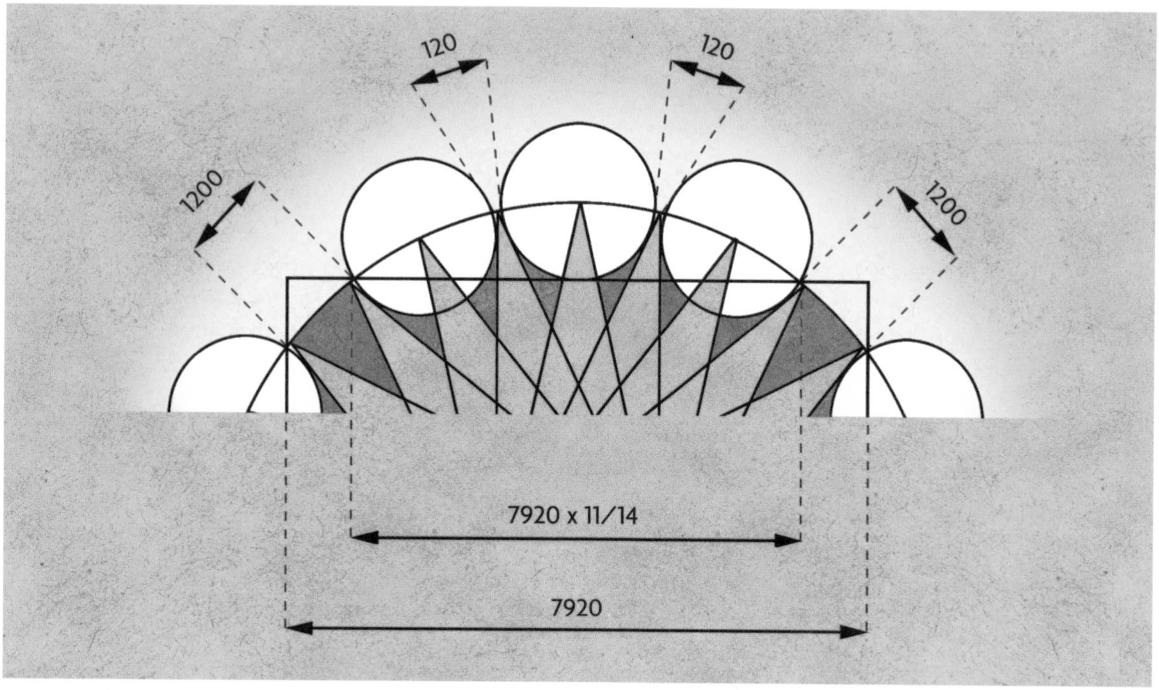

Fig. 28. For number fanciers the Heavenly City plan is a constant source of delightful ratios and harmonies. Here for example, the ratio 14:11 or 4/π (taking π as 22/7) appears in the divisions of the side of the square measuring 7920. Dividing it by 14 and multiplying by 11 gives the distance between the two square-circle meeting points on that side. This allows the calculation that the four gaps in the circle at the corners of the square each measure 1200, and the eight small gaps between the circles, marked by arms of the 28-pointed figure, are each 120. The circle of circumference 31680 is made up of 24 arcs covering 12 moon diameters (25920), 4 gaps (4800), and 8 small gaps (960).

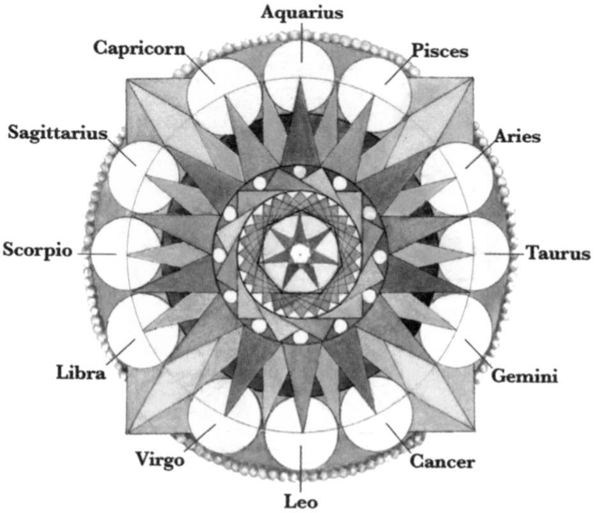

Fig. 29. The twelve lunar circles, diameter 2160 miles, also represent the twelve 'great' months, each of 2160 years, which the sun passes through in turn while completing its 25920-year circuit of the zodiac.

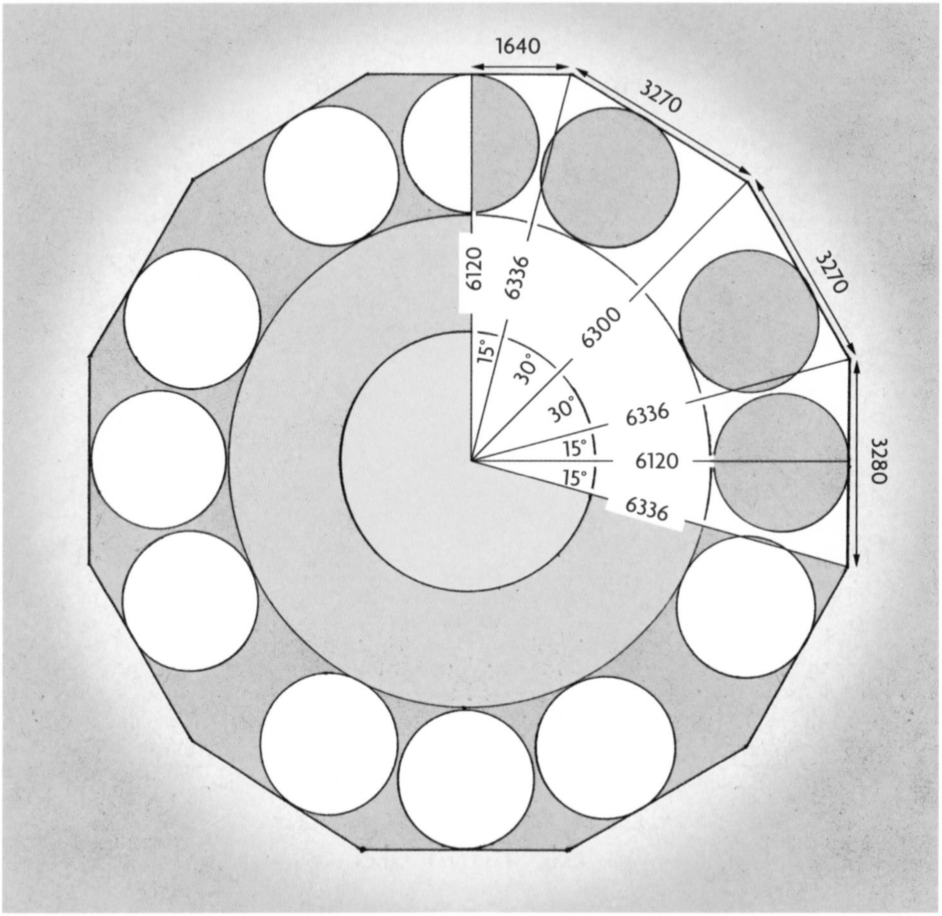

Fig. 30. An aspect of the Heavenly City plan that has attracted the attention of mathematicians is the dimensions of the 12-sided figure that can be drawn outside its lunar circles. First in the field was Ian Sommerville of 1960s' Beat Hotel fame. He noticed that this dodecagon is regular at its 'polar' sides (NSEW) but the other eight sides are slightly shorter due to the groupings of the circles they touch, and that the area enclosed by this figure is close to 120,000,000, emphasizing the characteristic Twelve in the cosmological scheme. Working to a tolerance of 1:2500 (about equal to the deviation of 22/7 from true π) he obtained whole numbers for the sides of the dodecagon, 3280 for the four longer and 3270 for the eight shorter sides, making the perimeter virtually equal to 36000 feet in terms of the old English foot that relates 12:11 to the current foot. Among other significant numbers in the scheme are the measures of the two radii to the decagon, 6336 and 6300, relating as 176:175, the first being a fifth part of the circumference of the cosmological circle, 31680. Sommerville's paper, "A Note on the Dimensions of the Irregular Dodecagon Associated with the New Jerusalem", was written in 1974.

Fig. 31. The practise of creative geometry is not materially rewarding: its attraction is that it is based on universal truth and goes beyond the fluctuating fads and fashions of scientific literalism. By combinations of shapes, beginning with the square and the circle, it aims to depict the pre-existent code of number behind all natural manifestations.

3 • The Circle, the Square

And the Meaning of Pi

What is this thing called pi? It is the Greek letter π, pronounced 'pie' (or by the Greeks 'pee') and denoting the periphery or circumference of a circle in relation to its diameter. $1:\pi$ is the first and most important ratio in geometry, but many of us leave school with no clear understanding of π or the definition of its length. That is not really surprising because no one has ever known the exact value of π and no one ever will. It has been called "a transcendental figure without resolution". Mathematicians from ancient times have worked it out to hundreds of decimal places and, with computers, to several billions, but without finding a regular pattern or any whole-number fraction between a circle's diameter and its circumference. There is, it has been proved, no such thing; π is a string of numbers beginning 3.141592654 . . . and going on forever.

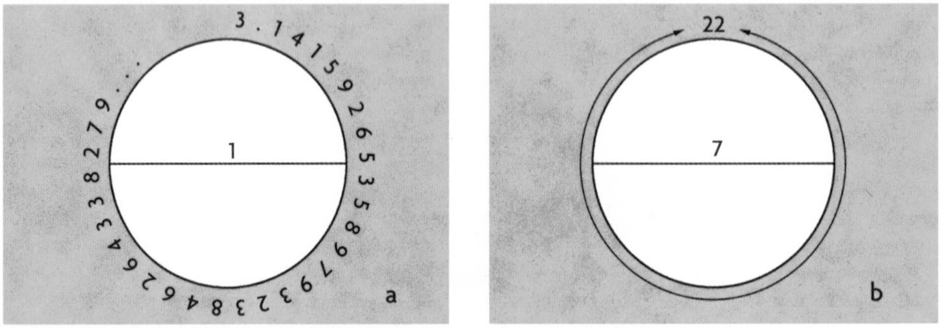

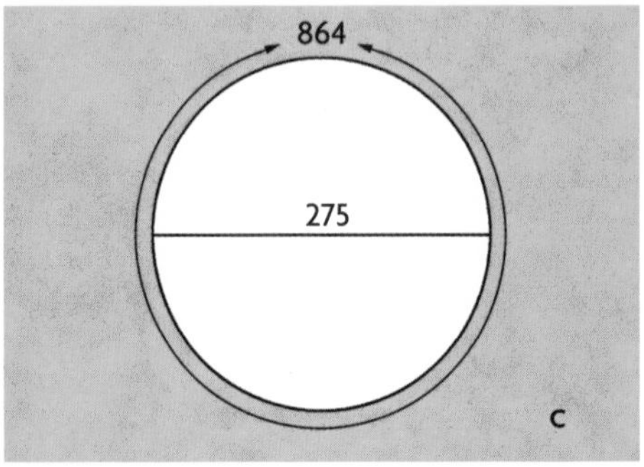

Fig. 32. (a) True pi, (b) conventional pi, and (c) Fibonacci's approximation

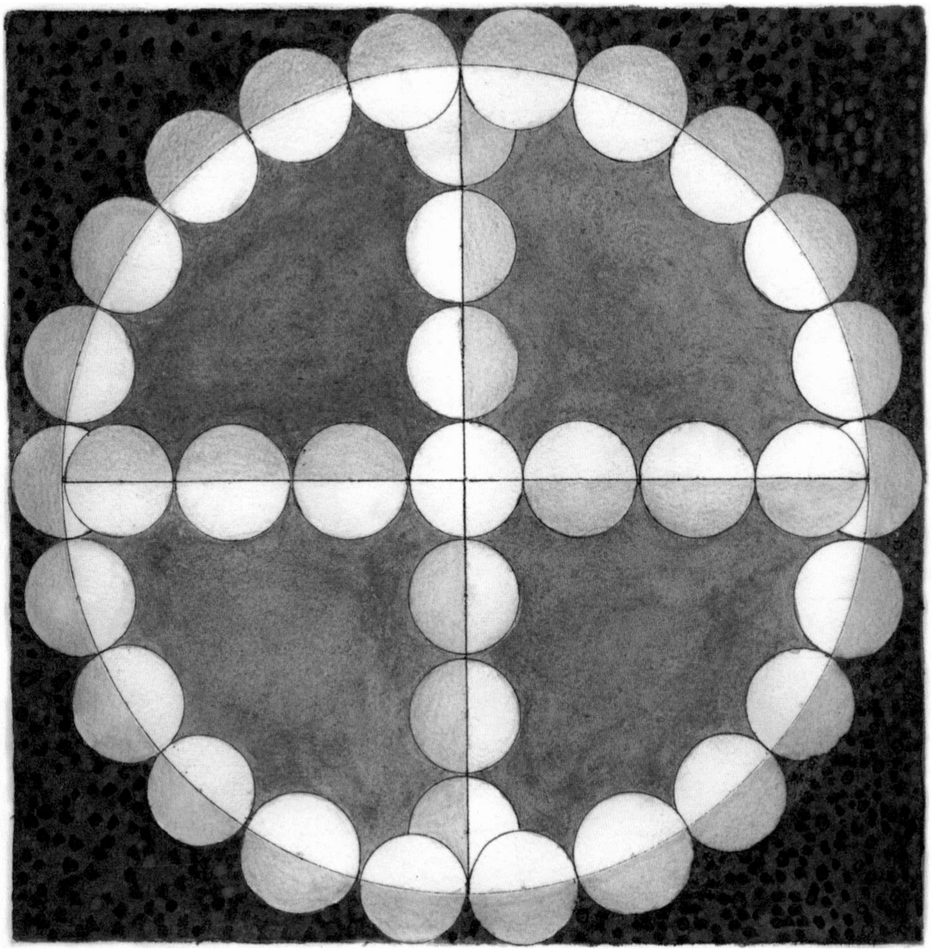

Fig. 33. As far as the eye can see and the hand can draw, the diameter of a circle is made up of 7 and the circumference of 22 equal intervals. The difference between this and true π is about 1 part in 2486 or about 2 ft. in a mile.

π *in Practice*

The fact that π is irrational and transcendental is no cause for despair. Perfect π may be unobtainable but it is never needed, because there is no such thing on earth as a perfect circle. The nearest thing we have is the equator, and the most accurate one we see is the disc of the sun. For all practical work π is given a fractional approximation. The Romans were satisfied with 3⅛ or 3.125 because they found the eighth part simpler than the more accurate 3¹⁄₇, but that value, 22/7, is commonly used today as it was in ancient times. Also of prehistoric origins is the slightly more accurate π of 864/275 or 3.14181818. This was the version adopted by Fibonacci (Leonardo of Pisa) in the thirteenth century. Earlier, in fifth-century China, learned astronomers recorded the most accurate small-number value for π, 355/113 or 3.14159292 . . . which is correct to several millionth parts of one percent. Who could ask for anything more? Only those literalists who wish for a universe that is describable in rational, whole numbers. But according to our myth, what we have is merely the best possible universe, a material copy of the transcendental reality in which alone can be found pure reason or pure anything.

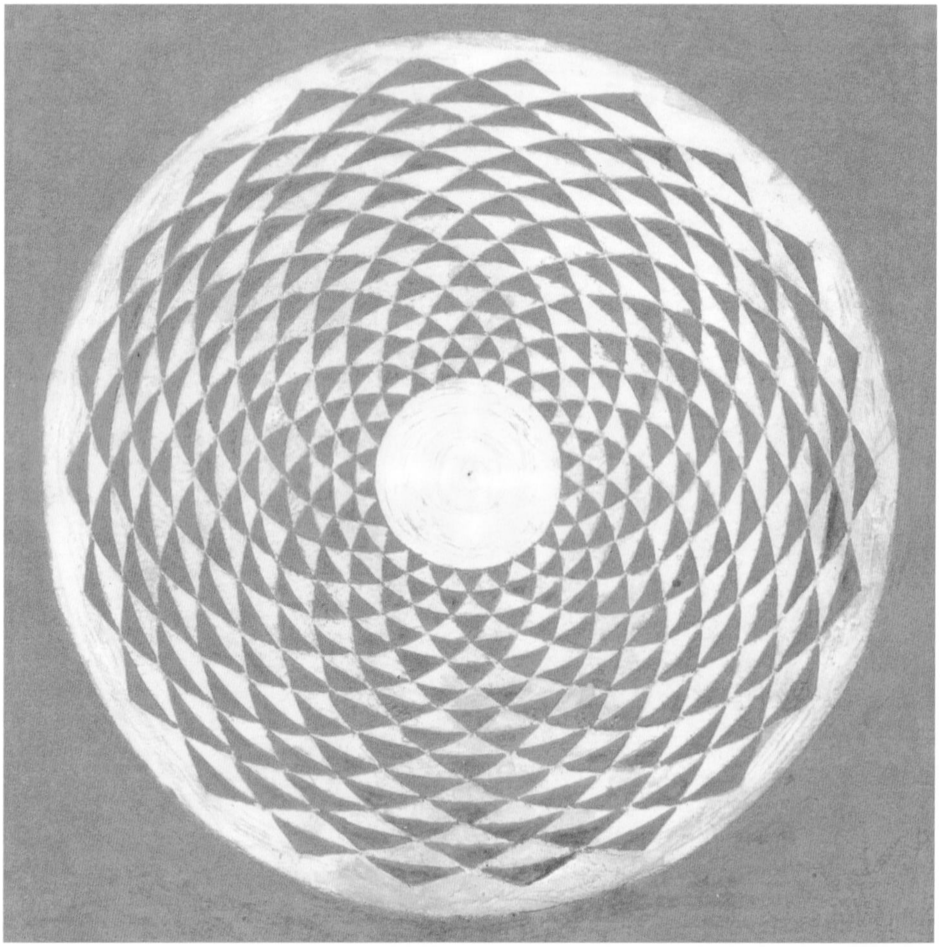

Fig. 34. The pi fraction, 22/7, is neatly expressed in this crop circle, 250 ft. wide, at Woodborough Hill, Wiltshire, in 2000. The circumference is divided by 44 points, and the 308 triangles form 14 concentric rings (44/14 = 22/7).

A curious piece of research that caught the interest of Einstein, because it involves a spontaneous appearance of π in nature, was carried out by Hans-Hendrik Stølum, professor of earth sciences at Cambridge. He measured the lengths of the earth's longer rivers, first in a straight line from their sources to their mouths and then, laboriously, along the course of their meanderings, and found that the ratio of the first length to the second tends to be 1 to 3.14, an approximation to π. Marc-Alain Ouaknin, who reports on this in *The Mystery of Number,* suggests that this recurring deviation of rivers from the straight course represents the ratio between order and entropy or chaos. Or perhaps, since everything that moves in nature tends to perform circles, rivers too have that 'desire', and though their destiny is to enter the ocean, they would rather proceed by the circular route than straight along the diameter. By such pleasant thoughts we are seduced away from the aridity of scientific literalism into the glories of animistic imagination.

π *in the Pyramid*

Histories of Western science generally take an evolutionary line. They begin with the Greek philosophers from about 500 BC, describing their attempts to define π and thereby square the circle, and tracing the rise of knowledge through medieval superstition to the present state of enlightenment.

That is one way of looking at things; but the trouble with it is that, long before any Western civilization, there is evidence of a superior, universal science which has left its mark in the monuments of later times. Well-known examples are the Egyptian pyramids, Stonehenge, and the ritual complexes of Mexico and the East. The purpose they served is no longer recognized because it was a form of state magic. It was based on the recognition of spirit and the process of rebirth, and all its institutions were governed by a code of universal law, a canon of harmonies expressed musically and through number. This knowledge, by all traditional accounts, originated in divine revelation. From time to time, in different parts of the world, the gods appear, show us the laws of nature that we should live by, and then depart, leaving with us the code of science upon which successive civilizations have been founded, everywhere.

The Great Pyramid of Egypt seems to have had many functions in connection with the ancient mystical sciences. Now it is in a state of ruin, but it still maintains one of its original purposes, to provide a record for posterity. It states in monumental form the numerical, harmonic standards that were at the foundation of Egyptian culture. Many codes and formulas are woven into its proportions and measures. The first of these, blatantly displayed in the height and girth of the Pyramid, is the 22/7 value for π.

The original height of the Great Pyramid is 280 Egyptian cubits of 1.7181818 ft., and the measured length of its base is 440 cubits. In units of feet that is:

height = 481.09091; side of base = 756; perimeter of base = 3024 ft.

If the height is taken as the radius of a circle, the circumference of that circle is equal to the measure round the four sides of the pyramid.

height, $481.09091 \times 44/7 = 3024$ ft. = perimeter

The wealth of numerical and scientific knowledge encoded in the structure of the pyramid is considered anachronistic. It is so far beyond the supposed capacity of its age that respectable scholars shy away from studying it. Others have hailed it as an alien artefact, the work of gods or space-beings. These reactions have a common source, ignorance of the ancient science. The pyramid retains many mysteries, most obviously in its construction; its standards of craft and engineering are inexplicable to modern experts. As a monumental record, however, it is a true product of its age, a summary of the esoteric code of numbers and proportions that, according to Plato in the *Laws,* maintained the high civilization of Egypt unchanged "for at least ten thousand years". That sounds like a science worthy of the name.

The ancient monument-builders of Egypt and elsewhere were obviously

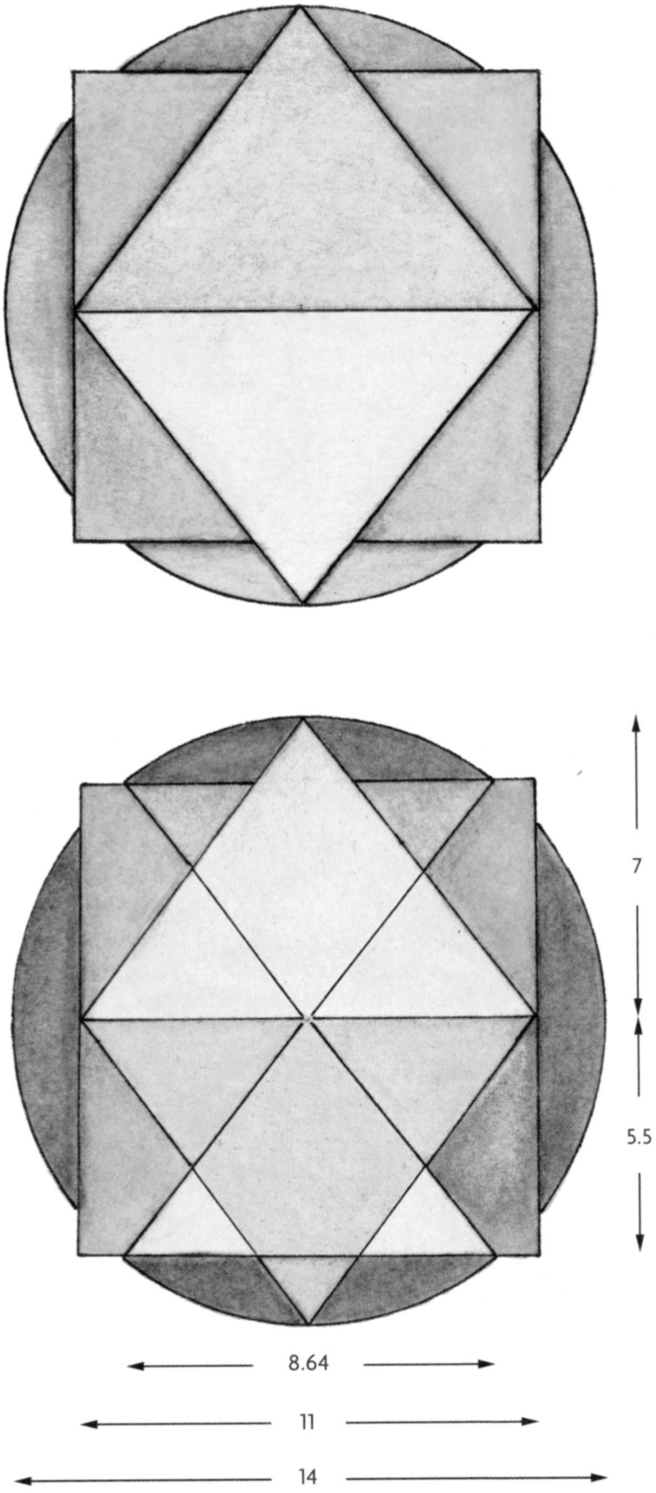

Figs. 35 and **36.** The Great Pyramid with 7:11 ratio between its height and baseline is a product of the squared circle.

familiar with the mathematical constants such as π and Φ and in their units of measurement is clear proof that they had precise knowledge of the earth's dimensions. In that they were far ahead of the eighteenth-century French scientists whose inaccurate measuring of the meridian led to a metre that is sadly deficient by ancient standards. The question that haunts this subject is this: how is it that the high science of antiquity became so neglected and forgotten that, in the early days of Western science, learned men were groping for the value of π and had no apparent knowledge of the ancient scientific tradition?

The probable answer is that, after the collapse of the old order, followed by the rule of tyrants, the old tradition went underground and was imparted only in

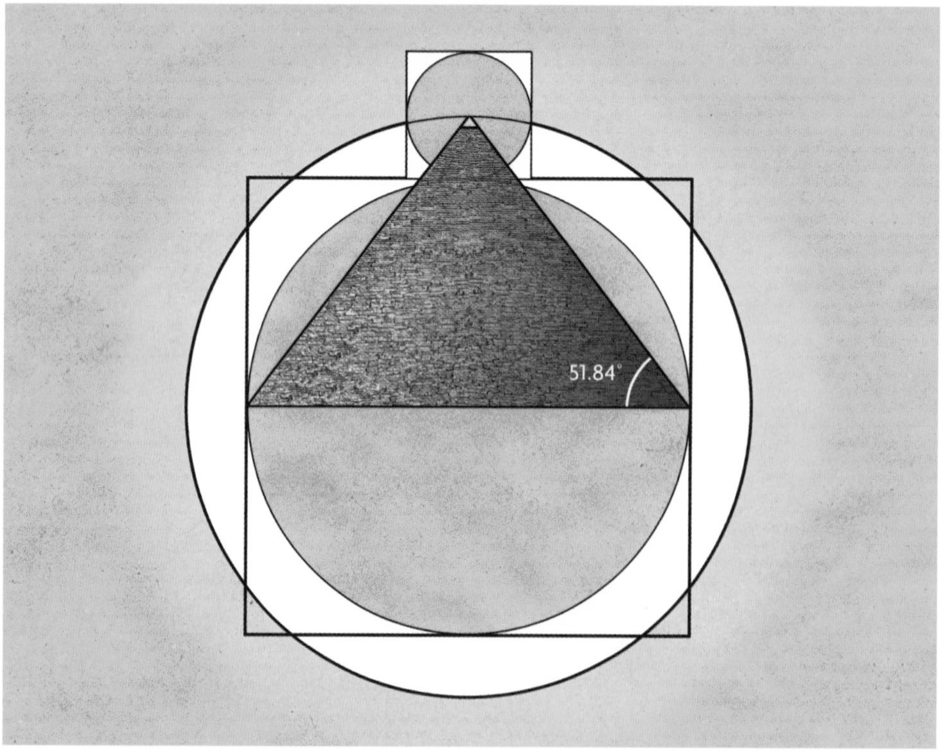

Fig. 37. The elevation of the Great Pyramid produced by the squared circle. Its height forms the radius of the outer circle, and its base is the width of the square with perimeter equal to the circle's circumference. In the pyramid the base measures 756 ft., so the perimeter of both square and circle is 3024 ft. These dimensions are 21 : 22 with those of the cosmological diagram in which the perimeters of both square and circle are 3168 and the base of the triangle is 792. This 21 : 22 ratio between two circles is illustrated again in fig. 39.

private, through ritual initiation. Many religions preserved the esoteric learning they had inherited. Plato in his academy taught it to chosen youths under an oath of secrecy; and it was present in early Christianity through the Gnostics. These masters of the old science were suppressed by the Church, as also were all successive schools of mystical revivalists and 'heretics'. As a result, Christianity lost touch with the ancient tradition and deprived itself of the mystical science and theology that inspired all previous religions. All Western religions today share that ignorance. Originally founded on truth, reason, and the ancient scientific tradition, they have lapsed into corruption and dogmatic superstitions. There are many good souls, even initiated ones, in Jewry, Christianity, and the Muslim faith, but their voices are barely heard amid the clamour of ignorant fanatics.

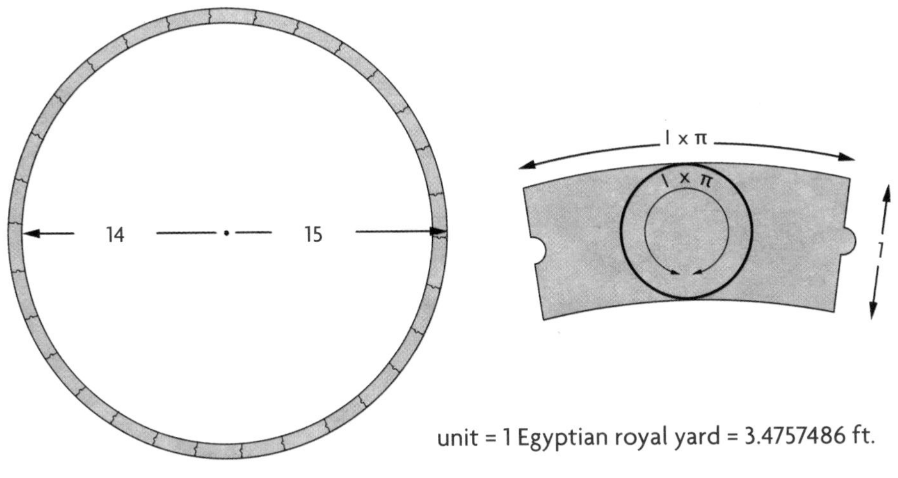

Fig. 38. A visual image of π is in the lintel stones of the Stonehenge sarsen circle. There were 30 of them in a ring, held together by tongue-and-groove joints. If the outer rim of a lintel stone were folded inwards to form a circle, the circle's diameter would be equal to the width of the stone. So its width relates to its outer rim as 1 to π. The width of a lintel stone is a thirtieth part of the outer diameter of the lintel ring.

The unit here is the yard, or 3 feet of the Egyptian royal foot. The length of this unit is 3.4757486, a six-millionth part of the earth's polar radius. There are 14 of these units in the inner radius of the lintel ring and 15 in the outer radius.

π Equals 3? An Antiquarian Fantasy

The evolutionist, rise-of-man historians often claim that the ancients were ignorant and believed the earth is flat and that $\pi = 3$. Any reading of classical authors will dispel the first claim; it has long been recognized that the earth is an 'oblate spheroid'. As to the second, it is obvious nonsense to say that $\pi = 3$, because the six sides of a hexagon inscribed within a circle are three times the circle's diameter and the circumference is clearly longer. Archimedes in the second century BC tried to discover π by doubling and redoubling the sides of the inscribed hexagon until it approached a true circle, and at the same time he circumscribed similar polygons around the circle. The average between them, he reckoned, would give him something like π. It gave him 3.141851, slightly better than 22/7.

Those who like to think that the ancients believed $\pi = 3$ point to sacred texts, including the Bible, where this seems to be stated. In I Kings 7:23 is described the great bowl or "molten sea" that Hiram of Tyre, King Solomon's architect, constructed at the Temple of Jerusalem in the ninth century BC.

> He made a molten sea, ten cubits from the one brim to the other: and a line of thirty cubits did compass it round about.

With the diameter 10 cubits and the circumference 30, the great architect must surely have thought that $\pi = 3$. But this reckons without the brim of the bowl which was a handsbreadth wide. The molten sea had two sets of dimensions, inner and outer, so two different cubits are involved, relating to each other as 21:22. Thus if cubit **A** is 22, cubit **B** is 21 units.

Ten cubits **A** or 220 units measure the outer diameter of the bowl and 10 cubits **B** or 210 units the inner. Three times the outer diameter is 660 units, and 660 divided by 22/7 is 210 or 10 cubits **B**. Half the difference between the two cubits, 5 units, is the width of the rim.

If cubit **A** is 1.5 ft., the width of the rim is about 4.1 inches, the approximate handbreadth of a 6 ft. man.

By this account, Hiram designed the molten sea so that its inner circumference was 3 times its overall diameter. The π he used was 22/7.

Inner diameter = 10 × cubit **B**

Outer diameter = 10 × cubit **A**

Inner circumference = 30 × cubit **A** = 22/7 × cubit **B**

Outer circumference = 22/7 × cubit **A**

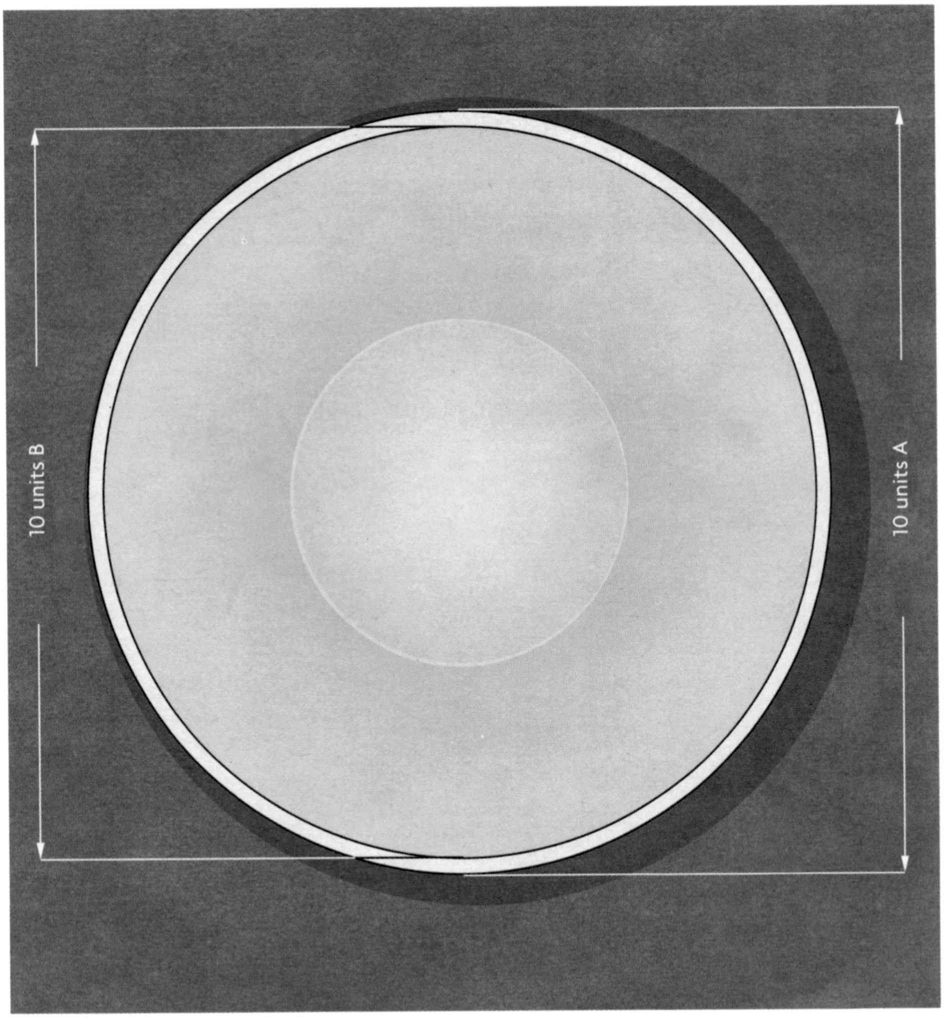

Fig. 39. Hiram of Tyre's great bowl, or "molten sea".

The π Patterns

Numbers have their own kind of beauty but, as in the notes of music, it is not easily apparent when they are written down in symbols. That is certainly the case with π. As an endless chain of meaningless figures it is an irrational monster. But when rationalized as 22/7, the beauty of π is made visible in the patterns created by the $4/\pi$ or 14 : 11 ratio between the circle and the square. Shown opposite are the four principal relationships between these two basic shapes.

a. A circle containing a square. The area of the square is 14, of the circle 22. The sum of these two areas is 36, allowing them to be displayed together in a two-toned square 6×6.
b. A square and circle with equal perimeters. The area of the square is 11, of the circle 14. These areas together ($11 + 14 = 25$) are shown in a square 5×5.
c. A circle within a square. If the area of the square is 14, that of the circle is 11. This is the reverse of b, so the same 5×5 square illustrates both, with tones reversed.
d. A square and a circle with equal areas, both taken as 11. Together they do not add up to a square number, so the relationship of their areas can not be illustrated like the others.

This last combination, of equal square and circle, is somewhat neglected by modern geometers, but it was well known to the ancients, whose exercises in circle-squaring concentrated more upon this type of union than on the square and circle with equal perimeters. There are various known approximations to squaring the circle in terms of equal areas, but none of them is very accurate. The method shown in figure 41 (see page 48) gives the best result by far. It is laborious in practise, but it brings the square and circle with equal areas into scale with the other combinations.

The key to this construction is that the square of area 11 has a side of $\sqrt{11}$,

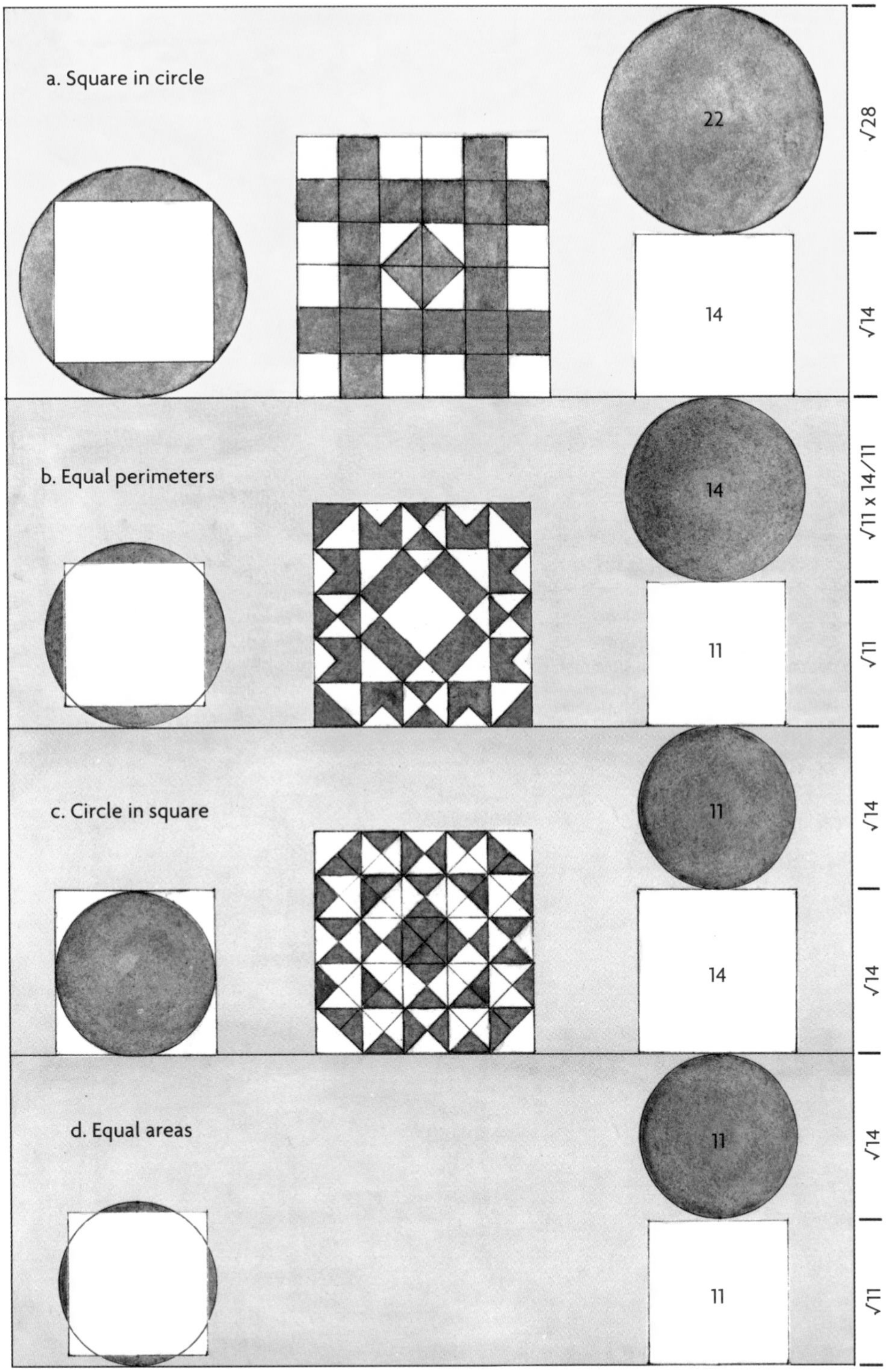

Fig. 40. The four types of square-circle relationships, drawn on the same scale

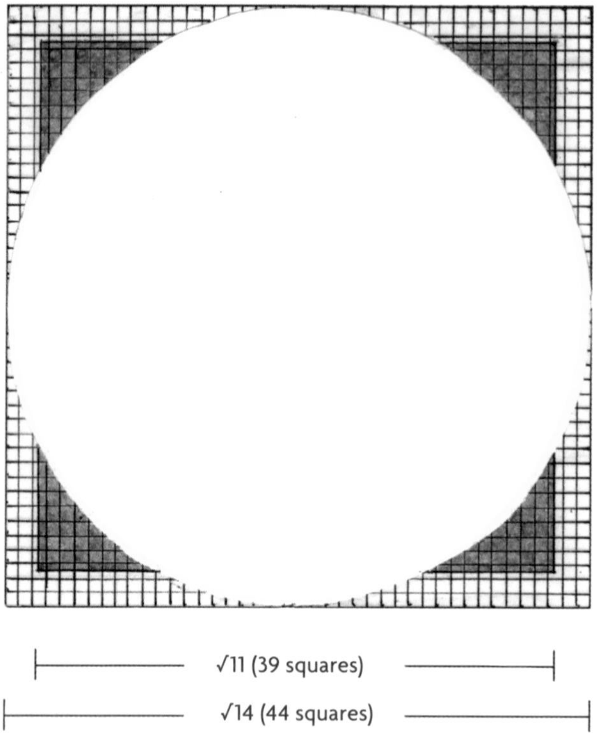

Fig. 41. Square and circle with equal areas. The ratio between the side of a square and the diameter of a circle equal to it in area is √11 to √14, very close to 39 to 44. In the measure round their perimeters the ratio is reversed, the distance around the four sides of the square being longer by 44 to 39 than the circumference of the circle. In this construction the square of 44 x 44 divisions contains the circle. The blue square 39 x 39 has the same area as the circle. This figure is repeated opposite in the synthesis of square-circle relationships.

and the diameter of a circle of area 11 is √14. The ratio between √11 and √14 is virtually 39 to 44. So, to draw a circle and square with equal areas, make a square with its side divided into 11 parts (by the construction in figure 26 on page 31) and divide each part into quarters, making a length of 44. Deduct 2½ parts from each end, obtaining a square of 39. A square of side 39 and a circle of diameter 44 have equal areas to an accuracy of about 1 in 3000—rather better than 22/7 as π.

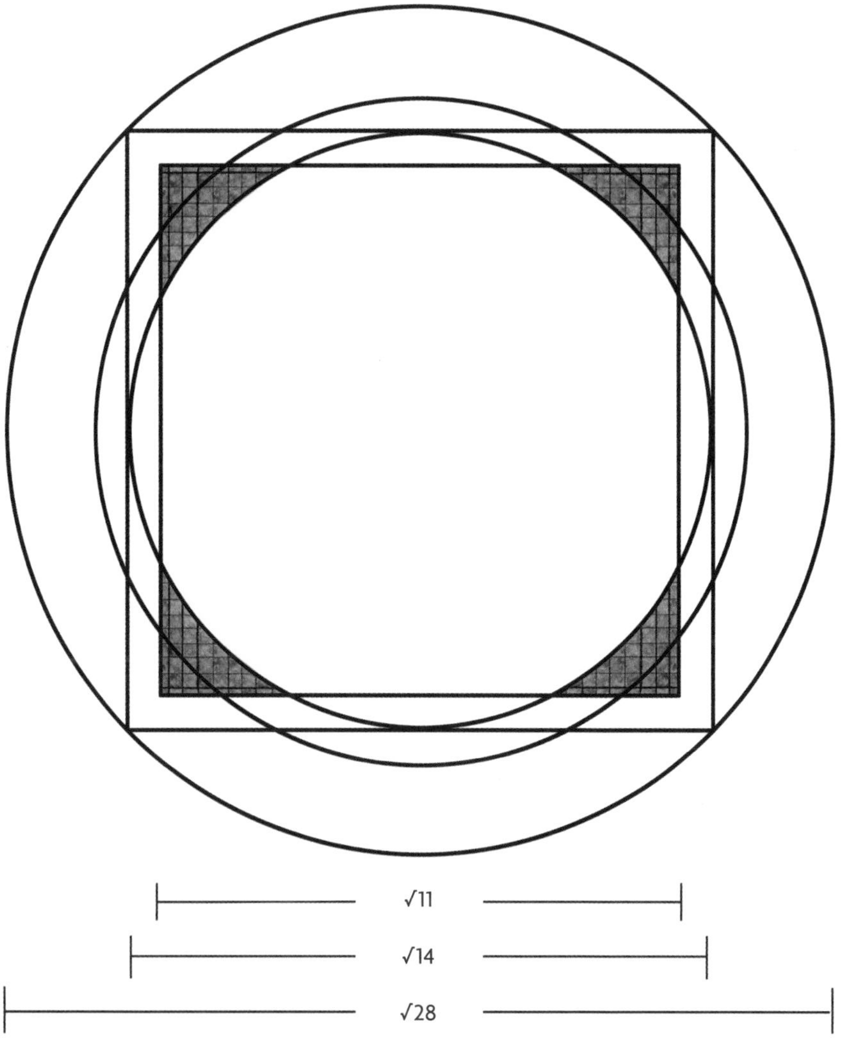

Fig. 42. The four types of square-circle combinations, drawn to the same scale, are assembled within one diagram. The areas of the five concentric shapes that comprise it are, starting at the outside, circles: 22, 14, 11, and squares: 14 and 11.

In this synthesis can be found: circle containing square; square containing circle; square and circle with equal perimeters; square and circle with equal areas (twice).

Finally in figure 42, the four types of square-circle relationships are brought together in one simple figure, using just two squares and three circles.

Fig. 43. The squared circle with equal areas. In Michael Maier's *Atalanta Fugiens,* a book of alchemical engravings by Johann de Bry, published in 1618, is this puzzle-picture of a geometer constructing a figure through a combination of square, circle, and triangle. He has only got so far in his work and two main components in the scheme are still undone. They are added here in red. When the figure is complete it shows that the geometer's purpose is to square the circle by constructing a square and circle with equal areas.

The geometer begins by drawing the small circle containing a man and woman and enclosing it in a square. He then places the point of his compass on each of the two bottom corners of the square in turn and swings arcs, with radius equal to the square's diagonal, to cut the extended base line of the square. This gives him the base line for his triangle, which is drawn through the upper corners of the square. Then, with the point of his compass placed halfway along the square's upper side, he draws two circles. In de Bry's picture he is just completing the first circle, drawn through the base corners of the triangle. The second circle (red) is drawn through the apex of the triangle. Finally the geometer draws a square to enclose the second circle. The area of this circle is supposed to be the same as the area of the outer circle square, but actually it is smaller than the square by about 1 percent.

The pi pattern appears in two different squares 5 x 5 and 6 x 6. The 5 x 5 grid here contains 14 dark and 11 light areas, showing the 14 : 11 ratio between a square and the circle it contains, or it has 11 dark and 14 light, corresponding to the 11 : 14 ratio between the areas of the square and circle in the squared-circle diagram.

Fig. 44 (above). Pi pattern of four 5 x 5 squares

Fig. 45. 11 to 14 pi pattern depicting the pi symbol

Fig. 46. Six 5 x 5 squares showing the 11:14 ratio between dark and light areas

Fig. 47. Six types of 5 x 5 squares, each with 11 red and 14 yellow areas

Fig. 48. The 6 x 6 square set out on the right is divided mostly into half-squares, the ratio between its blue and white areas being 14 to 22. Twenty-five of these squares produce this beautifully woven and bordered pattern.

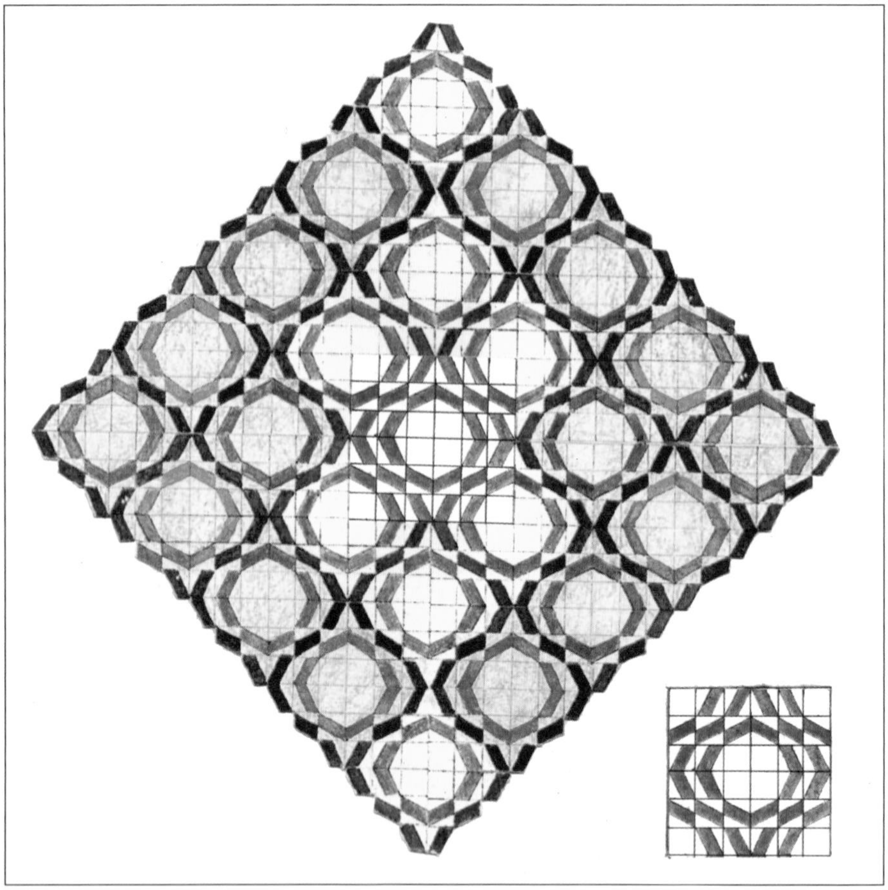

Fig. 49. Eight 6 x 6 squares make this pi-pattern pavement.

Fig. 50. An octagonal form of the pi pattern is made of nine 6 x 6 squares, each containing 14 dark and 22 light brown squares.

Fig. 51. The pi symbol in a square 6 x 6 with 14 red and 22 yellow squares

Fig. 52. The 6 x 6 square pi pattern is here subdivided to be 12 x 12, containing 88 light squares and 56 dark. Four of these 12 x 12 squares are set together above.

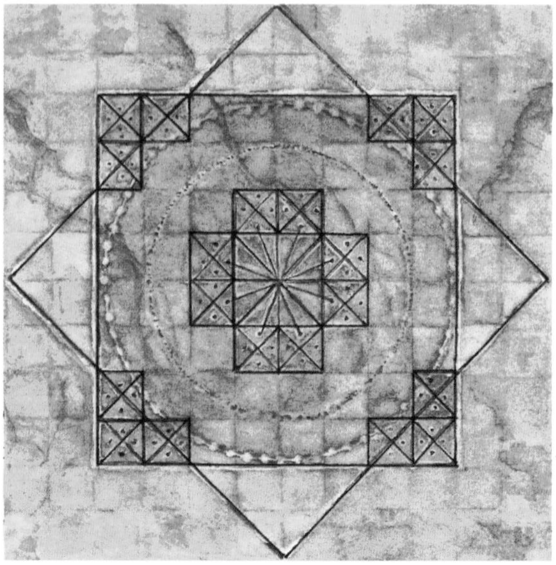

Fig. 53. The same type of octagon discovered from the air in the ancient Peruvian landscape (see also fig. 130).

Cosmological Revelations in Crop Circles

The initiate's path is said to be lighted up by revelations. These range from flashes or moments of insight to the ultimate vision of the heavenly order, as experienced by St John. The ancients attributed these inspirations to a god, Thoth, Hermes, Mercurius, the communicator of divine intelligence and sometimes a deceiver, as subtle and elusive as his corresponding metal, quicksilver. C. G. Jung in his last, most prophetic book, on the UFO phenomenon, published in 1959, interpreted the signs and wonders reported in the skies as portents of world-changing revelations to come. These, as he well knew, would not come through official channels or by human decision, but through strange irrationalities that the modern mind disdains and ignores—mercurial effects such as miracles, apparitions, encounters with 'aliens', spontaneous initiations, and the revelations in crop circles.

Some of the watercolours in this book were copied from designs that have appeared mysteriously, overnight, as large-scale impressions on fields of wheat and other crops, remaining there, open for inspection, until the harvest. In Wiltshire and the counties of southern England, where the phenomenon has been most active, crop circles came to public attention around 1990. From the beginning they attracted pranksters and hoaxers, and no one to this day (in 2008) can say to what extent these enthusiasts amplified the evidence, by copying the designs or inventing their own. Every summer new designs occur, sometimes with references to the traditional code of number and geometry that we are here following. Behind the glamour and trickery in the crop circle enigma is a serious, subtle mind and, evidently, a serious, high-level purpose.

The alchemical writer Patrick Harpur sees in crop circles the signature of Mercurius, joker and initiator. His mysteries are not riddles to be solved but are exhibited to delight and stimulate the mind. Those who have followed the crop circle mystery have been led on to interest in other subjects and to heightened appreciation of existence. If crop circles have a purpose, it must be evident in their actual effect. That imputes them benevolence and a source which, if you reject gods and space-beings, can be called the Good, το αγαθον, whose number is 504.

Fig. 54. This pi pattern, one of the many possible versions, consists of 36 squares, each 6 x 6, making 1296 squares of which 504 are dark and 792 light coloured (ratio 7 : 11). The same pattern can be transferred onto a circular grid, still displaying the same canonical numbers, 504, 792, and their sum, 1296.

The Revelation at Crooked Soley

A full account of the amazing crop circle that occurred in a Wiltshire wheat field in 2002 can be found in a small publication, *Crooked Soley, a Crop Circle Revelation,* by Allan Brown and John Michell. The purpose of writing it was to record an otherwise disregarded event, the brief appearance of a design in which the key numbers of traditional cosmology were woven into the form of a DNA strip. Within a wide ring of selectively laid-down wheat stalks, the area was divided by 72 arcs into 1296 little sections, in 792 of which the crop was laid to the ground, while 504 clumps of wheat were left standing (figure 55). This is a version of the pi pattern, for 792 to 504 is 7 : 11.

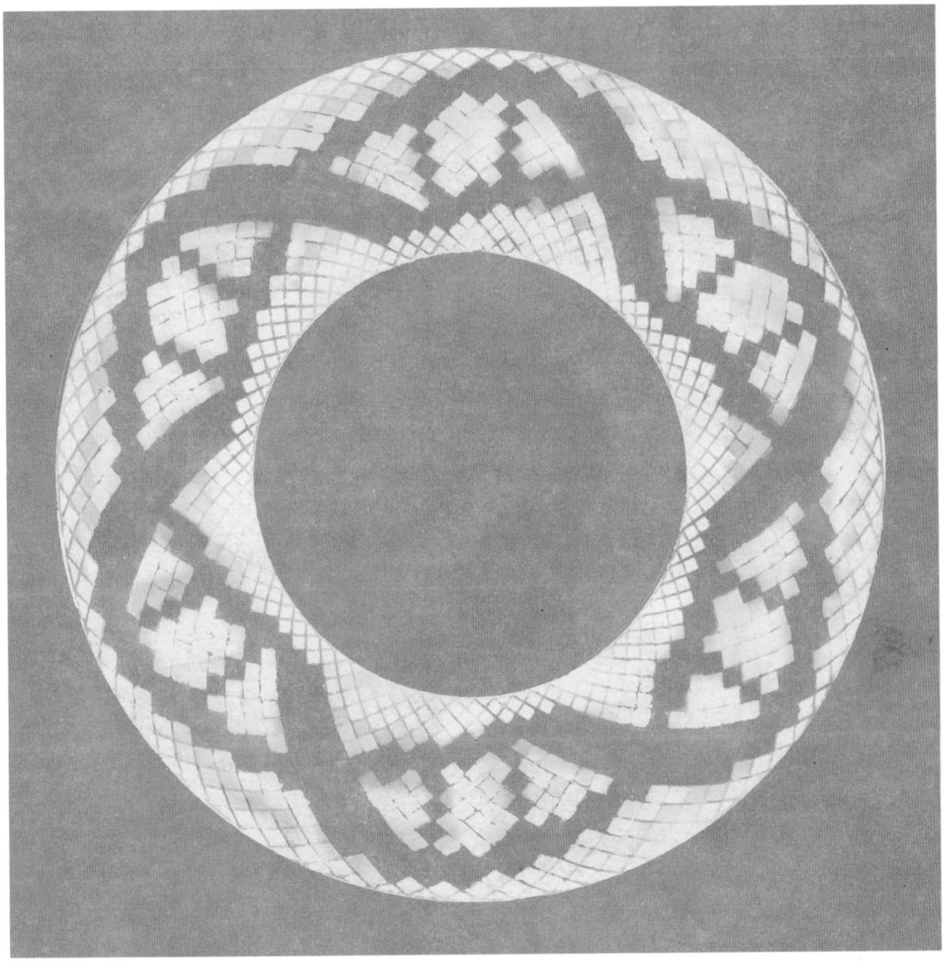

Fig. 55. The Crooked Soley crop circle. The extraordinary design of a DNA strand weaves together the primary canonical numbers, 504 and 792, in 1296 areas of standing and laid-down wheat. In this drawing the standing 'squares' of wheat are shown in orange, the laid-down areas in light yellow.

The wheat field was at a rustic hamlet, Crooked Soley near Hungerford, Berks. It was harvested the same day that the circle was reported. No one inspected the design on the ground, and the only records of it are Steve Alexander's photographs, taken from the air on the morning of its appearance. No one claims to have made it or even to know how it could have been done. And beyond the technical mystery is the even greater one, the mystery of the mind and purpose behind this significant design.

The numbers displayed at Crooked Soley, 504, 792, and their sum, 1296, or $6 \times 6 \times 6 \times 6$, are the principal components in the canon of number and the cosmological diagram upon which this book is structured. They are prominent on different scales throughout number and the numerical sciences, not for any human reasons but simply through the law of number. As 5040 and 7920 they measure the squared circle formed by moon and earth, providing the framework for the geometer's story of creation.

There is no need to look for any coded message in the beautiful design. Clearly and openly it draws attention to that long-lost standard of cosmology which, whenever it reappears, brings light and comfort to those who receive it.

The principal symbolic numbers, 72, 504, 792, 1296, expressed in the Crooked Soley design, are ten times smaller than the familiar 720, 5040, etc., in the cosmological diagram. These decimal changes of scale give the numbers different mathematical properties, but their symbolism is the same in every dimension. When scale demands it, as at Crooked Soley where a design incorporating 5040 and 7920 would be an impractical monstrosity, 504 and 792 have to stand in. It is the same at Stonehenge where the mean radius of the sarsen circle with lintels measures 50.4 feet. And in gematria, when only a lengthy phrase would contain letters to the value of 5040, its tenth part, 504, occurs instead.

The gematria of 504 is highly distinguished. It is the number of number itself in that η αριθμετικα, arithmetic, is 504. Also expressed by that number are the two principles most valued by the Greek philosophers, goodness and holiness.

504 = το αγαθον, the Good
= το αγιον, the Holy

As shown in the diagrams on page 73, 504 is the radius of a circle with 3168, the number of Lord Jesus Christ, in its circumference.

Another token of its virtue is that 504 unites the first pair of 'amicable numbers', highly regarded in the school of Pythagoras. Amicable numbers are those whose factors add up to each other. The first pair are 220, whose factors add up to 284, and 284 whose factors add up to 220. The sum of this agreeable pair of numbers is 504.

The other prominent numbers at Crooked Soley have striking gematria. 720 gives νους, *nous,* or divine intelligence, and 1296 stands for the feminine principle that rules nature—in both its pagan and Christian forms:

1296 = θεα παντων, Goddess of all
= Μαρια μητηρ Ιησου, Mary, mother of Jesus

4 • Initiation

And the Vision of the Heavenly Order

Geometry has many practical uses, in land surveying (*geometry* means literally "earth measuring"), architecture, engineering, military science, and everyday matters such as laying a carpet or parking a car. Its proper use, however, is for cosmological purposes, for investigating nature and bringing to light the wonderful range of patterns and types within the fabric of the Creator's universe. The study of number has a similar object. The ancient Greeks and all philosophers in the old tradition emphasized the importance of number, not for commercial or secular advantage but because numerical studies, philosophically directed, lead the mind into a world of abstract order and towards a state of understanding that the Greeks called *nous,* meaning 'divine intelligence'.

In the days of the old Mystery schools *nous* was achieved through a process of ritual initiation by those who had been educated and made ready for it. Their preparation included long, disciplined studies in number, music, and geometry along with astronomy, navigation, surveying, philosophy, philology, and the other canonical arts and sciences. There was little writing in those schools; instruction was verbal and practical, much of it imparted through chants, verses, and rhythmic recitations that lodged it forever in youthful memories.

Geometry and number were the main instruments by which candidates for initiation were led up towards the climactic ordeal when the Mysteries were unveiled before them. Initiation is a spiritual rebirth, an entry into a new world, illuminated by *nous.* It is the same old world but seen with new eyes and recognized for what it really is, a divine paradise. That perception has been gained by many people, spontaneously. But the old initiates were made ready for it, and when they experienced the vision of true reality, they saw in all its glory the pattern of universal order that was familiar to them through their studies. "There is a pattern in the heavens", said Socrates (*Republic* 592), "where those who want to can see it and establish it in their own hearts."

Fig. 56. Entrance to Plato's Academy in Athens, fourth century BC, a fanciful view featuring his imaginary cat, Nous. Nailed to the door is his recorded notice, "No one who is ignorant of geometry may enter".

An Initiate's Vision: St John and the Heavenly Jerusalem

"And I saw a new heaven and a new earth". Thus begins St John's account of his initiatory vision in the twenty-first chapter of Revelation. This book, the last in the Christian Bible, is rooted in the Mysteries. Many of its scenes and images relate to the ordeal of death and rebirth during the initiation process. Mystics and imaginative people have always been attracted to the dramas and enigmas of St John's book, but modern theologians tend to avoid it on the grounds that it is beyond rational understanding.

As an initiate of the Mystery schools that flourished in the early days of Christianity, St John was a profound scholar in the Gnostic tradition, well versed in the language of apocalyptic. It is a language of symbols and allegories, used in the historical and prophetic writings of all ancient religions. Two images, paired together, are recurrent in sacred histories. They illustrate a constant theme, the process of rise and fall, death and rebirth, that occurs on all levels of nature and is represented in the apocalyptic language by two cities. In Revelation these cities are called Babylon the Great and the New Jerusalem. The first is a grand, imperial, mercantile city, grown rich and decadent and ripe for its fall. This duly takes place and is vividly described in Revelation 18. As Babylon meets its doom and is destroyed amidst fire and tempest, the rich men and the whores weep and wail while the righteous rejoice. Then comes the centrepiece of St John's vision. An angel leads him up to a high mountain, meaning in the esoteric language a state of high vision, and shows him the 'heavenly pattern', the perfect order of creation. Following tradition, St John pictured it as an ideal city, the New Jerusalem.

It was a glorious city, radiant with golden light, glowing and sparkling like a jasper stone and with twelve facets. The wall of the city was studded with twelve different gemstones and it had twelve gates, three each to north, south, east, and west. The twelve gates were also twelve lustrous pearls, guarded by twelve angels and bearing the names of the twelve tribes of Israel. In the twelve foundations of the wall were the names of the twelve apostles of Jesus. As a cosmological

Fig. 57. The Heavenly City

image the Heavenly City was complete in all its parts, containing the shapes, sounds, colours, movements, and every other element in creation. It was wonderful beyond description, far lovelier than any object of normal, earthly vision. Yet its outward appearance was a reflection of something even more wonderful. From the course of esoteric studies that preceded his initiation, St John was aware of the numerical and geometric structure of creation, and he referred to it in his account of the Heavenly City.

The framework of the New Jerusalem pattern is duodecimal, organized by the number Twelve, with twelve gates, corners, and other features arranged in four groups of three to face the four directions. Twelve is the first numerical symbol of universal order. Its dominant position in the field of number itself is the reason for our twelve-fold divisions of concepts and phenomena, such as the zodiac with its 12 signs or gods, the 12 months of the year, the 12 notes of music, and the 360 degrees in a circle. The duodecimal theme is continued in the dimensions of the Heavenly City. In St John's allegory the angel who had induced his vision gave him a "reed like a rod" and told him to measure the New Jerusalem. The result of his survey is summed up by the basic duodecimal numbers, 12 and 144. The overall shape of the city is a cube, measuring 12 thousand furlongs on each side, and it had a high wall 144 cubits round.

These measures are on completely different scales, implying that the pattern exists on all dimensions from the astronomical to the microcosmic. Twelve thousand furlongs (660 feet = 1 furlong; 8 furlongs = 1 mile) means 7,920,000 ft. or 1500 miles, whereas the measure round the wall is only 144 cubits. The cubit indicated here is the unit of 1.728 ft., associated with ancient Egypt and prominent in the ground plan of the temple at Jerusalem. It is also a duodecimal unit, for 1.728 is a thousandth part of 12^3. The wall of St John's city is therefore five times duodecimal, for its circuit is 144×1.728 or a thousandth part of $12 \times 12 \times 12 \times 12 \times 12$ ft.

Reconciliation between the 248.832 ft. in the measure round the wall and the 7920000 ft. in the side of the cube (a square in plane geometry) is achieved when they are brought to the same scale. That can be done by multiplying the first by a hundred and dividing the second by a thousand, making them 24883.2 and 7920. The reference is then plain, for:

7920 miles = earth's mean diameter
24883.2 miles = earth's meridian circumference

The value for π in this calculation, 864/275 or 3.141818 . . . , is slightly better than the more convenient 22/7. It occurs in the ratios of traditional cosmology and was adopted by Fibonacci in 1220. It can therefore be called the Fibonacci pi. By its use the earth's dimensions are set out in figures of equal accuracy to those quoted today and superior to those obtained by the French scientists who measured the meridian at the end of the eighteenth century. The length they established was deficient, and the metre they derived from it, intended to be a ten-millionth part of a quadrant of the meridian, was too short to be truly geodetic. The ancient, canonical length of the meridian, a tenth part of 12 × 12 × 12 × 12 × 12 miles, is virtually the same as the figure (40,045,000 metres) from recent satellite surveys.

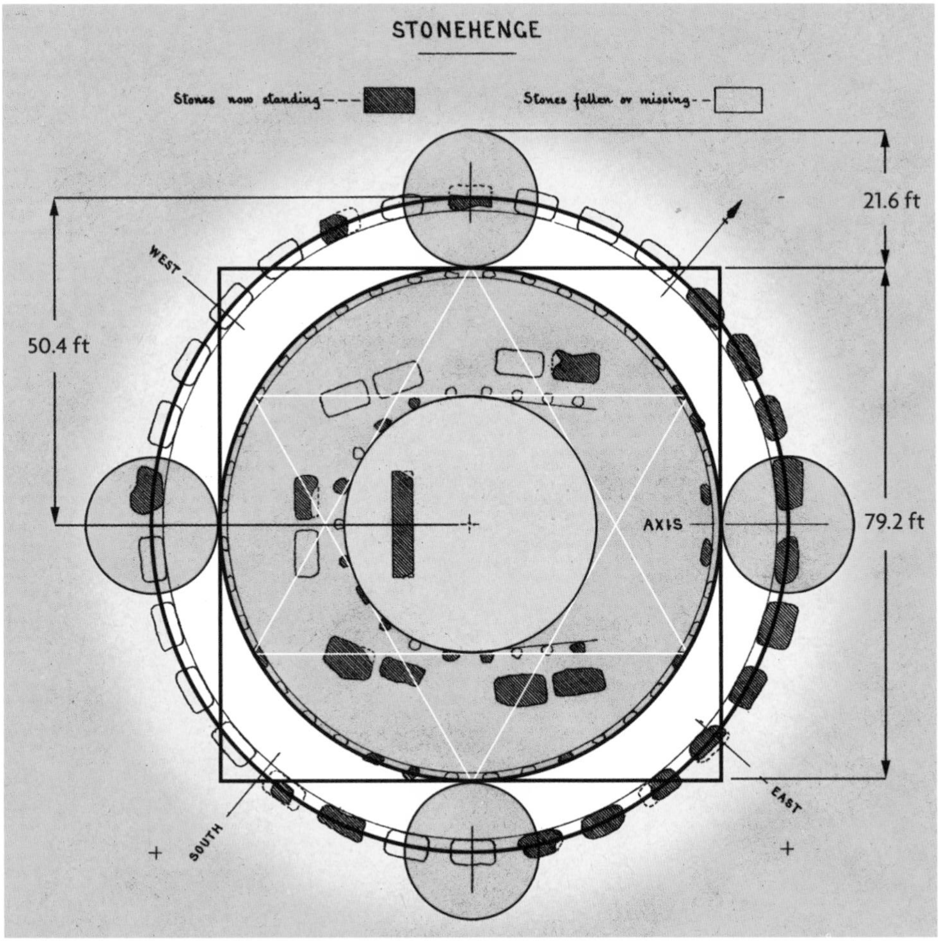

Fig. 58. The basic dimensions of Stonehenge are the same as those of the Heavenly City diagram on a scale of 1 to 100. The mean radius and the circumference round the centre of the outer ring measure 50.4 and 316.8 ft., and 316.8 is also the measure round the square containing the circle of bluestones, making its diameter 79.2 ft.

By these numbers and dimensions the meaning of St John's luminous city is made clear. His vision was of the earth as paradise, a divine creation reflecting the glory of its Creator and as perfect as any reflection or copy of the Ideal can ever be. It was not just a flash of vision, a transient moment of insight, but a lasting perception of the truth that St John and other initiates acquired at their experience of rebirth. They saw "the new heaven and the new earth" and were free to dwell in it. Thereafter they had no fear of death and lived according to their vision in a state of love and understanding.

Both Plato and his master, Socrates, spoke openly about the post-initiation state of *nous* and the perception of paradise on earth. It is, insisted Plato, the real earth behind the dull, murky version that is apparent to our physical senses. Like St John and in the same symbolic language, he speaks of gemstones. In the real world of high vision and imagination, emeralds, rubies, and all natural phenomena have more colour and sparkle than those we normally behold. There is, taught Socrates, a way into that world that anyone can take without undergoing ritual initiation. It is by cultivating belief in truth and justice and living by them. That, of course, is very hard to do. The laborious initiation process could prove to be an easier option.

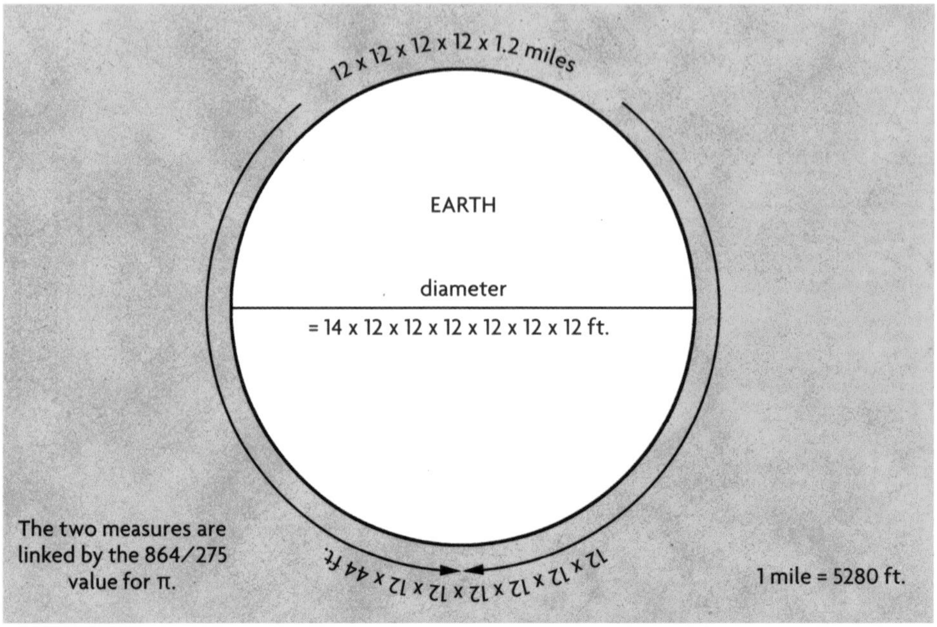

Fig. 59. The duodecimal numbers in the earth's mean diameter and meridian circumference

Heaven on Earth: The Pattern of the Sanctuary

The plan of Magnesia, Plato's ideal community described in the *Laws,* was based on his first principle, that "no state can find happiness unless the artist drawing it uses a divine pattern". The pattern he used was the central feature of the traditional Heavenly City diagram, the circle of earth within a square. The width of both square and circle in the cosmological model is 7920 miles, and in the holy city or sanctuary model 7920 ft.

In both versions of Magnesia—the ideal heavenly circle and the practical, earthly square—the whole area, minus the lands set aside for shrines, roads, and utilities, is divided between the 5040 households, 420 in each of the 12 sections. The areas held by each tribe in the square pattern (figure 61 on page 71) can be measured simply in acres, but in measuring the area of the circular sanctuary a different unit applies. It is defined as the area of a circle with radius 12 ft. This area is a seventh part of 3168 sq. ft. In the traditional sanctuary pattern, the circle 24 ft. in diameter is the ground plan of the central, circular shrine, enclosing the symbolic world pole. Its floor area provides the unit by which the whole scheme is measured. In *The Dimensions of Paradise,* chapter 4 (where the subject is more fully explored), it is called the NJ unit.

In figure 60 (page 70) the circular area, minus the strips of common land, is similarly distributed between the 5040 households, 420 to each tribe. Plato gives many other details of the land divisions, bringing out further numerical subtleties in the scheme. No doubt he used it in his academy to develop the minds of his pupils, which, he said, is best done through the study of number. The first exercise would have been: calculate the amount of land allotted to each of the 5040 households in both the square and the circular pattern. Expressed in the NJ unit of 3168/7 sq. ft., the answers are:

	Circular plan (fig. 60)	Square plan (fig. 61)
in the smaller sections	17.28 = 12 x 12 x .12 units	22 units
in the larger sections	21.60 = 6 x 6 x .6 units	27.5 units

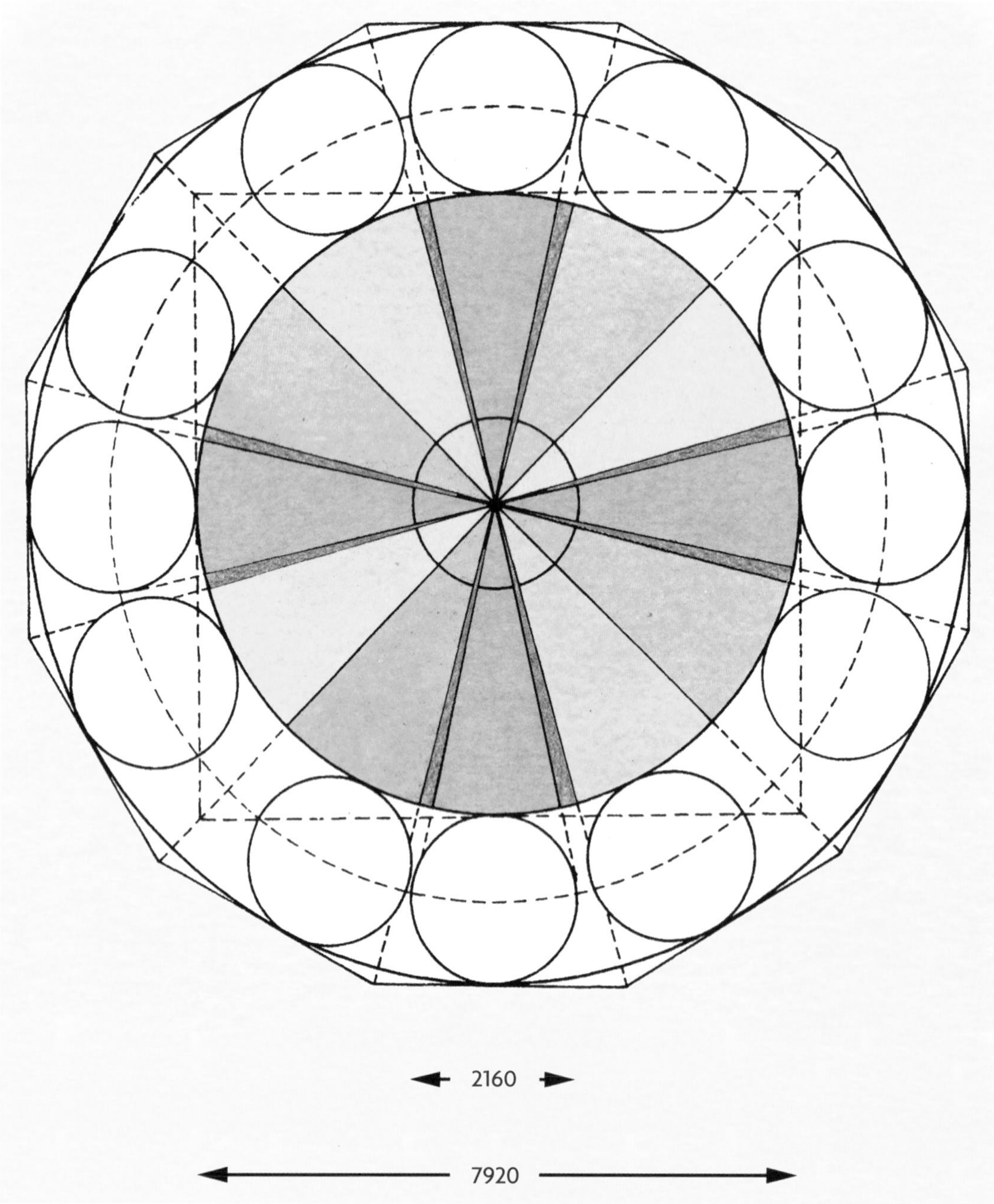

Fig. 60. The sanctified earth at the centre of the Heavenly City diagram is divided between the 12 tribes separated by 8 strips of common land. Plato's elaborate arithmetic allows four holdings to each family, two in the city (inner ring) and two in the country beyond, everyone having their fair share. This is the ideal pattern, made practical in the square version opposite.

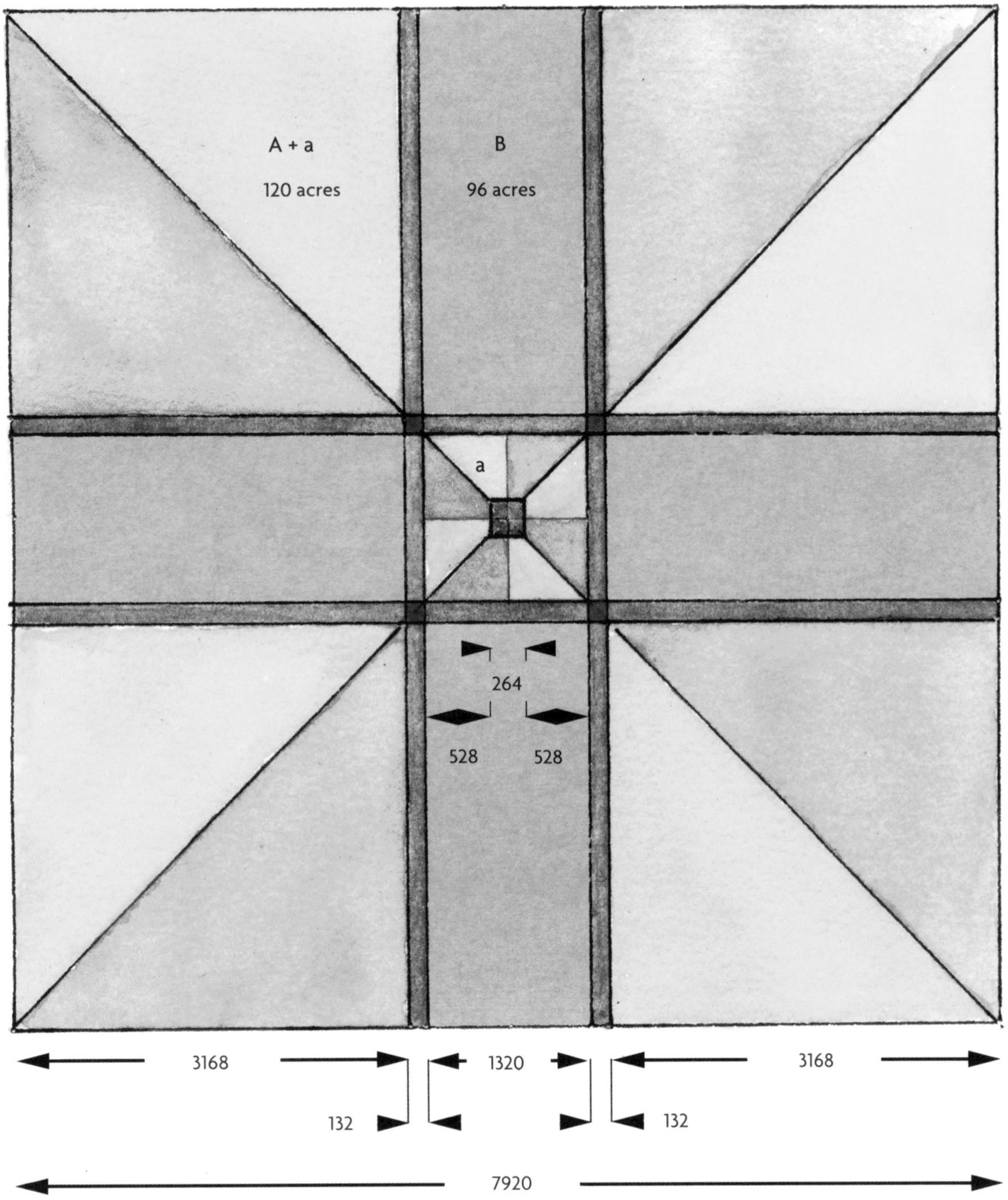

Fig. 61. The square, practical form of the traditional cosmological pattern, is measured rationally in acres (1 acre = 66 x 660 ft.). The strips of common land (blue) are deducted from the green sections.

The Numbers of the Holy City and Their Meanings

Every dimension in the cosmological diagram or holy city has its canonical number, and these all have certain meanings. By the mystical techniques of 'gematria' numbers can be expressed by letters of the alphabet and interpreted by names and phrases made up of those letters. The Hebrew and Arabic alphabets are adapted to this practise, and so is the Greek of the New Testament. The early Christian initiates, the Gnostics, followed tradition in composing the holy names of the new religion in accordance with numbers. Correspondences between Greek letters and numbers are set out below.

The number of any name, word, or phrase is obtained by adding together the numbers of the letters comprising it. Thus Jesus, written Ιησους in the New Testament, is Ι (10) + η (8) + σ (200) + ο (70) + υ (400) + s (200) = 888, and Mithras, Μειθρας, the solar deity known as lord of the 365 days in a year, has the appropriate number, for Μειθρας is 40 + 5 + 10 + 9 + 100 + 1 + 200 = 365. The same number is discovered also in the name of Abraxas, Αβραξας, 365. These examples were quoted by St Irenaeus, the heresy-hunting Bishop of Lyons in the second century. He was a leader of the campaign by the Church to extirpate Gnosticism on the grounds of its mystical outlook and its perpetuation of the pagan sciences such as gematria. St John, on the other hand, was a thorough Gnostic. His use of numbers as letters is demonstrated in Revelation 13, where he gives "the number of the beast" as Χξs or 600 + 60 + 6 = 666.

Greek Alphabet and numbers

Αα 1	Ββ 2	Γγ 3	Δδ 4	Εε 5	Ζζ 7	Ηη 8	Θθ 9
Ιι 10	Κκ 20	Λλ 30	Μμ 40	Νν 50	Ξξ 60	Οο 70	Ππ 80
Ρρ 100	Σσ,ς 200	Ττ 300	Υυ 400	Φφ 500	Χχ 600	Ψψ 700	Ωω 800

3168, the Number of Our Lord Jesus Christ

One of the reasons why the Gnostic scholars and mystical theologians who founded the Christian religion were so cruelly persecuted by the authorities of the early Church was because of names. Jesus is not a Jewish name; the historical Saviour was called something like Joshua. The name Ιησους was adopted so as to bring out the number 888, a number that would have applied to a corresponding figure in pagan religion. The number 888 is still regarded as a number of good fortune in the divinatory codes of China and the East. The addition to Jesus, 888, of Christ, 1480, makes Jesus Christ, 2368, and the third term, Κυριος, Lord, 800, produces the full title of the Christian principal, Lord Jesus Christ, Κυριος Ιησους Χριστος, whose number is therefore 800 + 888 + 1480 = 3168. This number is curiously linked to 666 because 6660 is the sum of all the factors of 3168.

Bound together with 31680 is the number 5040, these two measuring the circumference and the radius of the cosmological circle. A quarter of 31680 is 7920, the number of miles in the earth's mean diameter and the key number, along with 5040, in the numerical scheme of the Heavenly City.

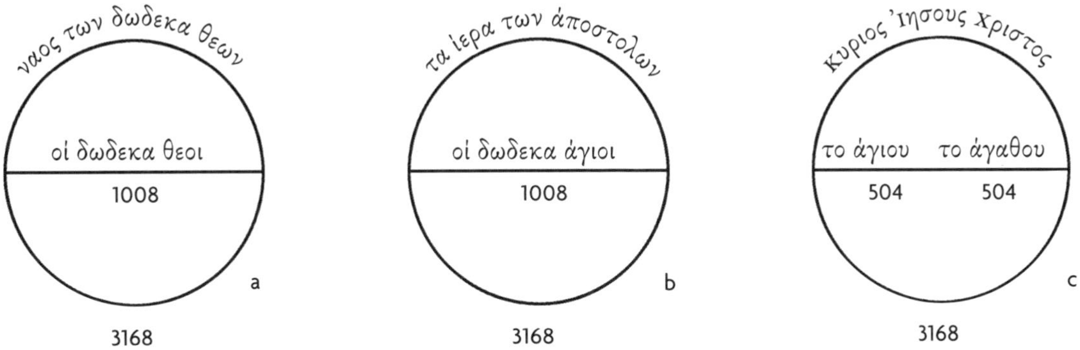

a. Diameter: The 12 Gods (1008)
Circumference: Temple of the 12 Gods (3168)

b. Diameter: The 12 Saints (1008)
Circumference: The Sanctuaries of the Apostles (3168)

c. Radius (left): The Holy (504); Radius (right): The Good (504)
Circumference: Lord Jesus Christ (3168)

1080, the Lunar Number, the Solar 666, and Their Sum, 1746

These three primary symbolic numbers together represent the trinity of powers. It is an elemental trinity, not personified, as in the Christian Father, Son, and Holy Spirit, but combining the solar, generative element (666), its lunar, reflective opposite (1080), and their sum, 1746, number of the universal spirit.

The number 1080, the number of miles in the moon's radius, is an important element in the numerical scheme of the Heavenly City diagram. It is perhaps the most widely known of all sacred, symbolic numbers, producing for example the 108 beads in the Buddhist or Hindu rosary, the 10800 stanzas in the Rigveda, each of 40 syllables, the 10800 bricks in the Zoroastrian fire-altar, the 1080 pillars round the Odinists' hall of Valhalla, the 1080 minims that make up the Jewish hour, and the 10800 years in each of the four seasons of the Hindu Kali Yuga. Civilization, said Heraclitus, is destroyed every 10800 years. This, according to modern reckoning, is the approximate interval between successive ice ages. In astronomy, 108 is the mean distance between the earth and the sun, measured by the sun's diameter (864,000 miles), and the same distance is equal to 4 × 10800 diameters of the moon (whose radius is 1080 miles). The old astronomers were familiar with this number. Hipparchus gave 1080 as the number of stars of first-magnitude brightness, and Galileo reckoned that the sun's radius is 1080 times longer that the diameter of a sixth-magnitude star.

Other appearances of this number are as 108, the atomic weight of silver, the 108-degree angles of the pentagon, the geometer's emblem of life, and the 1080 breaths normally taken in one hour. From these and other applications of 1080 in its various dimensions comes an image of the silvery moon. In contrast to its symbolic opposite, the sun, the moon has a quiet, subtle influence on our sublunary world. It draws the tides of oceans and stirs up the earth's vital currents, the periods of the female, the intuitive part of the mind, and the spirit that moves oracles. In traditional philosophy the moon is called the source of measure. Its cycle produces the 28 days of the lunar calendar used by nomadic people, and its dimensions set the standards in the canon of number that orders the solar system.

The number that arranges the first seven polygons in symmetrical and equal pairs is 1080. This is one of those 'magic' numbers that occurs in different contexts throughout the field of number and is recognized in all societies based on the number canon. Two pentagons, each containing the sum of 540 degrees, have 1080 degrees together, and the other figures pair off to produce the same number.

To illustrate this symmetry one has to include a 0-sided shape. It is the point or dot, visible in geometric practise as the indentation made by the compass point at the centre of a construction, but classically defined as having no dimensions. It therefore has no sides. The pair to the octagon with its combined angles of 1080° must be a figure with no internal angles. It is represented by the first figure in geometry, the dot within a circle.

Table of Combined Internal Angles of Polygons

dot	0°	triangle	180°	square	360°	pentagon	540°
octagon	1080°	heptagon	900°	hexagon	720°	pentagon	540°
sum of angles	1080°		1080°		1080°		1080°

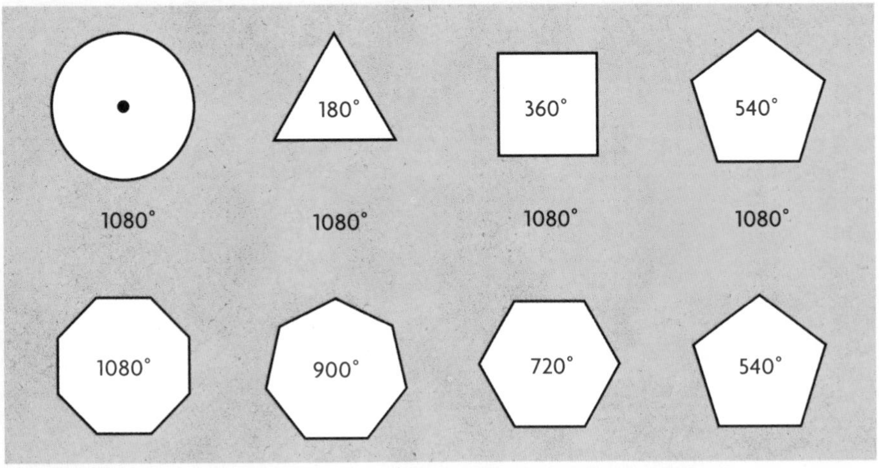

Fig. 62. The number 1080 in the internal angles of the first seven polygons

The gematria of 1080 confirms the character of that number as the primary symbol of the spiritual, mystical 'night side of nature', the yin or female aspect, associated with the underworld, the imagination, the gift of prophecy, and springs of healing and inspiration. The importance of 1080 in Christianity is as the number of the Holy Spirit, corresponding to the Earth Spirit of pagan religion. Their two names in Greek have the same letters with only one transposition, and therefore the same number, emphasizing their common meaning.

1080 = το αγιον πνευμα, the Holy Spirit
= το γαιον πνευμα, the Earth Spirit

Other appropriate phrases with the number 1080 are:

1080 = πηγη σοφιας, fountain of wisdom
= η Ταρταρος, Tartarus, the nether world
= ο θεος παθενος γης, the virgin god of earth
= η αρμονια κοσμου, the universal harmony

By the convention of gematria one unit can be added to or omitted from the number of a word without altering its meaning. Thus, the number 1081 = η αβυσσος, the Abyss, and Σατυροι, satyrs or regional spirits. The number 1079 gives ο Χθονιος, the god of the underworld, and 1082 numbers η προφετεια, prophecy, ουροβορος, the ouroboros serpent, and η πηγη υδατος, the "well of water springing up into everlasting life" (John 4:14). All these symbols and images have a common reference to the mystical number 1080.

On the opposite pole to 1080 is 666, a number regarded with superstitious awe by those who associate it with the Devil. This idea goes back to St John and Revelation 13 where he identified the "number of the Beast" by the three Greek letters, Chi (Χ), Xi (ξ), and Sigma (Σ) that stand for 600, 60, and 6. Before going into this delicate subject, the true nature of 666 is explored through its arithmetic properties.

The number 666 is the thirty-sixth triangular number. Triangular numbers, set out on the next page up to 666, begin with 1, the next is 3 (= 1 + 2), then come 6 (= 1 + 2 + 3), 10 (= 1 + 2 + 3 + 4), and so on. The numeral 666 is the sum of all numbers up to 36. These numbers 1 to 36 also form a 'magic square' (see figure 64), where each line, column, and diagonal adds up to 111 and the whole to 666. The traditional name for this, the magic square of the Sun, acknowledges the solar symbolism of 666. The number also occurs as the sum of the first six Roman number symbols, I + V + X + L + C + D, the values of which, 1 + 5 + 10 + 50 + 100 + 500, amount to 666.

The first twelve numbers, split into two halves, are curiously productive of the solar number, for:

$$
\begin{array}{lcr}
1 \times 2 \times 3 \times 4 \times 5 \times 6 & = & 720 \\
7 \times 8 \times 9 \times 10 \times 11 \times 12 & = & \underline{665280} \\
 & & 666000
\end{array}
$$

In St John's account there are actually two beasts. The first one he sees rising up from the sea, and the second is born from the earth. The second beast sets up the first as an idol, an object of compulsory worship, and decrees that "no man might buy or sell, save that he had the mark or the name of the beast, or the number of his name". To discover the name of the first beast, St John tells his readers to work out his number, for it is the number of a man, "and his number is 666" (και ο αριθμος αυτου Χξϛ).

This passage has perplexed the learned for almost two millennia, while generations of fanatics have laboured to identify the man with the number 666 as the Antichrist or the person who they think best fits that description. The second beast, who establishes the first as the object of a worldwide cult, is clearly some ruling authority. That in St John's time would have been the Roman empire or the Roman Church that succeeded it. As to the first beast, whose image, marked with a deadly wound, was made the chief emblem of the cult, he must have been a religious leader, officially venerated but disdained as an idol by St John and the early Christian Gnostics.

The answer to this conundrum is made plain through the esoteric code of symbolic number that St John makes use of throughout his book. In the last verse of Revelation 13 he wrote: "Here is wisdom. Let him that hath understanding (nous) count the number of the beast: for it is the number of a man". Then comes the key phrase: "And his number is 666". In that phrase, given in Greek on page 77, is concealed a number, not the exoteric 666 that needs no counting, but a number that emerges by adding up the numerical values of the letters in the phrase. They amount to 2368. The name with that number can be found among the holy names introduced with the number 3168 on page 73. Readers can find it for themselves and draw their own conclusions, and then it will be seen why orthodox theologians draw away from the subject. But St John warns that only those with understanding—meaning those initiated into the mysteries of symbolic number—should count the number. The name has been published, with proper obscurity, within the discourse on 666 in *The Dimensions of Paradise,* where those who are truly motivated can study the matter further.

The word 'beast' (therion), used in old-fashioned translations of the New

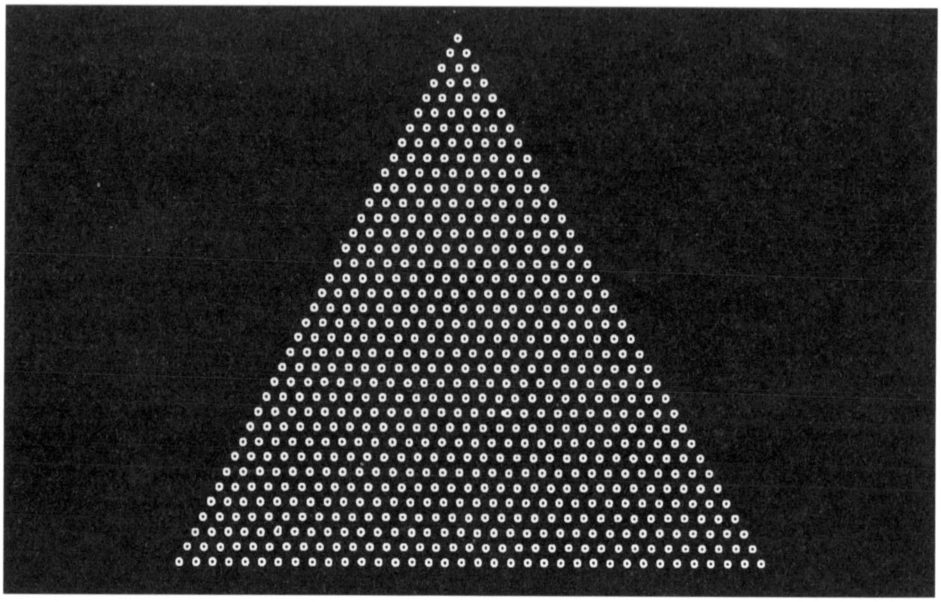

Fig. 63. The number 666 is the thirty-sixth triangular number, meaning that it is the sum of numbers from 1 to 36. The first 36 triangular numbers, beginning 1, 3, 6, 10 . . . up to 666, make up the pyramid.

6	32	3	34	35	1
7	11	27	28	8	30
19	14	16	15	23	24
18	20	22	21	17	13
25	29	10	9	26	12
36	5	33	4	2	31

Fig. 64. Magic square of the sun. The sum of all its numbers 1–36 is 666.

Testament, means simply a wild animal; there is nothing 'beastly' about the number 666. Numbers symbolize natural principles which in themselves are neither good nor evil. The number 666 is the polar opposite of 1080, and it is also its complement and partner. The number 1080 is the essential lunar number, applying to the world of imagination and the gifts of the holy spirit, whereas 666 refers to pure solar energy. As the symbolic number of the sun, 666 implies male authority and the principle of reason. Princes of this world rule in the spirit of that number; and the influence of 666 is evident in the materialism that dominates modern economics. But were it not for 666 and what it stands for, the world would lose its vitality and grow sterile. In the names and phrases that yield this number through gematria can be seen its overall character.

666 = η φρην, the mind, understanding, reason
= παρα θεου, from God or from above

665 = οργη θεου, divine wrath
= οπλα θεου, weapons of God

Many of the characters and images in Revelation appear to be the direct opposites of each other. The whore and the 'beast' of Babylon are opposed to the bride and the lamb of the New Jerusalem, and the two cities are similarly contrasted. Yet in St John's allegory they are linked together and have similar names, as if to represent two sides of the same coin. The implication is that Babylon, the decadent, doomed city, is essentially no different from the holy Jerusalem. They are merely at different stages in the cycle of rise and fall that continues throughout history. And their citizens are the same good souls who inhabit every stage in the process. This is made clear in the names of the two cities, for numerically they are identical.

1285 = Βαβυλων, Babylon
= η αγια πολις η Ιερουαλημ, the holy city Jerusalem

The numbers 666 and 1080, solar and lunar respectively, are also bound together in a partnership of opposites which, when happily consummated (by adding the two together), generates the blissful state of unity and wholeness that follows the initiation ritual. In sacred or alchemical writing this state is described by such terms as the Glory of the God of Israel, the number of which is 666 + 1080 = 1746.

1746 is referred to as the 'number of fusion', being the sum of the two numbers that represent sun and moon or the two opposite poles in creation. It is the pivotal number in the cosmological diagram which is the framework of our geometer's creation myth, for 17460 measures the side of the square that stands within the universal circle (area 12!) and relates as $\sqrt{3}:1$ with the diameter of the circle representing the sublunary world. As a numerical symbol of the whole scheme, pictured as the Heavenly City, it has the appropriate gematria, for

1746 = Ιερουσαλημ, η πολις θεου, Jerusalem the city of God

The sublime symbolism of the 'number of fusion' is illustrated by the holy phrases, used in the New Testament or Gnostic texts, whose letters add up to that number. Many of them are to do with the Mysteries and the seed of mystical doctrine that was implanted in the initiate's mind and developed as the tree of knowledge. In three of the New Testament Gospels (e.g., Luke 13:19) it is called the "grain of mustard seed", supposedly the smallest of all seeds, and in Mark 4:30–34 it is used as an allegory for the secret knowledge that Jesus revealed to his disciples. In the Greek of the New Testament the grain of mustard seed has the number 1746, and 1747 gives 'the divine Gnosis', γνωσις θεου, meaning direct knowledge of God. With these names, below, are some of the others that have been discovered with the same number and similar meanings:

1746 = κοκκος σιναπεως, grain of mustard seed
= το κεκρυμεννον πνευμα, the hidden spirit
= το πνευμα κοσμου, the universal spirit
= ο θησαυρος Ιησου, the treasure of Jesus
= ο νομος ο πνευματικος, the spiritual law
= η θεοτης πνευματος, the divinity of spirit
= η δοξα του θεου Ισραηλ, the glory of the God of Israel

1747 = γνωσις θεου, knowledge of God, or divine Gnosis
= μυστηια Ιησου, Mysteries of Jesus

1745 = πατηρ, υιος ,πνευμα, Father, Son, Spirit

864, the Foundation Number

Ancient Athens, according to Plato in Critias, was founded by a divine pair, Athena and Hephaistos, representing the two opposite signs of the zodiac, Aries and Libra. Significantly, the combined numbers of their names, Αθηνα 69 + Ηφαιστος 795, add up to 864, called the 'foundation number'.

The number 864 is a foundation stone in the code of canonical numbers that formulates the universe. Its character is solar and orderly, and its most prominent appearance is in the sun whose diameter is 864000 miles. That is 400 times the diameter of the moon (2160 miles) and, strange though it be, the moon's distance from the sun is about 400 times its distance from earth. That is why the moon's disk fits neatly over the sun at a total eclipse.

The table of comparative sizes and distances of sun, moon, and earth, set out on page 83, shows the organizing function of 8640 and its fractions, 4320, 2160, 1080, often in conjunction with 11, reflecting the 11 : 3 ratio between the diameters of earth and moon. Notable appearances of 864 include the radius of the Grand Orb (the earth's circuit around the sun or vice versa in earth-centred cosmology), which is 93,312000 miles or 86400 × 1080, a tenth part of the sun's diameter multiplied by the radius of the moon.

The number 86400 is the number of seconds in a 24-hour day, and this number extends through all the vast ages covered by traditional chronology, culminating in the period of 8640 million years which the Hindus call a day and a night of Brahma. In the 12-note musical scale and in metrology 864 is a familiar number. The royal Egyptian half-cubit of .864 feet is a standard measure in the pyramids and in the former temple at Jerusalem.

The image of 864 that emerges from its symbolism in many different fields is a square altar or cornerstone, linking earth and heaven. It corresponds to the rock of foundation, placed at the earth's centre to hold down the waters of the abyss—providing the firm ground on which human institutions are founded. The altar is a cube of 12 feet, making its superficial area (the combined areas of its six sides) equal to 864 square feet. Half of it is buried, half on the surface, so its total volume, 12 × 12 × 12 or 1728 cubic feet, is in two parts, both of 864 cubic feet. The cube in which St John saw the Heavenly Jerusalem also measured 12 × 12 × 12, but in units of a thousand furlongs. Reduced to 12 furlongs or 7920 feet on each side, its six faces have a combined area of 864 square furlongs which is also 8640 acres (43560 square feet = 1 acre).

Every aspect of 864 is reflected in its gematria. Jerusalem is 864, and so is the cornerstone of which, in St John's account, there were twelve in the holy city. The number 864 is also the number of the thysiasterion, the altar. Other phrases, below, indicate the central position of 864 in the numerical cosmology.

864 = Ιερουσαλημ, Jerusalem
= γωνια, foundation, cornerstone
= θυσιαστηριον, altar
= αληθεια κοσμου, universal truth
= αγιων, holy of holies
= θεων, temple of the gods

As a solar number, measuring the sun and the solar system, 864 is related to the 365-day solar year, ruled by Abraxas from his central throne. The number of Abraxas is appropriately 365, and his seat, θρονος Αβραξας, is 864. Another name, signifying a bearer of solar intelligence, is Pythagoras, Πυθαγορας, 864.

More clearly than any other symbolic number, 864 reveals its essential meaning through its correspondences in astronomy, time-keeping, music, measurement, and gematria. It is indeed the foundation stone in studies of number and cosmology.

	Earth diameter	Moon diameter	Sun diameter	Distance Earth–Moon
Earth diameter 7,920 miles				
Moon diameter 2,160 miles	3 \ 11			
Sun diameter 864,000 miles	1200 \ 11	400 \ 1		
Earth–Moon distance 237,600 miles	30 \ 1	110 \ 1	11 \ 40	
Earth–Sun distance 93,312,000 miles	129,600 \ 11	43,200 \ 1	108 \ 1	4,320 \ 11

Fig. 65 (opposite). Traditionally, and from the geometer's point of view, this is a duodecimal universe. Its numerical structure is dominated by powers and multiples of Twelve, while twelve-fold geometry is the framework in which all other regular shapes are happily combined.

Part 2

THE PHYSICAL CREATION

The Geometries of 1, 2, 3, 4, 6, 8, 12

5 • The Dodecad

A Summary of the Numbers One to Twelve

The first twelve numbers, the basic components in the numerical cosmology, fall into three categories along with their respective types of geometry.

First come the structural numbers and the geometries that occur in the architecture of the universe. These numbers are Four and Eight ($\sqrt{2}$ proportion) and Three and Six ($\sqrt{3}$ proportion). Set above them, as the first symbol of universal order, is the number Twelve, whose geometry embraces them all.

Five and Ten pertain to life and growth and are the subject of part 3. Seven is the number of the soul and, though it has priority, is the last to be illustrated in the geometer's cosmogony. That is the tradition, and the reason for it is that Seven is a symbol of the initiatory process completed. It therefore comes at the end of the geometer's allegory. With Seven is placed the mystical Nine, another symbol of the Mysteries. Their natural associate is Eleven, because polygons with 7, 9, and 11 sides are the outsiders—the only ones in the Dodecad that cannot be constructed with ruler and compass.

Eleven is the number that bridges the gap between the Decad and the Dodecad. Mediating between the two complete systems, the sublunary Ten and the heavenly Twelve, Eleven has no distinct characteristic of its own. Its geometry is alienated from other systems and it has no place in architecture or music.

Yet in the realm of number Eleven is active in ratios and relationships, especially in partnership with Seven, as in 22 : 7 (π) and 99 : 70 ($\sqrt{2}$). An arithmetical function of Eleven is to sum up the numbers 1 to 9, both forwards and backwards, through a sequence beginning, $11 \times 11 = 121$, $111 \times 111 = 12321$ and culminating $111111111 \times 111111111 = 12345678987654321$.

In this series of units can be seen the rungs of a ladder from the Decad to the Dodecad—fanciful, of course, but a visible image to those who have the eye for it.

6 • The One and Only

Symbol of the Universe

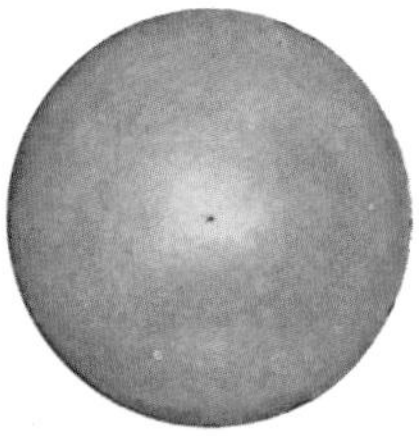

One is, obviously and by definition, unique. The Greek sophists with their pedagogic humour used to say that there are two classes of number, the first containing the number One and the second all the other numbers. The geometric image of One is a circle with its microcosm, the round dot at its centre made by the point of its creator's compass. The same image symbolizes the whole universe, the only true, self-sufficient representation of the One that is conceivable. On that scale, the central dot is a cross section of the world pole. Therein is the mystery that haunts physics and metaphysics alike. The earth spins on its axis, implying that there is an actual pole, however thin. Yet this pole must revolve, so where and what is the constant, unmoving centre? It seems to be devoured by infinite regression. Here the geometer's myth comes to the rescue. The dot at the centre of a diagram is called 'dimensionless' and taken to symbolize the unchanging element in Creation, on which everything revolves, that is, divine law.

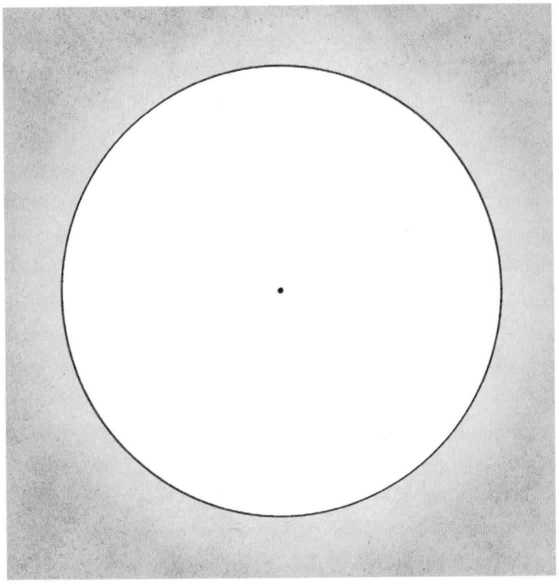

Fig. 66. This is the first figure in geometry, symbol of number One and the unique universe. The dot is dimensionless and conceptually non-existent. But it is the first and most essential element in this construction.

7 • The Geometry of Two

Duality and the World of Paradox

The geometric symbol of Two is two points joined by a line, for example the diameter of a circle, or the line that connects the two centres of a 'vesica piscis' (see The Geometry of Three, page 90). With this image enters the duality that runs through nature, gives two sides to every question, and makes this a world of paradox.

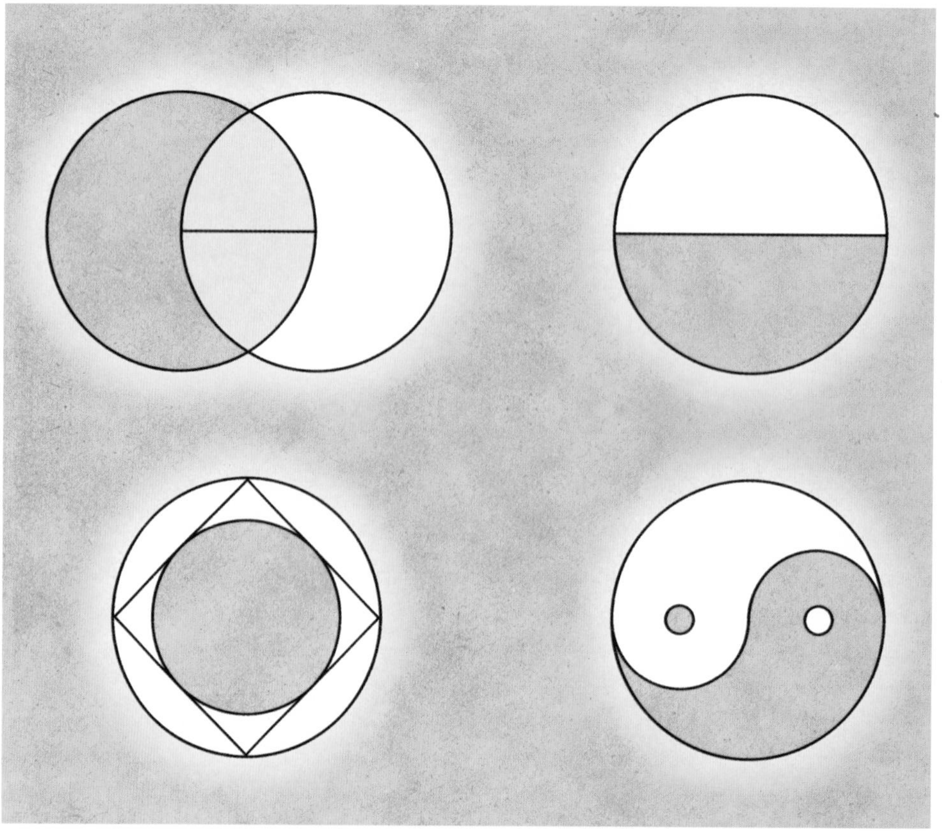

Fig. 67. Two is the line between two focal points and is seen in the division of a circle into two equal areas.

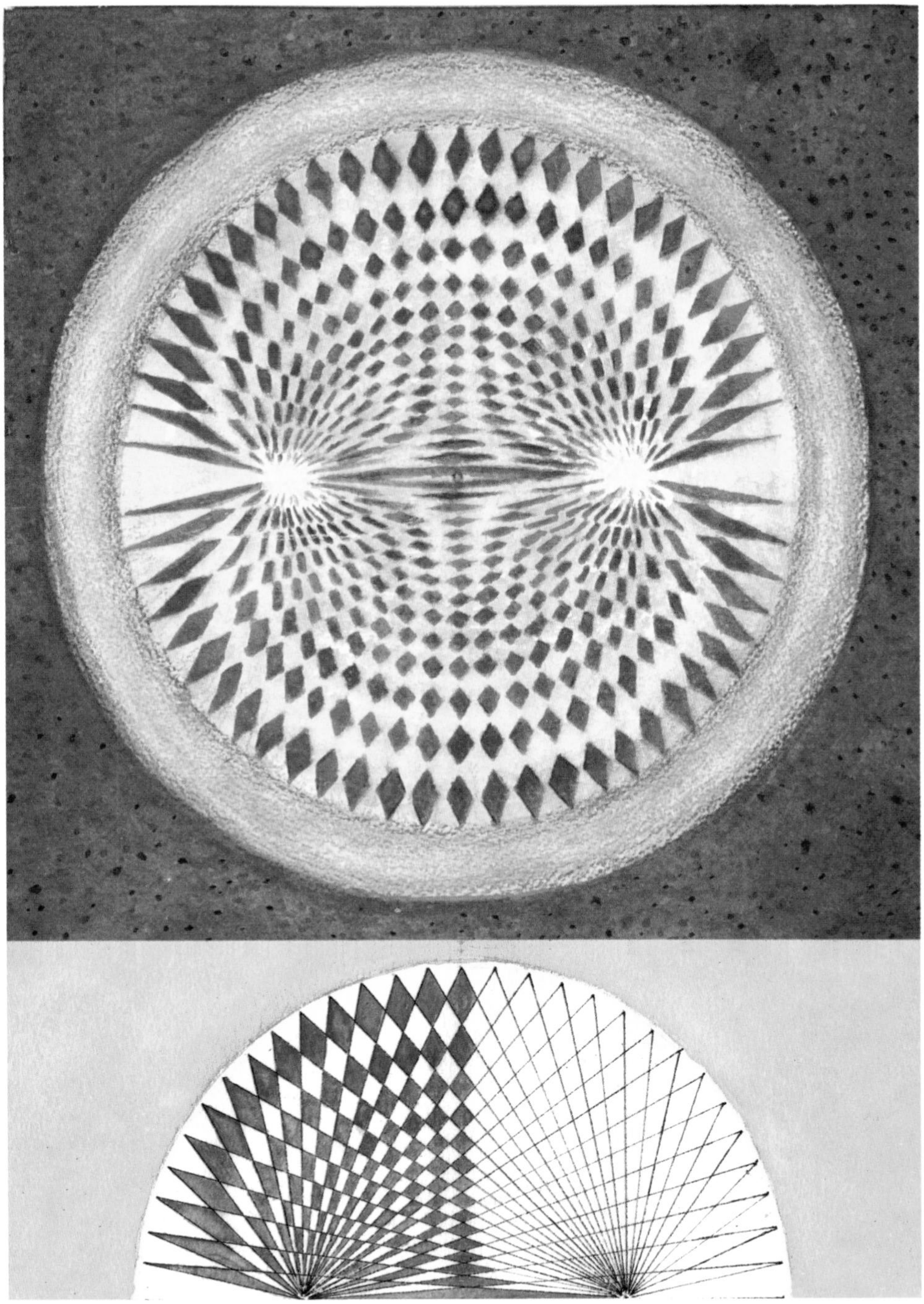

Fig. 68. The two poles of a magnet create an energy field, displayed in this crop circle from Avebury Trusloe, Wiltshire, at the end of July 2000. The outer circle is divided by 60 points (58 visible) and lines are drawn from each point to each of the two foci—as in the diagram below the figure.

8 • The Geometry of Three

The Vesica Piscis and Material Creation

The Vesica Piscis and the Marriage Made in Heaven

Symbols of the material creation begin with the first composite figure in geometry—made up of two separate shapes. It is the union of two equal circles, each circle passing through the centre of the other. The shape made by the two overlapping circles has been given many names, usually implying that it is a source or mother of geometric forms. In creative geometry it is commonly known as the 'vesica piscis', the fish vessel, because it looks something like a fish.

This productive union of two circles is the first and most perfect of geometric marriages. In alchemical terms it represents the conjunction of two opposites, two of the same kind who finally come together after their separation and refinement apart. Without losing their individualities or merging into one, the two oppositely charged or sexed entities find their point of balance and are creative together. It is an ideal image—too good to be true, some would say—but it is constantly reflected in the processes of nature and it lights up our human dreams.

In the practice of geometry the vesica piscis appears at the very beginning, as the first construction that everyone makes after picking up a compass. Further experiments lead to the six-petal flower and the realization that the radius of a circle divides its circumference into exactly six parts. It is natural and easy to develop the figure further, bringing in all the shapes that conform to the $\sqrt{3}$ proportion—the triangle, rhomb, hexagon, and $\sqrt{3}$ rectangle.

The first product of the vesica is a twin pair of equilateral triangles standing base to base. This four-sided figure is called a rhomb or rhombus, which is also the name of a flat fish, like a turbot. The equal-sided triangle is the first regular polygon, so Three is the first number that encloses an area. It is often regarded by geometers as the first real number, One and Two being abstract principles.

Fig. 69. Two circles mate, each passing through the centre of the other. In the area where they overlap—the womb as geometers imagine it—is generated a rhombus. Its two halves, black and white like their parents, are set together point to point, and when they mate they slide over each other to form a hexagon.

Fig. 70. Geometric products of the √3 grid

Fig. 71. Circles closely packed produce the same diamond lattice pattern.

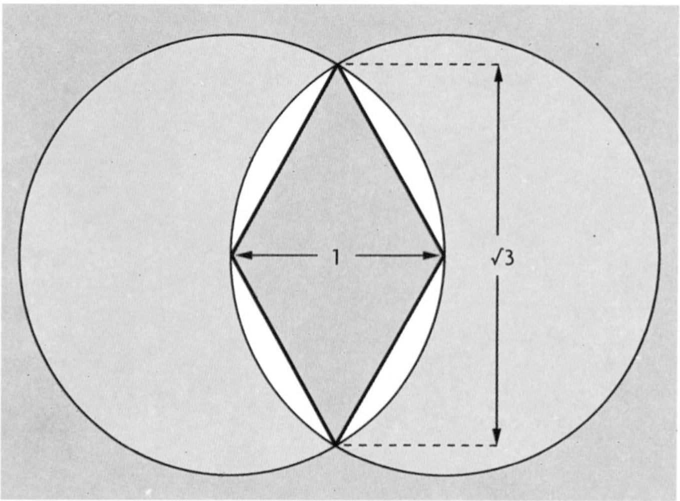

Fig. 72. Formed by the union of two equal circles, the vesica piscis gives birth to the rhombus, made of two equilateral triangles. If the width of this figure is 1, its height is √3, giving birth to the 'root 3' proportion that prevails throughout the physical world.

Fig. 73. The √3 grid with some of the designs it generates

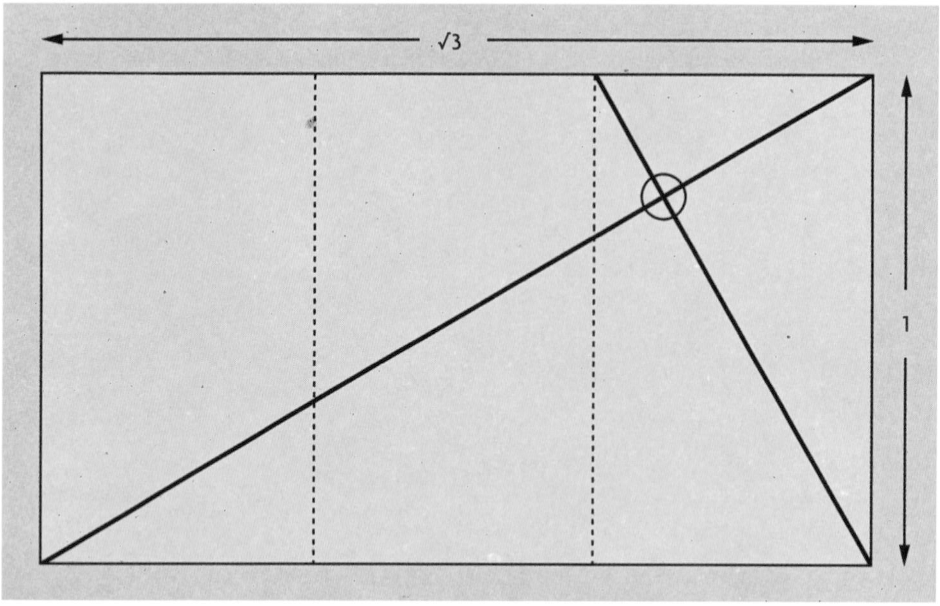

Fig. 74. The fish and the rhombus. The rhombus, first symbol of the √3 proportion, has given its name to flat fish, like the turbot, that have the same diamond-shaped outline. Tradition confirms its association with the fish. This is emphasised in the peculiar story of the "153 fishes in the net" that occurs in the last chapter of St John's gospel.

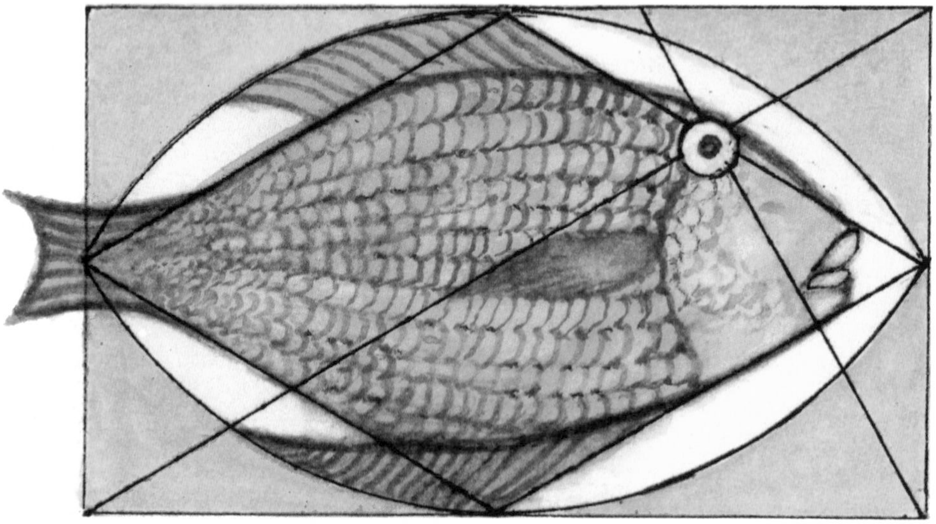

Fig. 75. The √3 'fish' geometry. The eye of the fish is located in the √3 rectangle at the point where its diagonal is intersected by the line drawn perpendicular to it from one of its corners. The point where the line meets the opposite side of the rectangle divides the figure into three equal parts.

Fig. 76. 144 fishes in a bowl (√3 grid)

Fig. 77. A piscine rhombus of 48 fishes, 24 blue, 24 red, in the √3 pattern of a church window

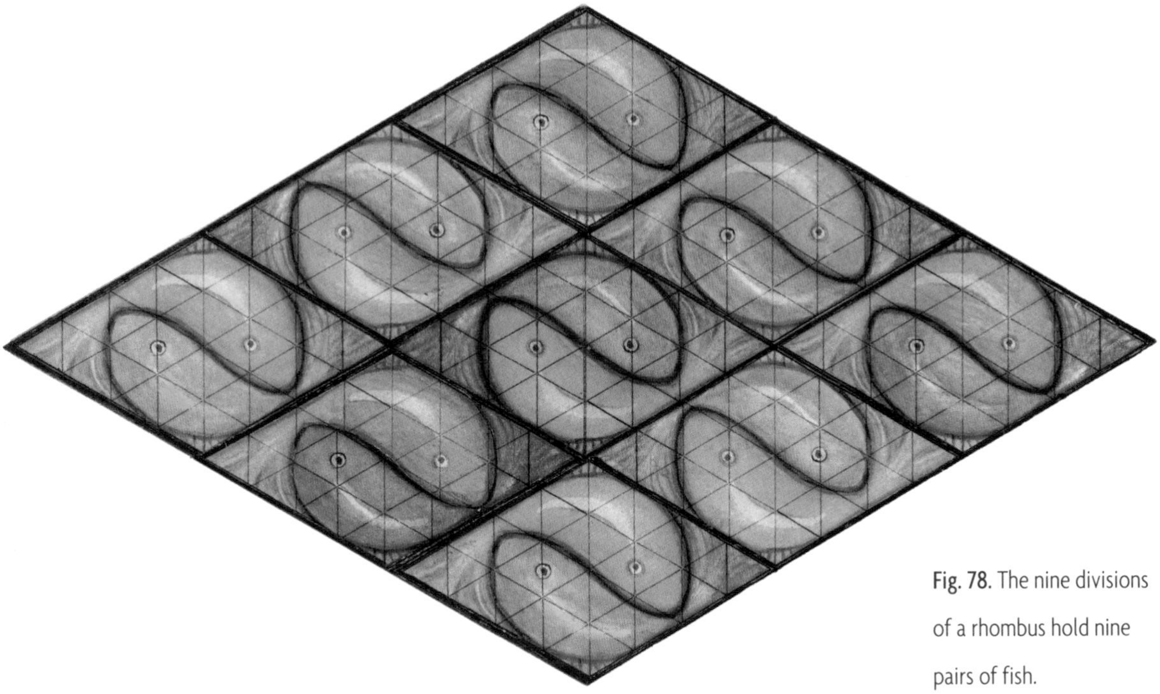

Fig. 78. The nine divisions of a rhombus hold nine pairs of fish.

The Net with 153 Fishes, a Geometer's Parable

Many of the stories and parables in the life of Jesus were repeated from earlier sources. Some of them have a numerical and geometric framework, for example the 'miracles of multiplication' summarized in Mark 8:19–20. These are the miracles, attributed to many saints and ascetics, both men and women, where a limited supply of food is made sufficient to feed a great many people. Jesus performed two such miracles, once when he fed the 5000 with 5 loaves and 2 fishes, and again when 4000 of his followers were satisfied by 7 loaves and a few fishes among them all. On the first occasion 12 baskets of food were left over and on the second 7 baskets remained. In these numbers, as Jesus emphasised, sacred allegories were concealed which the disciples failed to understand. Nor can they be understood today. There is, however, one miracle that is openly numerical and clearly refers to a scheme of geometry based on the √3 proportion—the story of the miraculous catch of precisely 153 fishes (John 21).

Why 153? It is a triangular number, the sum of all the numbers from 1 to 17. Eighty times 153 is 12240, a number that applies to the Heavenly City diagram as its outer diameter, being equal to the earth's diameter in miles plus two diameters of the moon. 1224 is the key to the story of the 153 fishes in the net. It is the number by gematria of both το δικτυον, the net, and ιχθυες, fishes.

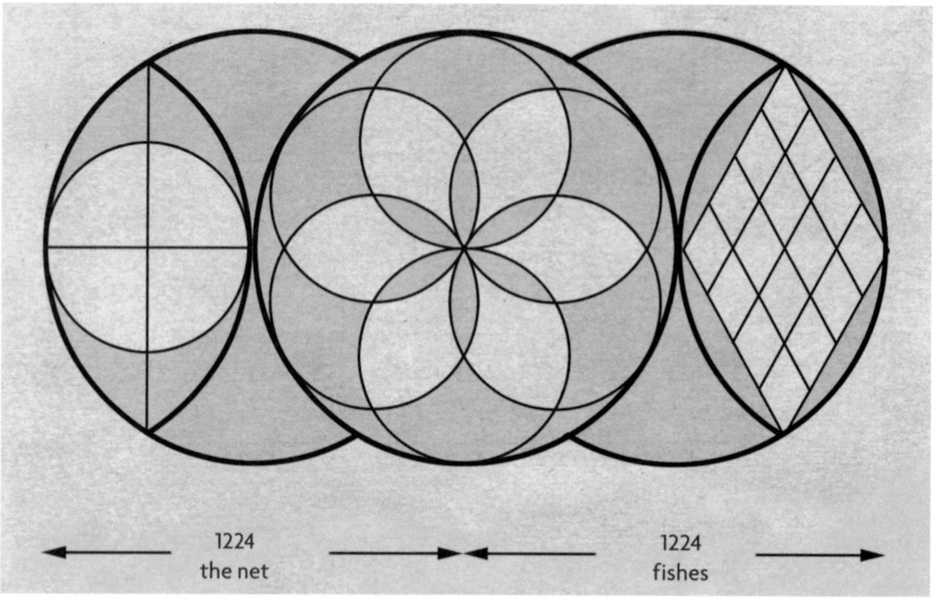

Fig. 79. The geometry and numbers of the 153 netted fishes

The gematria of 1224 ± 1 brings out phrases which identify 1224 as a numerical symbol of paradise on earth. These are some examples.

1224 = ο κυριος ο θεος, the Lord God
= κτισις θεου, God's Creation
= κυκλος θεου, divine circle
= η φυτεια, the plantation, an epithet of paradise
1223 = η οδος παραδεισου, the way of paradise
1225 = ο παραδεισος θεου, God's paradise, i.e., the Garden of Eden
= εγω ειμι η οδος, I am the way (John 14:6)
= η δικαιοσυνη θεου, the righteousness of God
= εν ολον ολων, the one Whole of wholes, Plato's name in *Timaeus* for the unique sphere of the cosmos

Here is how the geometry of the 153 fishes develops.

Fig. 80. The 153 fishes in the net (John 21)

St John's story begins when St Peter decides to go fishing by night in the Sea of Tiberias and takes six of the other disciples with him. They enter a boat, which can either be depicted as circular like a coracle or boat-shaped by enclosing the circle in a vesica. They pack in as six overlapping circles with the circle of St Peter in the middle (figure 80, page 99). The number of Σιμων ο Πετρος, Simon Peter as he is called in St John's account, is 1925, which is the circumference of a circle with diameter 612¹/₇, taken as 612. With 612 as the diameter of the central circle representing Simon Peter, the width of the circular boat is 1224.

The seven disciples plied their net all night but caught nothing. As dawn broke they saw a figure on the shore. At first they did not recognise Jesus, who had risen from the grave after his entombment. He advised them to cast their net on the right side of the boat, and when they did so the net was almost broken by the weight of the 153 fishes that filled it. Simon Peter jumped into the water and towed the boat to land, a distance of about 200 cubits, with the net of fishes behind it.

In the geometrical sense, the disciples cast the net on the right side of the boat by placing the point of their compass on the circumference of the circular boat and drawing an arc of another circle with the same radius, 612, containing a vesica piscis. The rhombus within the vesica is then divided by 6 lines into 16 smaller diamond shapes. The width of the vesica being 612, each of the 16 divisions is 153 in width. These represent 16 small fish or, together with the great fish that contains them, 17 fishes in all. Here again the number 153 comes in, for the sum of numbers 1 to 17 is 153. Each side of the greater rhombus fish measures $153 \times 4 = 612$, so the measure round its perimeter is 612×4 which is 2448 or $1224 + 1224$, the number of το δικτυον, the net, plus the number of ιχθυες, fishes.

The fish geometry and the number system based on 17 and 153 continues in the rest of St John's story. When Simon Peter sees the net bursting with fishes, he puts on his fisherman's coat and dives into the sea so as to pull the boat to land. The number of the fisherman's coat, η επενδυτης, is 1060 which is the height of a vesica whose width is 612, the same as the diameter of Simon Peter in the boat. The geometric image makes his coat long and hooded. The boat is 'about' 200 cubits from land. A cubit is 1.5 feet, so the distance is about 300 feet, allowing it to be 306 feet. That is the distance from the centre of the Simon Peter circle to the surrounding circle of land. The diameter of this all-enclosing circle is 2448 or 16 × 153, closely corresponding to the number of the sea of Tiberias or Galilee (θαλασσα Γαλιλαιας της Τιβεριαδος = 2446), where the miracle of the 153 fishes took place.

When the disciples come to land, the risen Jesus is awaiting them. He has lit a fire and is grilling fish for them to eat with the bread he has provided. There is much symbolism in this story, far beyond the numerical. Jesus was known esoterically as the Fish and was identified with the Age of Pisces, the Fishes, or ΙΧΘΥΕΣ, 1224. This name and number are given by the sum of the initial letters of his holy epithets. Jesus (Ι = 10), Christ (Χ = 600), of God (Θ = 9), son (Υ = 400), Emmanuel (Ε = 5), Saviour (Σ = 200) add up to 1224, the number of Pisces, the dominant sign in the Christian era.

The story of the 153 fishes provides a glimpse into the sacred code of geometry and number that was taught in the Mystery schools and adapted to the Christian myth by those who formulated the new religion.

Fig. 81. The large rhombus fish and the 16 smaller ones within it make 17 in all, a reference to 153, the sum of numbers 1 to 17.

The Triangles That Fill Up Space

The importance of the triangle in the structuring of space is demonstrated in the five regular figures of three-dimensional or solid geometry by which Plato in *Timaeus* (54–57) symbolizes the five elements, earth, air, fire, water, and the ether. Three of these, the tetrahedron (4 sides), the octahedron (8 sides), and the icosahedron (20 sides), are made up of equilateral triangles and represent in order fire, air, and water. The two other solids are the cube or hexahedron with six square sides, the symbol of earth, and the dodecahedron with twelve pentagonal sides which represents the 'ether' and orders the whole universe. Johann Kepler in the seventeenth century showed how these five regular solids, each contained in a sphere, fit together within the dodecahedron to create a geometer's world image.

There are two kinds of right-angle triangle. One is the isosceles with two equal sides and the other, the scalene, with three unequal sides. The first is half a square bisected along its diagonal, with angles of 90, 45, and 45 degrees, while the scalene has an infinite variety of shapes. The most perfect of these, said Plato, is half an equilateral triangle, with one side half the length of its hypotenuse and with angles of 90, 60, and 30 degrees. These two triangles, each united with its pair, are the building blocks of creation, forming the first four regular solids which, in the geometer's cosmology, correspond to atoms. As the basic components of fire, earth, air, and water, they are in constant motion, and as they knock and jostle each other they are broken up into separate triangles, which are then sub-divided into similar shapes on different scales. At the same time, the particles are reassembling, small triangles joining with others to make big ones and these combining to form new atoms or geometric solids. The scalene triangles can become parts of tetrahedrons, octahedrons, or icosahedrons, because these have sides made of equilateral triangles, whereas the isosceles can only fit into a cube, the element of earth.

As an essay in physics, Plato's account is strikingly odd, but he persists with it in detail, describing the interactions of the atoms and elements and illustrating the correspondences between earth, air, fire, and water and the four geometric shapes. For example, spicy dishes taste hot and burn like fire because the spice atoms are tetrahedrons, the smallest and most prickly of shapes. Sweet and creamy things, on the other hand, consist mainly of icosahedrons, whose rounded shape soothes and pleases the tongue. That sounds plausible enough, but no one today would take Plato's account literally, and no one was ever meant to. Plato is here elaborating on the traditional, geometric myth of creation. With high wit and beautiful imagery he is leading his students into the intricacies of solid geometry, not boring them with shapes, numbers, and figures but bringing life to the subject through the allegories attached to it. A noticeable omission from Plato's story is the fifth regular solid, the dodecahedron. It plays no part in the clashing and breaking-up to which the other four are subjected. All that Plato says in *Timaeus* is that "God used it for arranging the constellations on the whole heaven". Elsewhere (*Phaedrus* 110) he indicates that the dodecahedron is the earth's essential form—its etheric envelope perhaps. As a symbol the dodecahedron is uniquely significant, for with its twelve pentagonal faces, it provides an image of the ideal earth, where all twelve types of humanity dwell in harmony under the guidance of the twelve zodiacal gods. The reality of this image, if only on the level of ideals, is apparent in the dodecahedron, the most perfect and noble polyhedron in geometry.

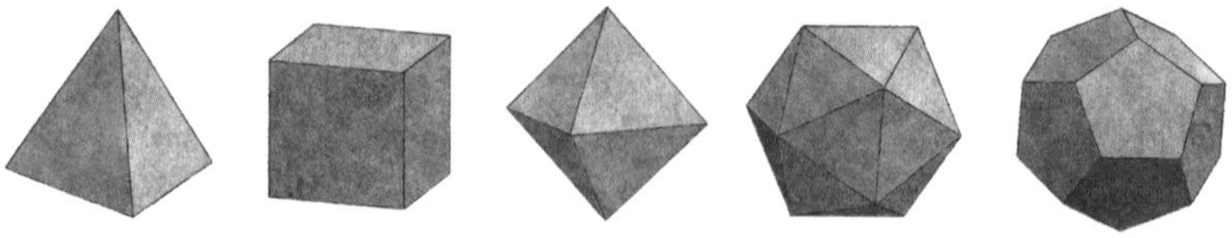

	Tetrahedron	Cube	Octahedron	Icosahedron	Dodecahedron
Shape of sides:	triangle	square	triangle	triangle	pentagon
Sides:	4	6	8	20	12
Corners:	4	8	6	12	20
Edges:	6	12	12	30	30
Element:	fire	earth	air	water	ether

Fig. 82. The five regular or Platonic solids

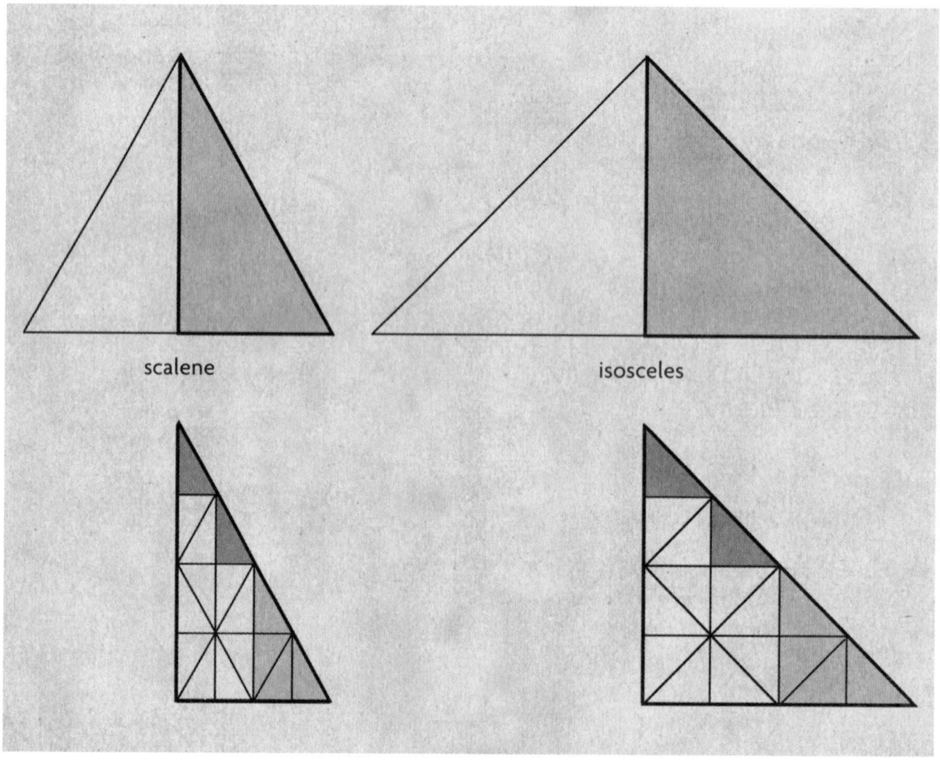

Fig. 83. The two triangles that feature in the sides of the first four regular solids. They can be subdivided endlessly into parts which are always similar to themselves, illustrating Plato's account of the dissolution and reconstitution of atoms.

Pythagorean Triangles

Pythagorean triangles have a right angle and whole numbers on each of their three sides. Though given the name of geometry's great hero, they were not his original discovery. The records of ancient Babylon show that these triangles and the systems behind them were perfectly known in that period. But he made good use of them to demonstrate the gist and core of his teaching—that the universe is a divinely born creature, perfect in all its parts because it is based on the most perfect of paradigms, number itself. As a means to persuading his pupils towards that perception, he revealed to them the order that prevails in the world of Pythagorean triangles.

A modern revealer of this order is the geometrical researcher Joan Moore of Weston-Super-Mare, whose analysis and identification of Pythagorean triangles results in two series, both starting with the basic triangle with sides 3 and 4 and hypotenuse 5. The two series, as here illustrated begin:

3–4–5	3–4–5
5–12–13	8–15–17
7–24–25	12–35–37
9–40–41	16–63–65

The regular progressions apparent in these terms bring to light an endless sequence of Pythagorean triangles. Some of them are prominent in ancient geometric designs, in temples and across landscapes.

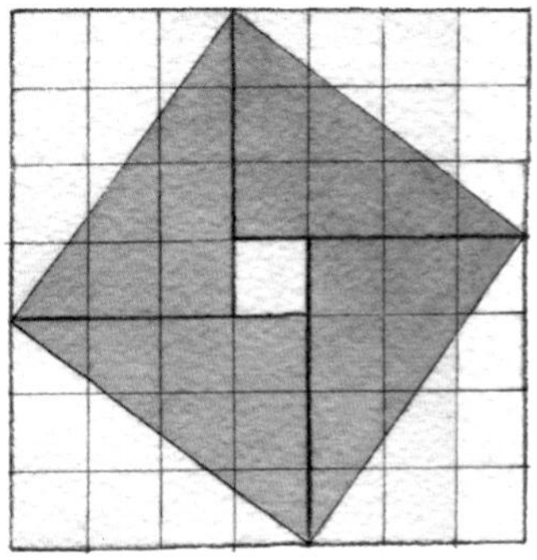

Fig. 84. A square 7 x 7 contains eight of the first type of Pythagorean triangle with sides of 3, 4, 5, leaving a blank square in the middle.

Fig. 85 (left). In the centre is the 7 x 7 square (previous page) containing eight 3–4–5 triangles around a small blank square. The next square contains eight 5–12–13 triangles, and the series continues 7–24–25, 9–40–41 . . .

Fig. 86 (right). The second series of Pythagorean triangles starts, like the first, with a blank square surrounded by eight 3–4–5 triangles, and the series continues 8–15–17, 12–35–37, and onwards.

The 5–12–13 Pythagorean Triangle

The oldest recognized example of the 5–12–13 Pythagorean triangle is the large-scale construction identified by Robin Heath. Its base line runs due west from Stonehenge to the centre of Lundy Island in the Bristol Channel where a right angle locates the third point of the triangle in the Prescelli hills of Wales, source of the Stonehenge bluestones. The 'station stone' rectangle at Stonehenge is part of this prehistoric scheme, for its sides of 5 and 12 with hypotenuse 13 repeat the larger triangle on the scale of 1 to 2500. The large 5–12–13 triangle has sides measuring each a seventh part of 360, 864, and 936 miles. From this data can be calculated the precise dimensions of the Stonehenge rectangle, leading to further discoveries in the field of ancient science. Details are in *The Measure of Albion* (Robin Heath and John Michell, 2004).

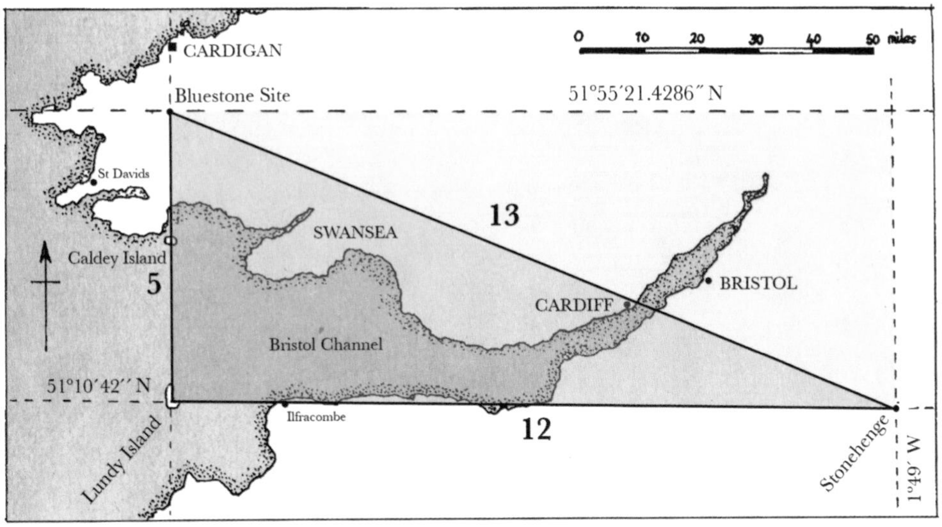

Fig. 87. The Stonehenge–Lundy triangle

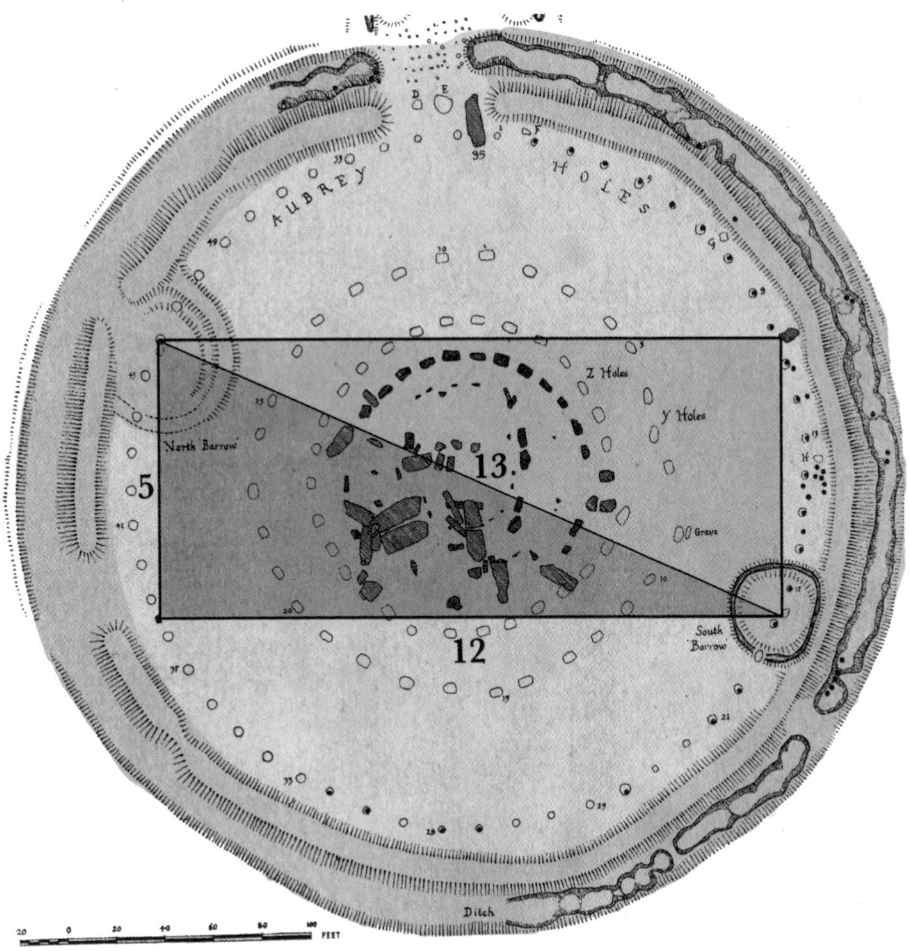

Fig. 88. The 'station stone' rectangle at Stonehenge

A rectangle made of two 5–12–13 triangles shaped the Temple at Jerusalem, founded by King Solomon in 961 BC and reconstructed on the same site in Roman times. Measuring 120 by 288 cubits it stood within the 'eschatological' temple prophesied by Isaiah, the dimensions of which are six times larger, i.e., 720 by 1728 cubits. This cubit is the same as that used by St John to measure the New Jerusalem, 1.728 ft., so the length in feet of the greater Jerusalem temple is 1728 × 1.728 ft., a thousandth part of 12 × 12 × 12 × 12 × 12 × 12 ft. The plan of the temple is said to have been a divine revelation to Solomon's father, King David.

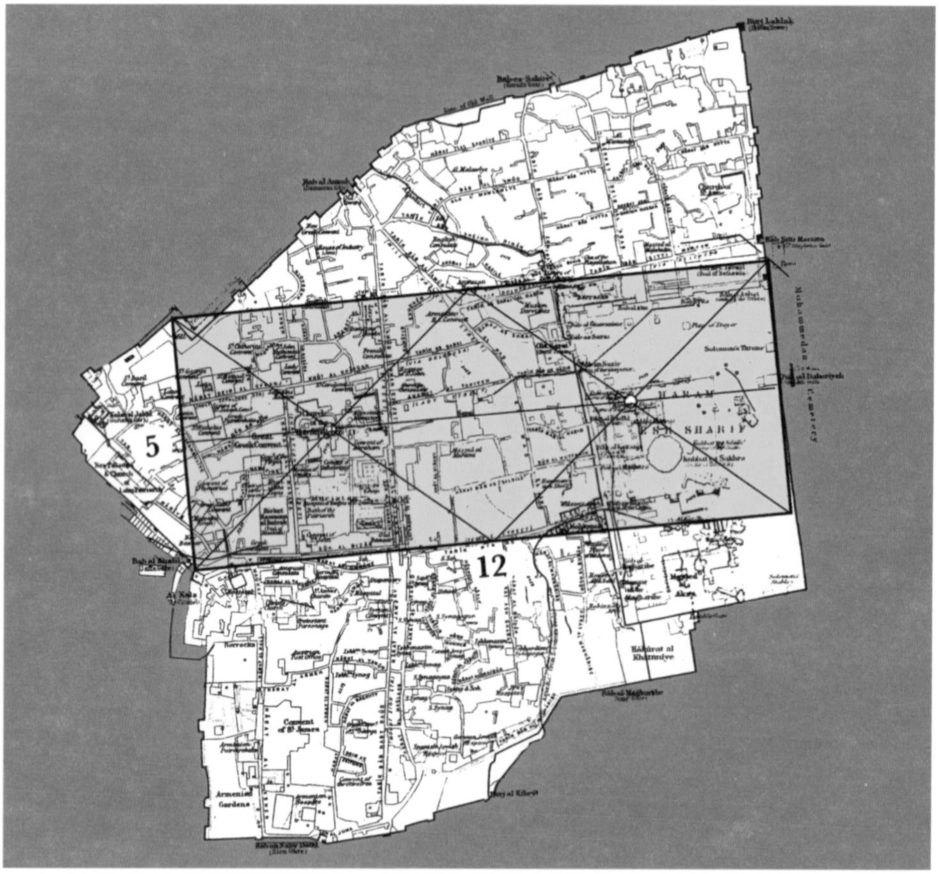

Fig. 89. The 5 by 12 rectangle containing the eschatological temple at Jerusalem is delineated by architectural landmarks, such as the Tomb of Absalom to the east. Within it, at the crossings of the diagonals, are the two sacred rocks of Jewry and Christianity. These are the Rock of Foundation in Solomon's Holy of Holies (east) and Golgotha, where Jesus was crucified (west). The distance between them is 864 cubits.

9 • Four and the Square

Reason, Stability, and Order

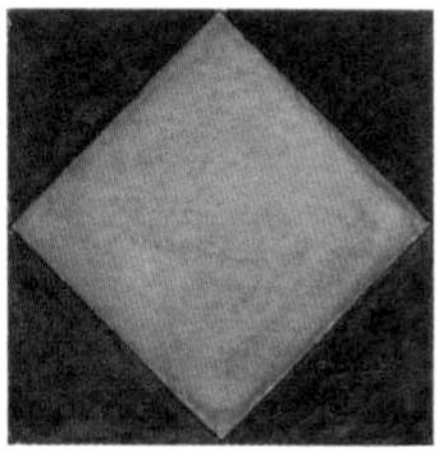

The Rational Square and the Root-2 Proportion

A further product of the vesica, the geometer's womb image, is the square, symbol of the number Four. If the Creator had the use of a T-square, as the Masonic emblem indicates, he could easily have drawn a square with his ready-made right angle. According to our myth, however, he had nothing but a compass and ruler, and when geometers talk of 'constructing' a figure, they mean drawing it with these instruments alone. The simplest way of constructing a square is to draw a circle with a diameter and enclose it in a vesica. Joining the two ends of the diameter to the two points where the longer axis of the vesica cuts the circle completes the square.

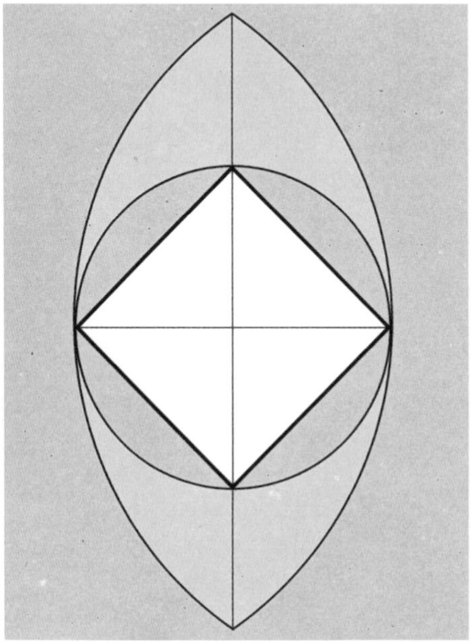

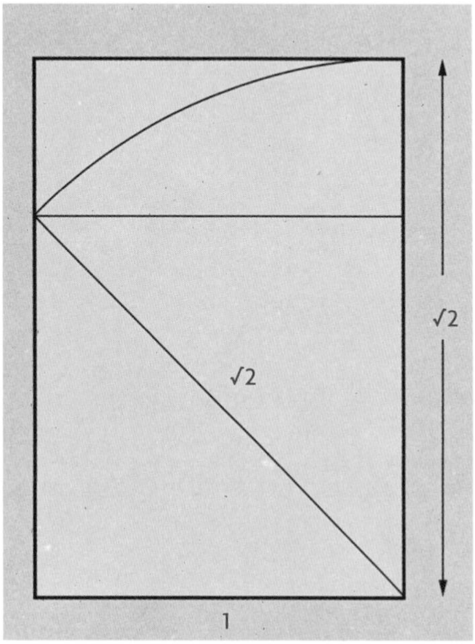

Fig. 90 (left). Constructing a square from a vesica piscis

Fig. 91 (right). The root-2 rectangle has its longer side equal to the diagonal of the square on its shorter side. For its practical advantages see figure 116.

In contrast to the circle, whose circumference is defined as its width times the irrational π, the square is a rational figure; the measure round its four sides is equal to four times its width. It stands for reason, stability, and order, as implied by such phrases as 'fair and square' and 'standing four-square'. The cube, the three-dimensional extension of the square, is the traditional symbol of earth and firm ground. Plato calls it the most stable of the geometric solids. Four or 2×2 is the first square number. With it the world acquired its four quarters and directions, four seasons, four primary colours, and the root-2 proportion favoured by rational administrators. The square is not often apparent in nature but dominates architecture and the works of man.

Doubling the Area of a Square: An Exercise in Recollection

The square, the most solid and material of geometric shapes, was used by Socrates to demonstrate the most highly ineffable of his philosophical doctrines, the immortality of the soul. We have, he observed, certain innate forms of knowledge which can be drawn out (educated) into our conscious minds. Knowledge, said Socrates, is recollection. The truths of number and geometry, for example, are within us, and we can either discover them for ourselves or, once they have been pointed out to us, we recognize them as old friends. If we have not been instructed in these things in this life, we must have learnt them in some other existence. In that case there is an immortal element in our beings—the soul.

In Plato's *Meno* is the extraordinary account of how Socrates claimed to prove his point. Meno, a rich man, was a disciple of Socrates, and at his house the master was speaking about virtue, what it really is and why and how one should attempt to acquire it. In the tradition of initiates, those who have learnt that reality is in our souls, he saw virtue as whatever feeds and cultivates the soul—which is nous, or total understanding. Everyone, he said, knows how to double the area of a square—if only they can remember it.

He asked Meno to bring forward one of his attendant slave boys, one who had been brought up in his household and had never received any form of

Fig. 92.

A quiet life

There's so much noise and bustle that
I've come to the decision
to go back to the place where I was born,
when nothing ever happened and,
instead of television,
we used to watch the blackbird on the lawn.

scholarly education. Socrates, probably using a sand tray, drew a square and asked the boy to draw another, double in size. That's easy, said the lad. He doubled the length of one side of the square and made a greater square upon it, but Socrates soon convinced him that the area of this square was not twice that of the original but four times larger. The base line must be 1½ times the side of the original square, suggested the boy, but that did not work either, and the poor youth, who had confidently asserted that he knew how to double a square, was reduced to confusion. That, said Socrates, is an excellent thing. If you once believed something and it is proved false, you are motivated to discover the truth. That is the first step towards knowledge.

If that boy had been given compasses or dividers, he could easily have doubled the square by swinging its diagonal onto its extended base line, thereby obtaining the $\sqrt{2}$ length needed to make a square of area 2. But in that case he would have needed to know the Pythagoras theorem. Socrates led him by an easier path. He took the boy's first square, measuring 2×2, and pointed out that, if you halved it, you would have the required area. The square is made up of four smaller squares, and when you divide each of them along its diagonal, you obtain a central square whose area is equal to four halves, which make two. Then you can see that the way to double the area of a given square is to draw a square on its diagonal.

Once the boy had seen that, thought Socrates, he would be drawn on to further studies and, if a normal, intelligent youth, would be set on the path towards initiation and nous.

As a type of messiah, who set out to purge the world of errors and bring both the individual and society into the state of nous, Socrates had to battle on two fronts. First he had to expose the false assumptions that are handed down by fathers, mothers, grandmothers, and generations of schoolmasters, and then, having broken down all beliefs and prejudices, to reconstitute minds with the truths that lie beyond opinion. Truths that lie? That is the paradox of earthly existence, where authorities proclaim great lies to be true, and truth resides, as ever, among the few who dare cultivate it. And that is why Socrates, who was executed for speaking truth several centuries before

Jesus, said in the *Republic* that a perfectly just man is bound to be crucified.

There is no doubt that Socrates, like all initiates, truly believed in the immortality of the soul, but it is hard to accept that he proved it by doubling the square with Meno's slave boy. In the first place he led him on blatantly, and it was not the boy but Socrates himself who solved the problem. Then again, is doubling the square a token of immortality? As faithful geometers, we can see this as a parable, an expression of truth in the guise of a good story.

Fig. 93. Doubling the square

The square that has to be doubled. For convenience Socrates makes it 2 x 2 with an area of 4.

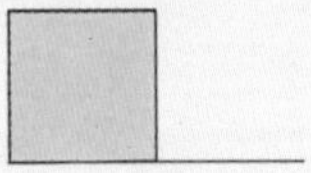

The boy's first effort. Doubling the base line . . .

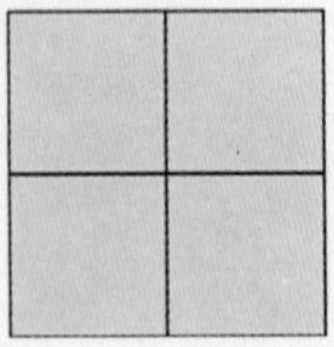

. . . produces a square that is not twice but four times the area of the original.

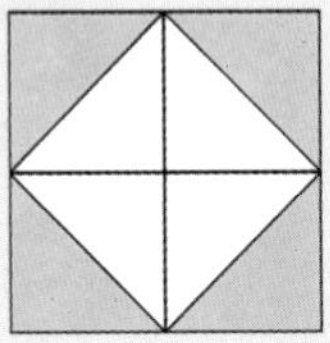

His second try, halving his original extension of the base line to make its length 3, gives a square of 9 rather than the required 8. The boy is confused and admits to not knowing the solution to the problem. But his curiosity is aroused and Socrates proceeds to engage his reason. By dividing all four squares into halves along their diagonals, he forms a central square containing four halves. He asks the boy to count them. In the original square there are two halves, and in the new square four halves. The boy is then congratulated on doubling the square!.

Fig. 94. This arrangement of squares looks like a letter rack or block of pigeon holes. It is one of the ingenious types of geometry used by the Cosmati, the guild of marblers and paviours who flourished in Italy in the Middle Ages.

Fig. 95. Another work by the Cosmati geometers is the marble pavement in Westminster Abbey, laid down in in 1268. Overall it is a symbolic picture of the universe. One of its features is the combination of square and triangle, illustrating together the √2 and √3 proportions.

Fig. 96. Three and Four are brought together under the aegis of Twelve. Starting from the central hexagram, the 6-sided geometry develops into a 12-sided polygon. On these 12 sides squares and triangles alternate, both inwards and outwards, and the gaps between the outer figures are filled with 12 similar triangles.

Fig. 97. Falling leaves: a pattern that combines the √2 (square) proportion with the √3 (rhombus). These figures illustrate the union of Three and Four, the first mixed marriage, i.e., between two different numbers.

Fig. 98. Another view of the 'falling leaves' pattern

10 • Six and the Hexagon

The Perfect Number

According to the story in the first chapter of Genesis, which is based on number and geometry, the universe was completed in six days. The number Six was allotted to the period of creation because it is the first perfect number. As St Augustine wrote in *The City of God,* "God, even though he could have created the world in an instant, decided to dedicate it to six days in order to reflect on the perfection of the universe".

A perfect number, as defined since ancient times, is a number that is the sum of its factors. The factors of 6 are 1, 2, and 3, and $1 + 2 + 3 = 6$. The next perfect number is 28 because the sum of its factors, $1 + 2 + 4 + 7 + 14$, equals 28. The third such number is 496, and after that perfect numbers become even rarer, 33,550,336 being only the fifth. Six is not only the first perfect number, it is unique in being doubly perfect because, as well as being the sum of its factors, it is their product also, for $1 \times 2 \times 3 = 6$.

Six is also called the marriage number because the hexagon is created by the union of the two equal triangles which are the first issue of the vesica piscis.

The hexagon and six-pointed star are easy to construct with the Creator's ruler and compass. The measure round the six sides of a hexagon is exactly six times the radius of the circle that contains it. Thus six pennies or plates or equal circles can be placed round an equal seventh so that each circle touches the central circle and its two neighbours. To construct a hexagon, draw a circle with its diameter, place the compass point on one end of the diameter and, without changing the compass opening, mark off two points on the circumference. Repeating the process from the other end of the diameter provides six equally spaced points around the circle.

From this can be drawn an endless succession of hexagonal patterns, the underlying grid being the diamond-shaped network produced by the $\sqrt{3}$ proportion.

The geometry of the number Six is regular and repetitive and occurs mainly in inorganic nature, such as the growth of crystals, the cells of a honeycomb, and the orderly structure of the universe. Hexagons will pack together endlessly, as also will triangles and squares, for they relate to matter rather than to life or spirit, which are represented by other orders of geometry.

Hexagonal geometry is so easy and rational that geometers tend to pass it by and move on to more challenging systems. But as every child with a compass knows, there is great satisfaction in the patterns to be found within the simple hexagonal order. And there are more subtleties and illusions in it than is immediately obvious. The perfection of Six is emphasized in Genesis for good reason. In the geometer's myth the Great Architect wanted the structure of his creation to be perfect, so he used the geometry of Six to make it so.

Fig. 99. The hexagonal rug. This classical hexagon pattern is one of nature's wonders. It is a 1:$\sqrt{3}$ rectangle containing 216 hexagons. Each hexagon consists of 3 diamond rhombs, differently toned to give the 3-D effect. The are 216 dark diamonds, and the other 4 tones are in pairs of 216 each. The numeral 216 is the appropriate hexagon number being 6 x 6 x 6. The 12 horizontal rows in the hexagon pattern show regular intervals between their 4 tones.

Fig. 100. This mat on a polished wooden floor displays the hexagon pattern and contains 1296 (= 6 x 6 x 6 x 6) diamond shapes.

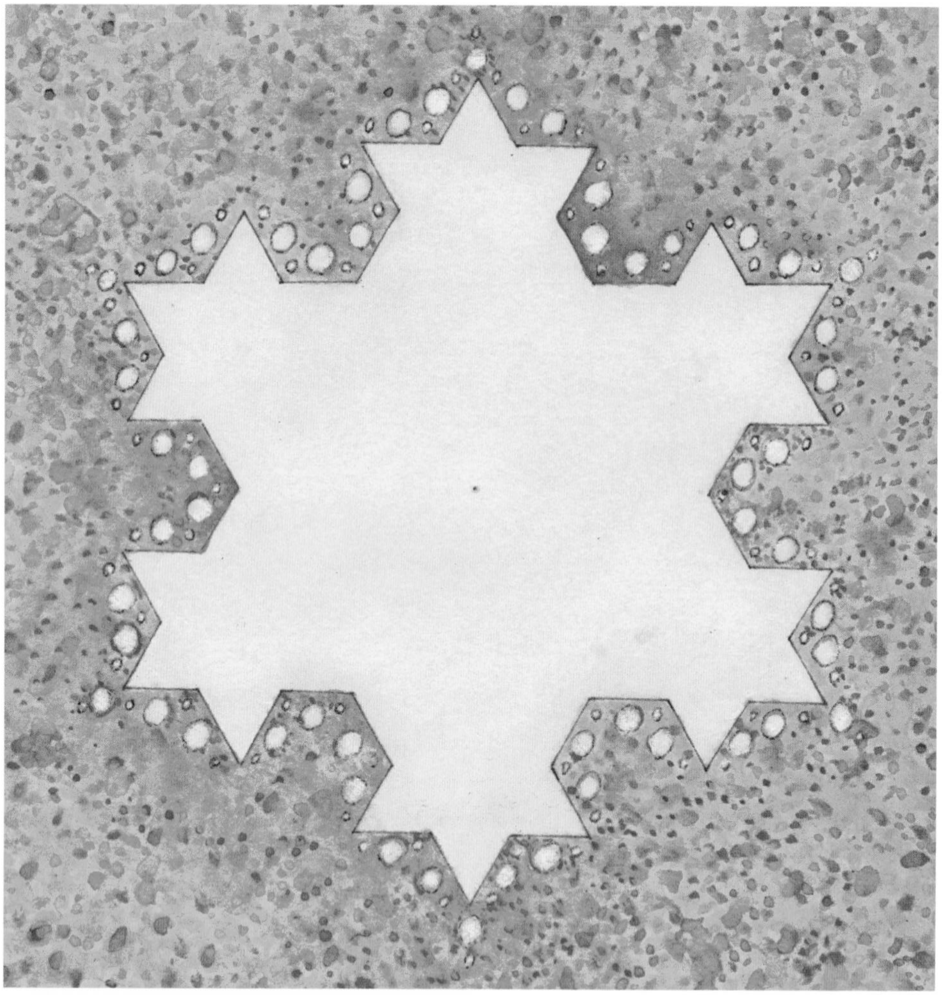

Fig. 101. Hexagonal geometry is often displayed in crop circles. This specimen, situated below Silbury Hill, Wiltshire, in 1997, has a fringe of 126 'gemstones' (54 large, 72 small).

Fig. 102. The crop circle with its precious geometry is cordoned off by the imaginary intertwining of a hexagon and a hexagram.

Fig. 103. The strange, baroque pattern formed by the lay of the wheat within the Silbury Hill formation is given colour to create a jewel-like effect.

11 • Eight and the Octagon

For Peace and Justice

Eight is the first cubic number (2 × 2 × 2). Like the cube the octagon has eight corners and is made up of squares. In the octagon is consummated the second of the sacred marriages in geometry, the union of two equal squares, overlapping diagonally. From these square associations the octagon derives the earthly side of its character. It conforms throughout to the $\sqrt{2}$ proportion.

Eight belongs to the class of numbers called 'evenly even' because they can be halved and halved again right down to 1. In the same way, a sheet of the ordinary A4-size typing paper, whose sides are in the $1:\sqrt{2}$ proportion, can be folded in half to make A5, half of which is A6, and so on, always retaining the same $\sqrt{2}$ ratio in its sides. The evenly even series begins 2, 4, 8, 16, 32, 64. . . . These numbers are popular with architects and were much used by the medieval masons. In churches and chapter houses throughout Europe their wonderful octagonal and sixteen-fold symmetries in stone delight the senses and at the same time are strictly functional in roofing and supporting their structures.

A common architectural use for the octagon is to bridge the gap between square and circle, as when a dome or a cylindrical spire, symbolizing the heavens, is set upon a square base, symbol of earth. The octagon that mediates between these two opposite shapes has the appropriate angelic symbolism. This is indicated by its characteristic number, given by the sum of its eight 135-degree interior angles, which is 1080, the number of the Holy Spirit. Octagons are often found in the bases of old stone crosses and holy fountains.

As evidence of their higher nature, octagons will not pack together like triangles, squares, and hexagons. In a crowd they line up and down in orderly fashion, leaving blank squares on four of their sides (figure 104, top). This is a common tiling pattern, a favourite for bathroom floors. 'Male' octagons with points on each of their eight sides stand farther away from each other, tip to tip, separated by an equal number of pointed crosses (figure 104, below). These cross shapes, for reasons to be explained, can be called hermaphrodite octagons. Despite their formality, octagons are highly adaptable, have many possible divisions, and generate a large number of patterns, both in themselves and in formation with others of their kind.

Fig. 104. Octagons, packed as closely as possible, produce the 'bathroom tile' pattern. Octagon stars, made by two squares in marriage, are divided from each other by pointed crosses.

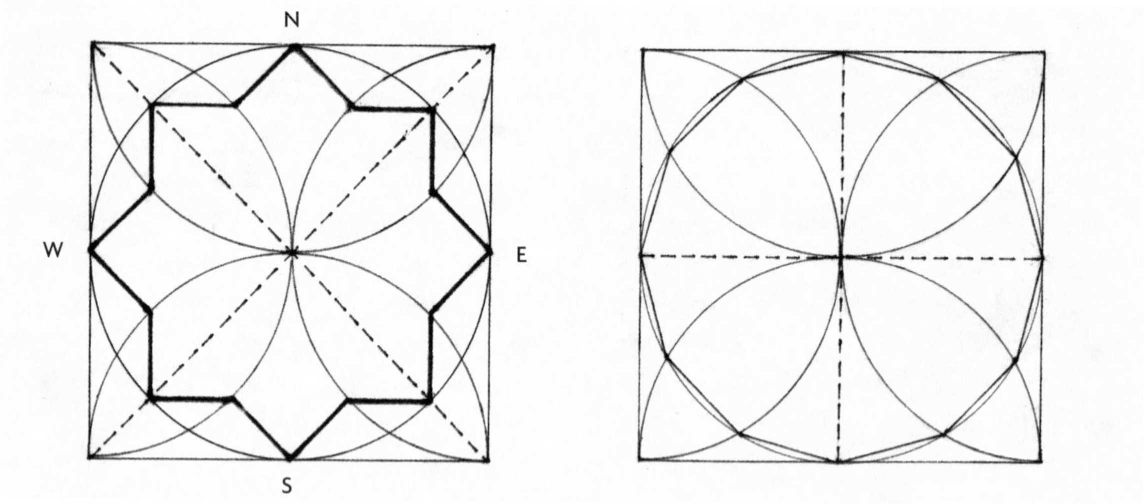

Fig. 105. An attractive construction of an octagon by arcs from the points of a given square, NSEW, passing through its centre. By this method the circle, through the points of the octagon, is divided into both eight and twelve parts.

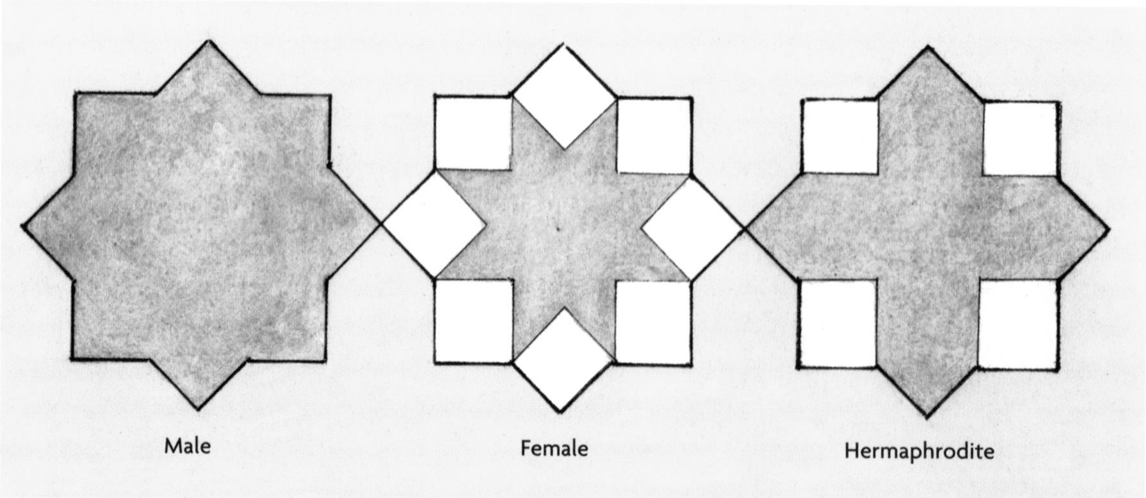

Fig. 106. The three octagonal sexes. In accordance with their reputation for fairness, octagonal figures have three sexes: male, female, and hermaphroditic. These three types constantly mingle with and transform into each other. The male octagon is so called because it has protruding points on all eight sides. In the female octagon the points are folded inwards to make eight recesses, and the hermaphrodite figure, cross shaped, has four protrusions and four recesses.

Fig. 107. Justice and equilibrium. As the architectural link between square and circle, the octagon stands for peace through reconciliation of heaven and earth. And since lasting peace is impossible without justice, that virtue is also demonstrated in the octagon. There are many ways of drawing eight-sided and eight-pointed figures and dividing their areas. Those that best depict the fair, even-handed nature of the octagon have areas equally divided between light and dark. These figures and their dominant number Eight are popular in eastern systems of divination and are considered lucky. These and the following examples of octagonal patterns begin with a selection that exhibit justice in their equal dark and light areas, and continue with unequal examples.

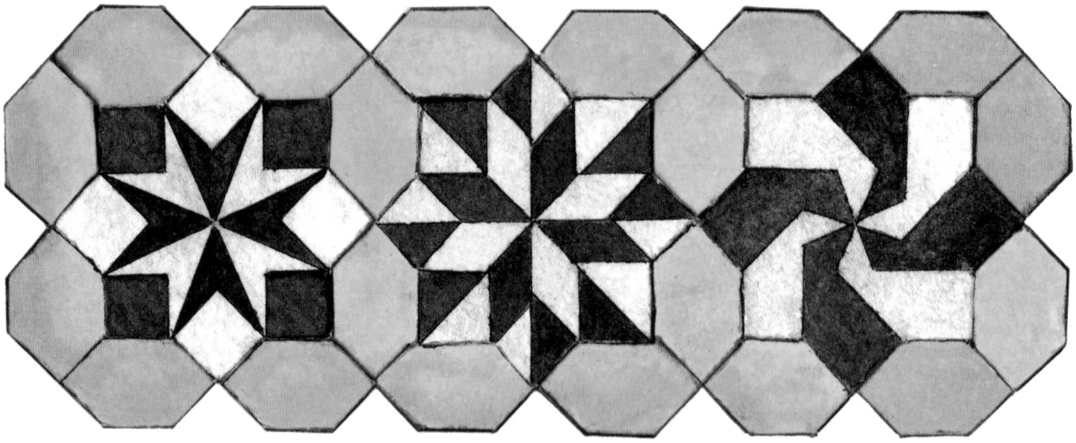

Fig. 108. Octagons, equal areas of dark and light, framed in six-sided lozenges

Fig. 109. Octagon types

Fig. 110. Octagon types (light and dark blue) in a colourful frame

Fig. 111. Octagonal spinners

Fig. 112. Octagons are a byword for dignified stability but here is a rare example of an octagonal dance.

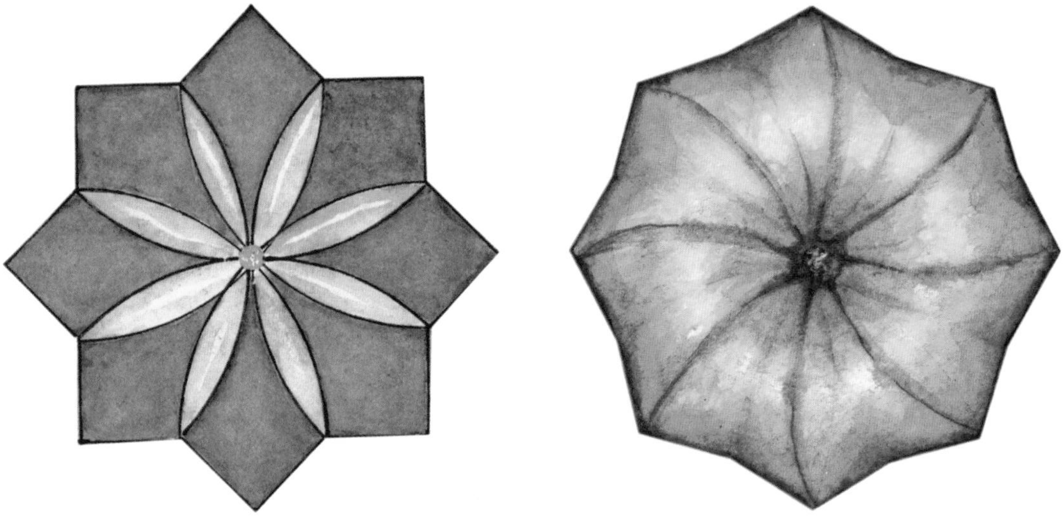

Fig. 113. Octagonal leaf and flower patterns

Fig. 114. Octagonal economy. Another illustration of justice in the octagon occurs in this method of constructing an octagon with sides equal to that of a given square. Four circles are drawn on the corners of the central square, passing through its centre. The points where the extended sides of the square cut the rims of the circles mark the eight angles of the octagon.

A circle is drawn to contain the four circles, and it is calculated that its area is equal to that of the four circles individually combined. That means that the areas where they overlap are equal to the areas they do not cover. Also equal are the two lengths of line that make up this figure. (There are twenty-four lines in all, including the four semi-diagonals.) If the four equal sides of the square and the eight sides of the octagon measure two units, the other twelve lines measure $\sqrt{2}$.

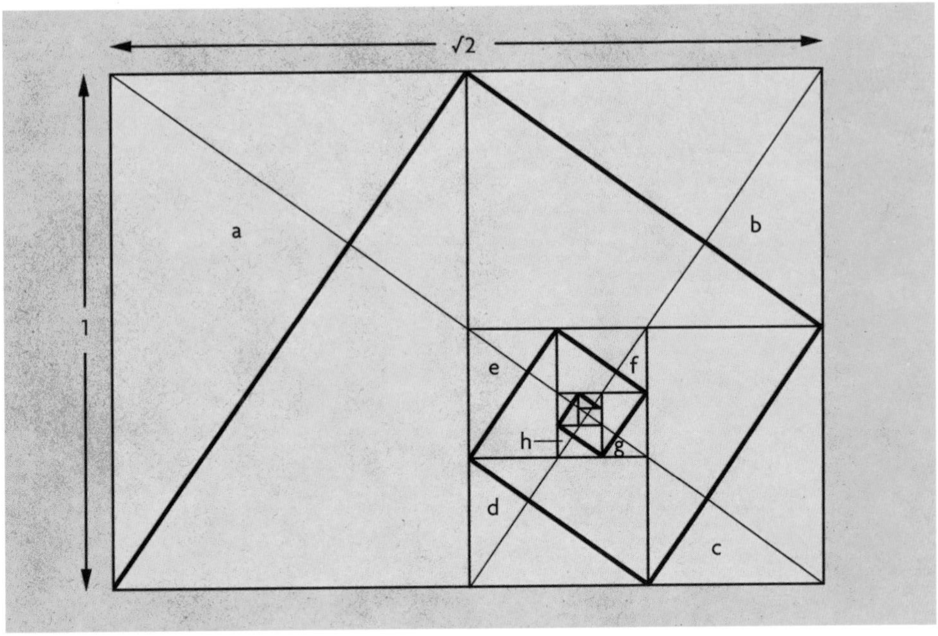

Fig. 115. The root-2 rectangle and its uses. The rectangle featured in the octagon, with sides of 1 x √2 (or 2 x √2 if the longer side is put first), has the unique property that, when it is divided into two, its half has the same proportion as the whole. This division is made by the thin line drawn perpendicular to its diagonal. The point where they intersect is the 'eye' of the rectangle around which successive root-2 rectangles spiral. This proportion, made rational as 99 x 70, was known by the ancient geometers and is used in the modern A4, A3, etc., paper sizes, A4 being 297 x 210mm or 3 times 99 x 70. These dimensions, about 11.7 x 8.3 inches, are too big for this book, as well as objectionably metric, but the root-2 proportion is attractive, so we have chosen the simple 9.9 x 7 inches.

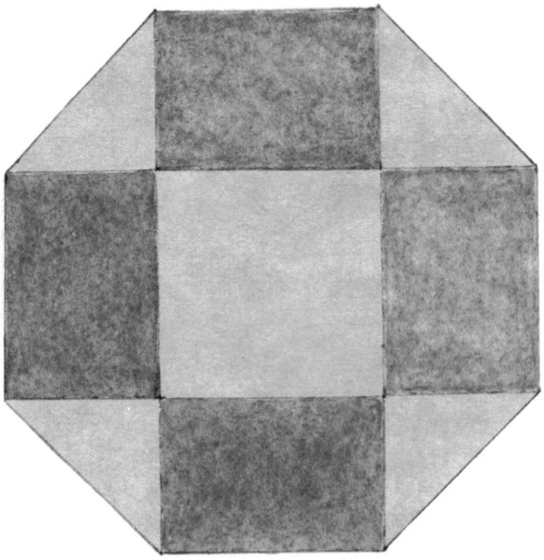

Fig. 116. Four root-2 rectangles form the greater part of an octagon. Their areas, taken together, exceed the other areas (blue) by √2 to 1.

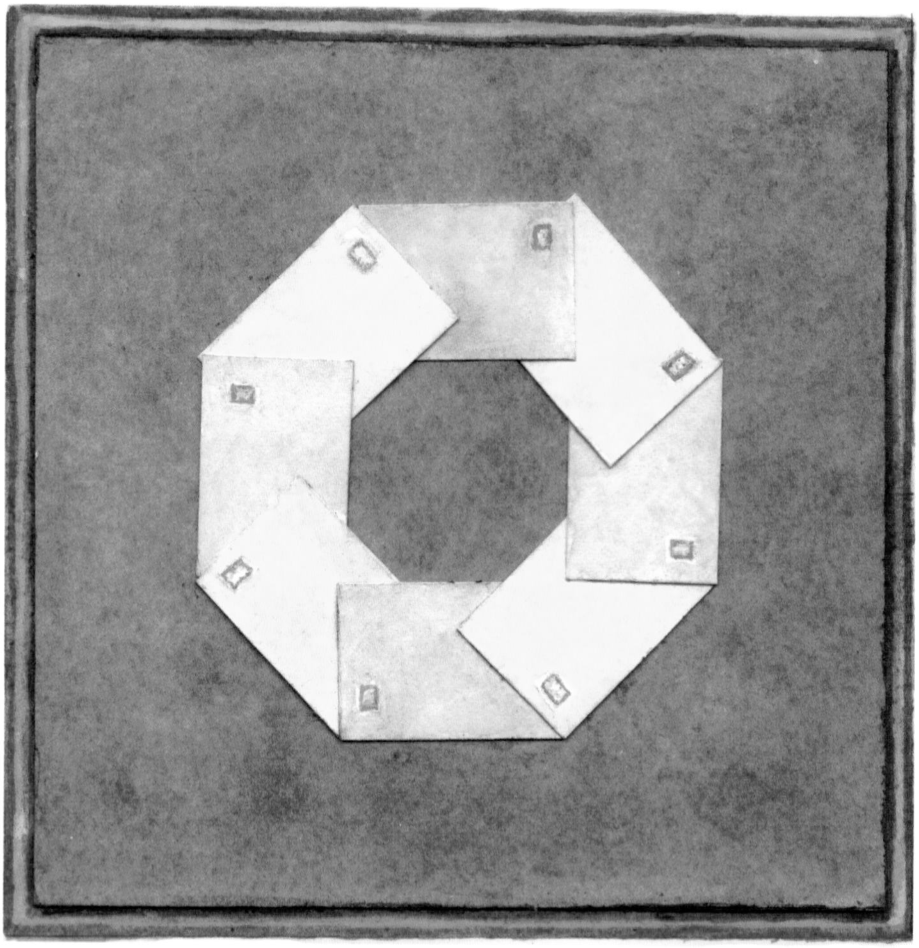

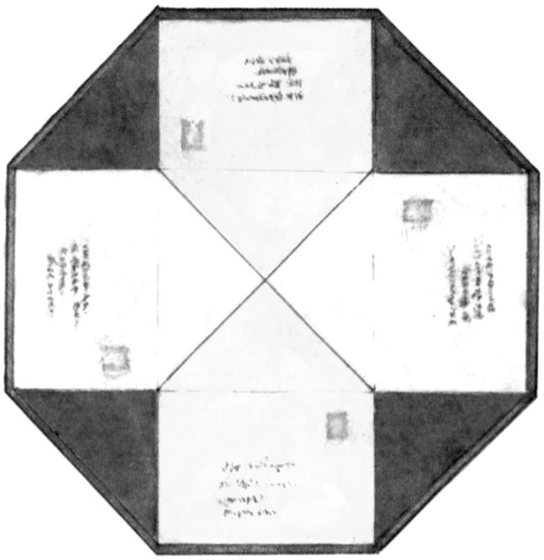

Fig. 117. Eight A-series envelopes, in the root-2 proportion, arranged on a card table, overlap to create an inner and an outer octagon.

Fig. 118. A-series envelopes, because of their root-2 proportion, lie together with their flaps open on an octagonal table.

Fig. 119. The root-2 overlapping rectangles are repeated within the central octagon and recede inwards towards infinity.

Fig. 120. The component parts of this octagon are rearranged to form the two strips above and below it.

Fig. 121. The twenty-four isosceles triangles that make up a hollow octagram are packed together in the rectangle below it.

Fig. 122. Octagonal kite in Sussex

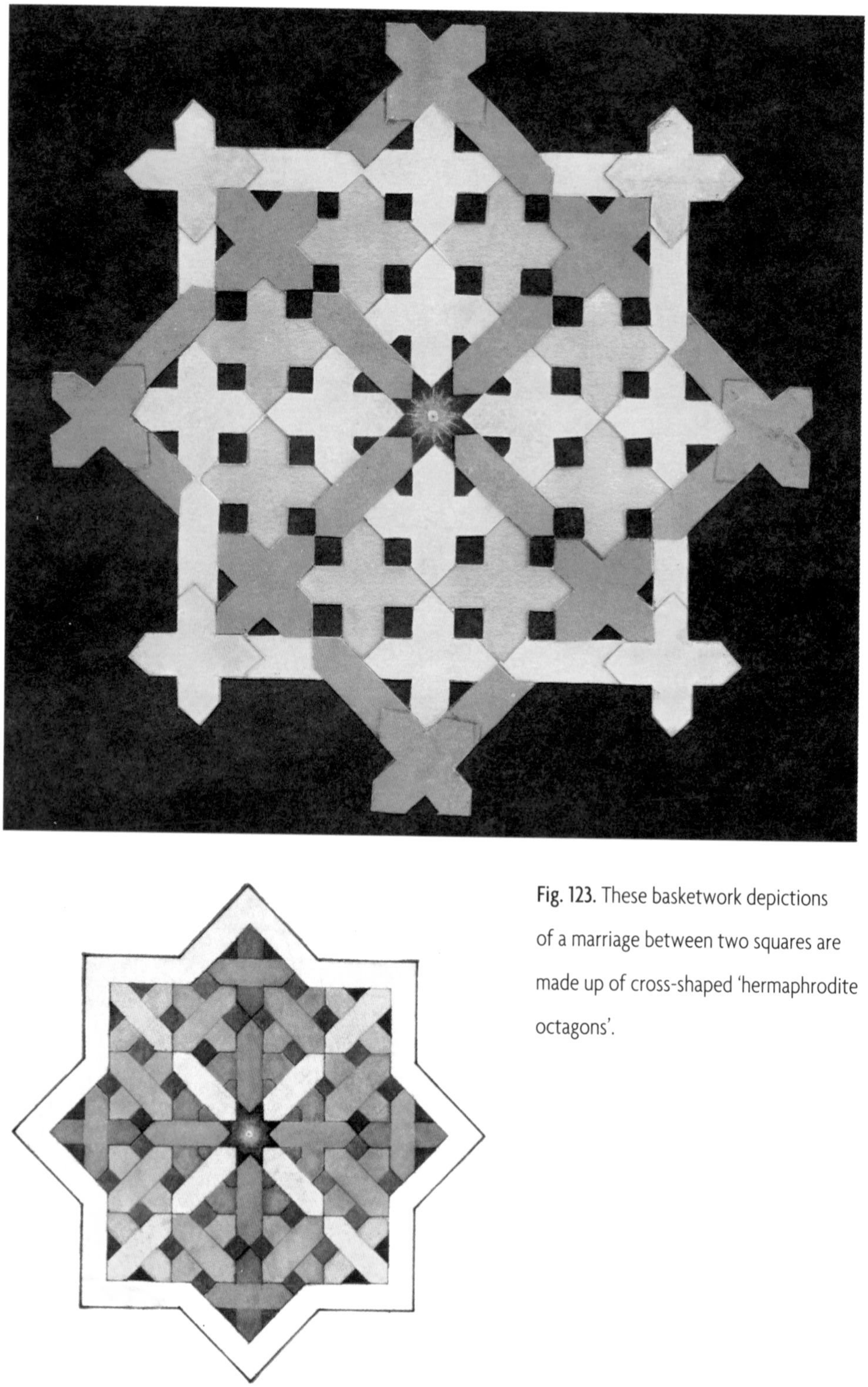

Fig. 123. These basketwork depictions of a marriage between two squares are made up of cross-shaped 'hermaphrodite octagons'.

Fig. 124. Octagonal economy: a forest settlement

Fig. 125. Octagonal illumination with wise counsel from Ecclesiastes 12

Fig. 126. A beautiful and geometrically ingenious octagon appeared in this crop formation at Alton Barnes, Wiltshire, in 2004. It is not difficult to draw and colour by hand, but on this scale, about 200 ft. across, it is a formidable night's work.

Fig. 127 (previous pages) and **128 (above).** Cursive octagonal patterns. A web of strips at right angles with octagonal holes is woven by repetitions of the octagonal types below.

Fig. 129. Octagonal details from the cursive octagonal pattern

Fig. 130. Huge geometric figures, accurately surveyed across the rough mountain landscape of Peru, can only be seen wholly from the air. This design in the Palpa mountains is a rational variation of the octagon, made up of two unequal squares within the overall grid of small squares. The respective areas of the squares forming the octagon are as 8 : 9, the interval of a musical tone. The dimensions of the whole figure can be calculated from the estimated length of one side of the little squares, 26.4 ft. See also figs. 52 and 53.

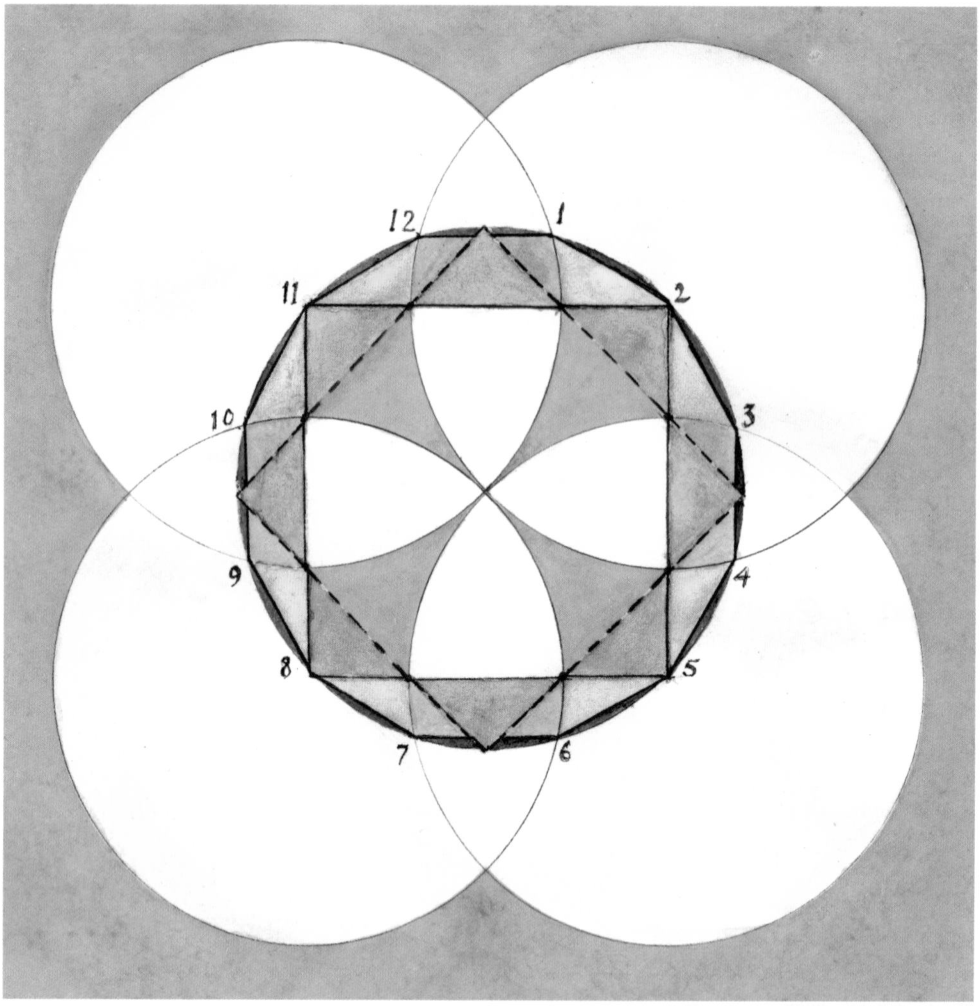

Figs. 131 (above) and **132 (left).** Eight and Twelve. The same construction, beginning with four arcs or (for the sake of completion) circles centred upon the four corners of a square, divides the circle around the square into both eight and twelve parts.

Fig. 133. The arithmetical progression 4, 8, 12 is illustrated by this combination of shapes corresponding to these numbers. By the widths of the strips making up the 12-pointed figure, the overlying square in the octagon is divided into 9 lesser squares.

Fig. 134. Combinations of Twelve and Eight with ruler and compass

12 • The Majestic Twelve

The Number of Universal Order and Harmony

In the field of number, Twelve is the ruler of all. The entire structure of number is basically duodecimal, and so is the cosmological diagram that depicts, through the paradigm of number, the entire universe. Twelve is above all the number of order. It is the root number in the code of proportions that governs the solar system, and it therefore plays the leading part in all aspects of cosmologically ordered societies, wherever they arise. It may be called the framework number.

Twelve is the first number to be called 'super-abundant', meaning that the sum of its factors is greater than itself. The factors of 12 are 1, 2, 3, 4, 6, adding up to 16. Its shape, the dodecagon, accommodates the geometries of the structural numbers Three, Four, Six, Eight, and also, as shown later, the geometry of Seven. The twelve-pointed figure is made up of three squares, four triangles, or two hexagons.

In three-dimensional geometry the number Twelve reigns supreme. Ever since Johann Kepler claimed to have packed all the five regular or Platonic solids into successive shells, corresponding to the planetary orbits, geometers and physicists have followed the same path towards the depiction of universal order, from the astronomical to the atomic scale. Our master-geometer, Keith Critchlow, in his book of 1969, *Order in Space,* emphasizes the twelve-sided dodecahedron as the all-embracing shape, and he shows how twelve spheres, compressed together, give rise to the other solid figures. (See also his *Islamic Patterns* where the regular solids are examined in detail.) A model of the five regular solids, fitted within each other and all enclosed by a dodecahedron, is exhibited by Stephen Wilmoth, architect and geometer of California. The twelve-sided figure, he concludes, is the matrix and generator of all the other shapes. On the sub-atomic level, where solid matter gives way to abstract geometry, Dr Robert J. Moon of the University of Chicago has analysed the nuclei of atoms comprising the various elements, showing how they conform to the shapes of the five regular and thirteen semi-regular or Archimedean solids. The puritan fundamentalists of science are suspicious of such approaches, seeing in them a gateway to deism—and perhaps they are right. Facts are indeed neutral, but perception of the same beautiful, rational organisation in every dimension of nature leads inevitably to meditation on its source.

The drawing (page 162) of the twelve spheres, each touching an equal thirteenth at the centre, depicts the geometric model for the entire range and variety of groups of twelve around a leader. Jesus and his disciples provide the most obvious example for Christians, but the pattern is endlessly repeated in the traditions of all nations, where a great teacher, hero, or religious founder is surrounded by a group of twelve knights or holy men, who divide the country around them into twelve zodiacal sections. Legendary examples include King Arthur, Charlemagne, Solomon and the twelve tribes of Israel, Odin who led the twelve gods to Scandinavia, and St Finian with the twelve scholar-saints of old Ireland. Sometimes the central thirteenth is replaced by a holy shrine or oratory, where twelve missionaries, like St Joseph and his followers in the Glastonbury legend, maintain a perpetual round of prayer and chant.

In recognition of the essentially duodecimal nature of number, the circle is traditionally divided into 60 degrees, each of 60 minutes or 3600 seconds. The French revolutionaries wanted a 400-degree circle to go with their metric system, but that made the angle of a triangle 66.666 . . . degrees rather than 60, so the idea was dropped. In some remote, unknown age, the zodiac was divided into twelve sections, so that the sun passed through one zodiacal house or sign in 2160 years, which is $6 \times 6 \times 60$, the same as the diameter of the moon in miles and ten times the number of minutes in a circle. Music was similarly adapted to the chromatic scale of twelve notes, and nations were divided accordingly into twelve tribes with twelve gods, each ruling one section of the zodiac.

Twelve Tribes and the Revelation of the Heavenly Order

Twelve is associated with Apollo, the solar deity whose dominance coincides with settlement, civilisation, and a social order designed to reflect the twelve-fold pattern of the cosmos. Like its model, the sublunary centre of the universal diagram, the nation was divided into two halves, four quarters, and twelve tribes, three to each quarter. Each tribe was placed under one of the twelve zodiacal gods, and each had its corresponding tone of music and celebrated one of the twelve episodes in the national saga—that of Gilgamesh for the Babylonians and the twelve-part Arthurian cycle in Celtic regions.

At the centre of these cosmological societies, making the thirteenth sphere amid the twelve, was the national sanctuary and the seat of the ruler, a sacred king who played the Sun in the ritual drama. It was rare that he actually sat there, because his whole life was a procession. Like the sun passing through the zodiac, the king with his court and retinue proceeded month by month through the circle of twelve tribes, holding law-courts in each and presiding over games and festivals. Dramas were enacted about the particular episode of the national saga that was located in the landscape of that tribe, and the festival music echoed their particular note in the twelve-part chant. At the end of the circuit, usually at midsummer, the whole nation came together at the ritual centre where the national parliament and the high court had their sessions. These were always in the open air, with twelve councillors, twelve judges, and the ever-traditional twelve jurymen to represent the twelve human types. It was a time of sports and contests, trading and treating, music, dancing, and all sorts of entertainments, and at the centre of it all was the serious business of upholding the nation's law-code, said to have been divinely given, together with its standards of culture.

Nation-states founded upon the cosmological pattern have been known in every part of the world. Their legendary origin is as perpetual choirs, where each tribe contributed its note to a sacred chant that passed continuously round the circuit of twelve. The first amphyctiony (league of twelve tribes or choristers around a common sanctuary) was established, according to the Greek tradition, by Orpheus and was centred upon Delphi. There, in the midst of the sanctuary, was the holy shrine, said to be the birthplace of the nation and also the spot where the world pole passed through the earth. This was a universal claim, attached to the centre of every cosmologically ordered society. It was demonstrated by siting the national sanctuary on the symbolic pole of each country, meaning the longest line, preferably north-south, that could be drawn through it. The ideal spot was halfway along the axis, but if the terrain there was unsuitable, compromises were necessary. Examples of this practice are collected in a previous book, *At the Centre of the World* (1994), and subsequent research (mostly confined to island realms where the boundaries are drawn by nature) has produced others. The present significance of this is that, wherever the national place of assembly has been located exactly or nearly halfway along the pole of a country, it was the hub and focus of a ritualised social order, based on the duodecimal pattern and the same traditional code of universal harmony.

All this, you may suppose, was long ago and far away. Even in Plato's time the old, Orphean, twelve-tribe choir and order of society were no longer in popular memory. His attempt to revive the old order was partly practical and political (in the model constitution he describes in *Laws*), but equally it was on the level of the mind. The code of knowledge behind these societies, said Plato, was divine revelation, a lighting-up of minds. Every nation that has adopted the cosmological pattern as its foundation claims to have received it from some god or goddess. Plato's story in *Laws* is that from time to time the gods appear on earth and rule over us—but so lightly and naturally that we do not even know that we are being governed. When they leave us, they impart the secrets of their rule to certain people, urging them to maintain the god-given laws and customs, never changing their modes of music or any aspect of their culture. As long as this is done all goes well. It is as if the gods were still ruling or, in another image, as if the Holy Grail were apparent on earth. But entropy is always at work and human nature is weak. Eventually the order established by the gods becomes diluted and the enchantment that held it is broken. That is when progress begins, the march of civilisation and the rise towards the great state of Babylon—or, in Plato's allegory, doomed Atlantis.

Most interesting here is Plato's assertion that revelations of the heavenly order occur at different times and always have done. Yet the content of these revelations, and their numerical core, is always the same. Sometimes it must happen that the revelation strikes someone who is in a position to institute it—a young, initiated ruler perhaps who can reform his people on cosmological principles. Far more often, of course, it is to individuals whose power extends little farther than their own minds. There, in the mind, is where Socrates said that the 'pattern in the heavens' might be established, and there, in the minds of his students and readers, Plato wanted to install the divine code of knowledge, the instrument of peace and understanding.

In supposing that revelations took place only in the remote past, we are evidently mistaken. Long after Plato's time the very same form of constitution that he described has been implemented in various parts of the world. It was enacted by the Norsemen in the ninth and tenth centuries, when they settled Iceland and the Faroes and divided both countries and each part of them in accordance with that same code of number and geometry. When the French colonizers seized Madagascar at the end of the nineteenth century, deposing its queen, they discovered a full-blown, cosmological state pattern and a ritual form of government through a council of the twelve kings of the twelve tribes into which the people were divided. Anthropologists were puzzled by how precisely the elaborate constitution and ceremonies of the Madagascan state paralleled those of old Iceland and of Ireland in the days of its high kings. The apparent conclusion is that these and all cosmological societies everywhere have been founded upon the same canon, code of knowledge, and symbolic world plan that Plato took as the basis of his ideal city and state of mind.

The most essential part of the revealed pattern of universal order is the number Twelve. As the symbol of the architecture behind the cosmos (whose total area in our universal diagram is 12!), it is a number to be respected. Its geometric forms are pleasingly complete and symmetrical. Its proportions accommodate all the structural orders of geometry, and it is divisible into halves, thirds, and quarters—unlike the simple, sublunary Ten. If a society, or its human unit, is to be orientated with reality, it should surely count and categorize everything in twelves. Yet Ten is a good, useful number, also to be respected, and it is duly combined with Twelve in the ancient number system. There is no obvious geometrical union between these two basic numbers, symbols respectively of structure and life, but it is provided on a lower level by their halves, Six and Five, whose combinations are illustrated later, beginning on page 202.

The most perfect of all geometric marriages must be that between Twelve and Seven, body and soul. The construction of this union is again not obvious, but it is the climax of the geometer's odyssey, and it is achieved with great rejoicing in the last part of this story.

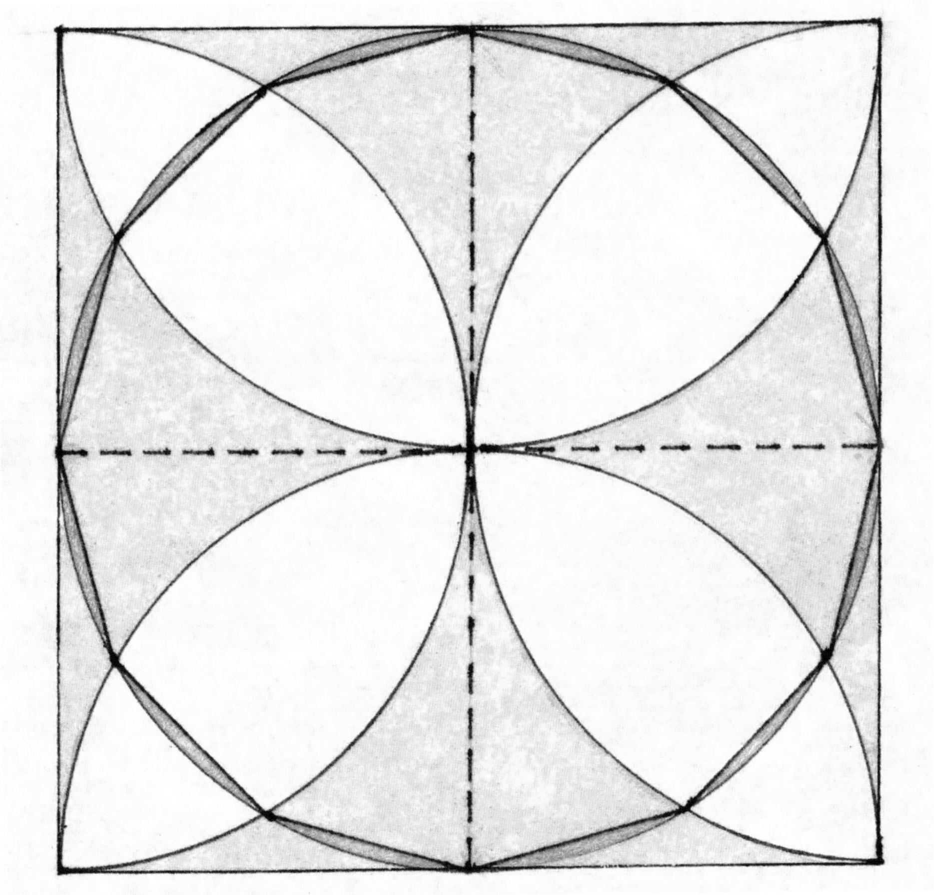

Fig. 135. Dividing a circle into 12 parts—method 1. Four arcs through the centre of the circle from each of its four quarters make the 12-part division.

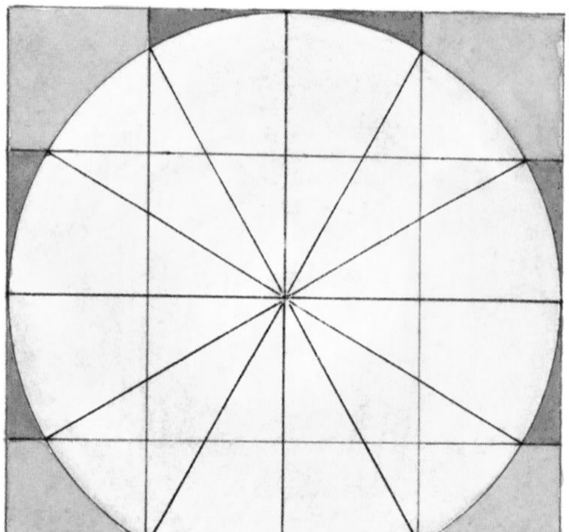

Fig. 136. Dividing a circle into 12—method 2. The circle is enclosed in a square divided into 16 lesser squares. Lines from the centre to the points where the circle meets the straight lines divide the circle into 12.

Fig. 137. Four triangles or three squares (here with another three squares inside them) combine to produce the 12-faceted figure that symbolizes perfect structure and the harmonious cycles of the cosmos.

Fig. 138. The 4 triangles that make up a 12-pointed figure create 90° angles, allowing 12 squares to fit around it and to overlap neatly around the centre.

Fig. 139. A whirling dodecagon, or twelve geese on a common, with a nut

Fig. 140. The famous 12-faceted east window of Chartres cathedral is based on the 12-pointed star which begins, conceptually, beyond the window itself (pale) and defines the sides of the 12 squares that tumble around its centre.

Fig. 141. This design, based on a Wiltshire crop circle, is made up of 12 circles struck from 12 regularly spaced points around the inner circle. The figure has 24 radii and 120 separate areas.

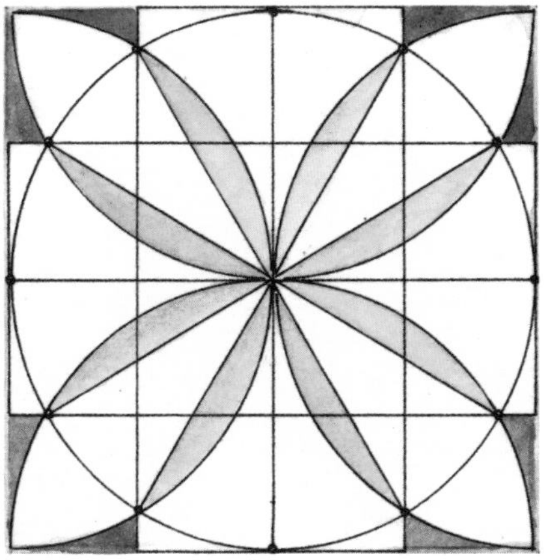

Fig. 142. Variations on the 12-part division

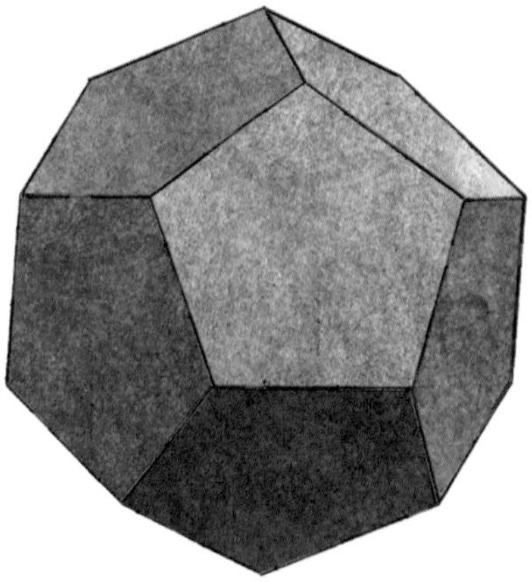

Fig. 143. The dodecahedron, the leader and most mystical of the five regular solid figures, has twelve sides, each of which is a pentagon. The pentagon star, as illustrated later, is a natural symbol of humanity, so the dodecahedron signifies the highest ideals, the twelve nations or types of personality united within the harmony of the number Twelve. It also illustrates the traditional, sacred pattern of twelve tribes around a common sanctuary or twelve saints or heroes with a thirteenth as leader.

There is another version of the legendary group of twelve, without the addition of a thirteenth. Examples include the eleven missionaries, together with St Joseph, who founded the church at Glastonbury, and the twelve tribes of Israel in their early days, who each presided in turn without a permanent central authority. These two groupings each have their own geometric prototype, shown in the drawings of Keith Critchlow and reproduced below from his 1966 book, *Order in Space*.

The first, where the twelve spheres all touch a thirteenth of equal size, is called a 'cuboctahedron'. In the second, the twelve spheres have no need for a central nucleus of equal size and the figure is categorized as an 'icosahedron', the Platonic dual of the dodecahedron. This figure, like the dodecahedron, has twelve faces.

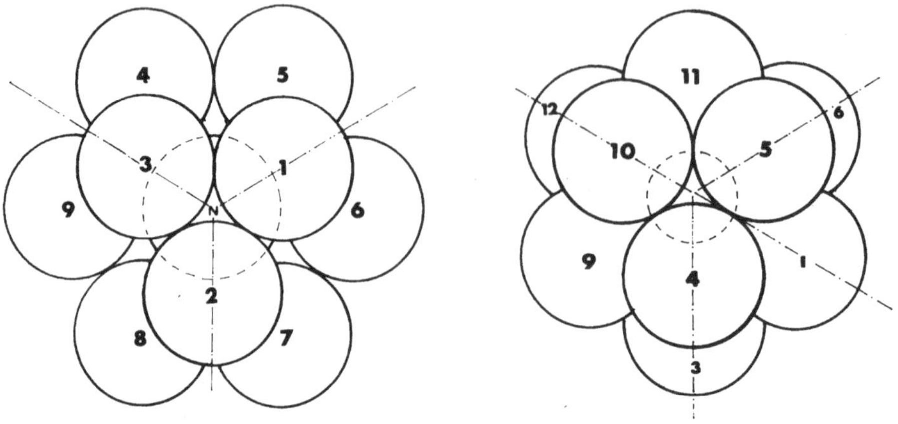

Fig. 144. Twelve spheres around a thirteenth of equal proportions (cuboctahedron, left) and twelve spheres without a centre (icosahedron, right)

Fig. 145. The Heavenly City

Fig. 146 (opposite). The marriage of two pentagrams, five-pointed stars, generates this firework display of pentagonal geometry.

Part 3

THE CREATION OF LIFE

The Geometry of Five and Ten

13 • Five and Ten

Numbers of Life and Growth

Life and the Pentagon

On the third day of creation, according to Genesis, the Creator, having separated earth from ocean and provided dry land, began seeding it with grass, herbs, fruit trees, and plants of all kinds. For this new stage in his work, the introduction of life, the Creator needed another kind of geometry, the pentagonal, illustrating the Pentad, the number Five, the primary symbol of life and the living spirit.

Five has left its signature throughout nature. Briar roses and most other wildflowers have five petals with pentagonal stamens and tiny geometrical patterns around their centres, reflecting the number Five. All trees and shrubs that bear edible fruit have five-sided flowers, and their pentagonal geometry is continued in the fruit itself. Cutting an apple in two along its equator exposes the delicate little pentagram formed by its seeds. The same pentagonal shapes and details occur in starfish and many other marine creatures of all sizes, down to the microscopic level. The wonders of natural geometry are endlessly varied, yet in every case so apt and ingenious that geometers are made humble by an art so far beyond their own abilities. The old clergyman-naturalists of days gone by were drawn irresistibly towards the conclusion that behind nature's artwork is the mind and purpose of a great Artist. "Consider the lilies of the field", cried Jesus. "They toil not neither do they spin: and yet I say unto you, that even Solomon in all his glory was not arrayed like one of these."

Darwin's revolution burst the bubble. The Creator was torn from his throne and demoted to a figment of imagination, while Evolution was set up in his place. Yet at the same time, the development of photography and science opened a new perspective on nature's geometry. Artists, scientists, mystics, and anyone who has been struck by the phenomenon of artistic design in nature are united in praise of it. Whatever the cause may be, the beauty and wit in the designs of living forms is apparent to all who care to look.

In our geometrical creation story, the Creator is a mythic character, named as the leading player in the drama, but otherwise unknown. He is not the dogmatic, humanized God of religious creationism, and he is not encumbered with the literalism that evolutionists apply to their First Principle. We call him the Great Geometer, just for the sake of our story. But without him and his wonderful Creation there would not be any story to tell.

In the Pythagoreans' colleges where numbers were studied as individual entities, Five was held in great honour and the pentagram was made the emblem of their brotherhood. Their mystic sigils showed its five points each with the letter of an appropriate virtue or deity, such as Υγεια, Health, or Ερμης, Hermes, the god most closely identified with the number Five. Five was called the marriage number—not just because it unites Two and Three, but from its link with humanity and all other creatures that breed in pairs. You cannot go far into pentagonal geometry without seeing that, in order fully to develop its patterns, the pentagon has to find another of its kind to link up with, forming a ten-sided figure, the decagon, which enables it to reproduce. In the *Symposium* Plato repeats the strange, geometric fable of how human beings were once happily joined together in pairs and rolled along the ground like hoops. But even then they behaved badly, and God punished them by splitting up the pairs. Ever since then, we have been trying to find our natural partners, our other halves, and join up with them to regain the former bliss. "The Desire and Pursuit of the Whole" is Plato's name for this process. The geometric clues to the diagrams that must have illustrated the *Symposium* story are too obscure for certain interpretation, but the figure the storyteller had in mind was evidently a decagon or ten-pointed star, made up of two pentagrams in union. When torn apart (probably by some technique like origami paper-folding and cutting) the two pentagons are geometrically sterile and yearn for reunion. Their styles of marriage and separation are displayed in some of the following illustrations.

Five and the Golden Section

With the number Five and the appearance of life on earth, the Creator brought into play the last of the four principal ratios in geometry, the ratio of 1 to 1.618033989 . . . Commonly known as the golden cut or section, this ratio governs the whole field of pentagonal geometry, beginning with the pentagram itself which conforms to the golden section in all its limbs and parts.

Fig. 147. The beautiful necessity. A fact of nature, mundane or wonderous as you care to see it, is that ten pentagons stand side by side in a perfect ring, while the ten pentagrams they contain touch each other's limbs, as in a dance.

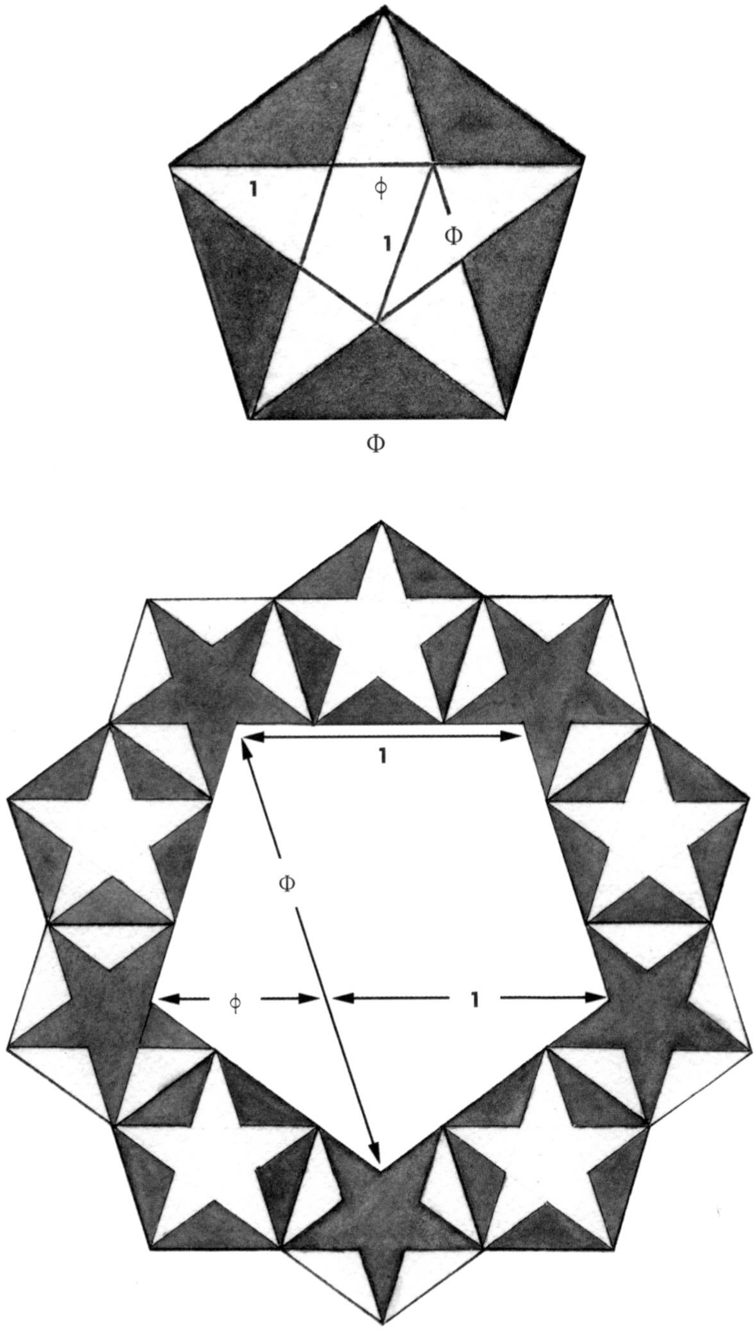

Fig. 148. Like all pentagonal and decagonal figures, the ring of pentagons is dominated by the phi (Φ) ratio, 1 : 1.618 or 0.618 : 1. This is the ratio known as the golden section, much prized by mystical geometers because, through its influence on the shape and proportions of phenomena throughout nature, it indicates the pre-existence of a numerical law-code. In these diagrams Φ denotes 1.618 . . . and ϕ is 0.618 . . .

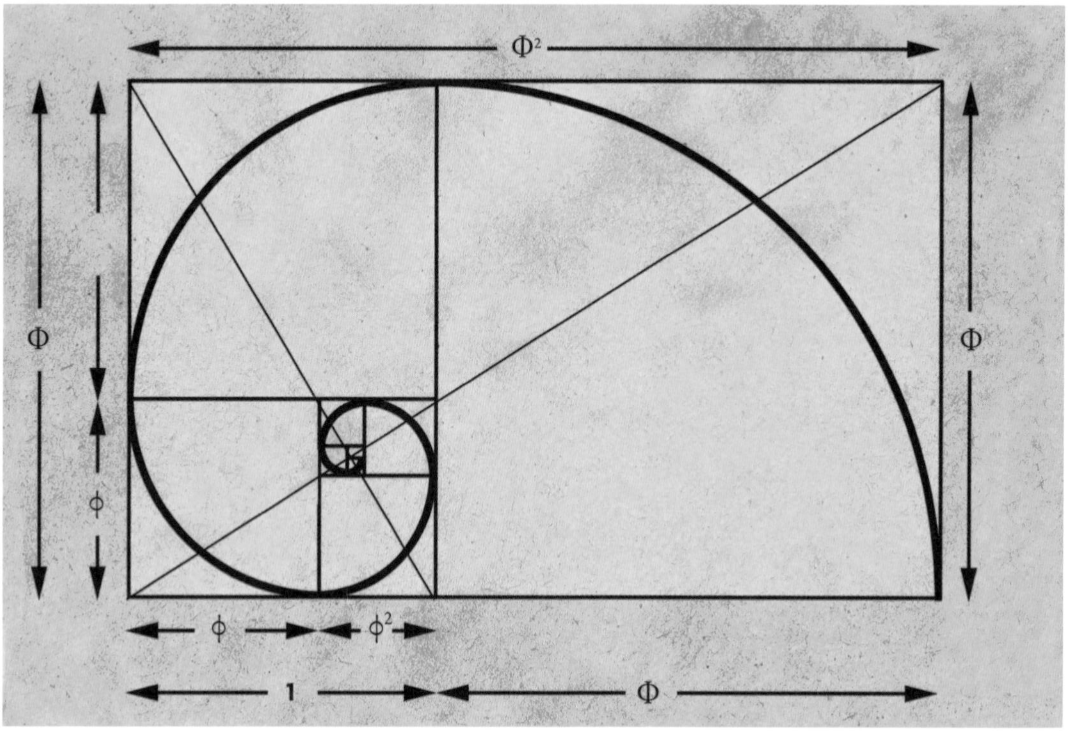

Fig. 149. The workings of the golden section are illustrated by the rectangle with sides in the ratio $1:\Phi$. Here they are $\Phi:\Phi^2$, a ratio that can be also expressed as $(1+\phi):(1+\Phi)$ or 1.618 : 2.618 which are all the same thing. The 'eye' of the rectangle (the point where its diagonal is cut at right angles by a line from its corner) is the pivot on which successively smaller golden section rectangles revolve. It is also the focus of the golden section spiral which governs the growth and form of ferns, shells, and organisms throughout nature.

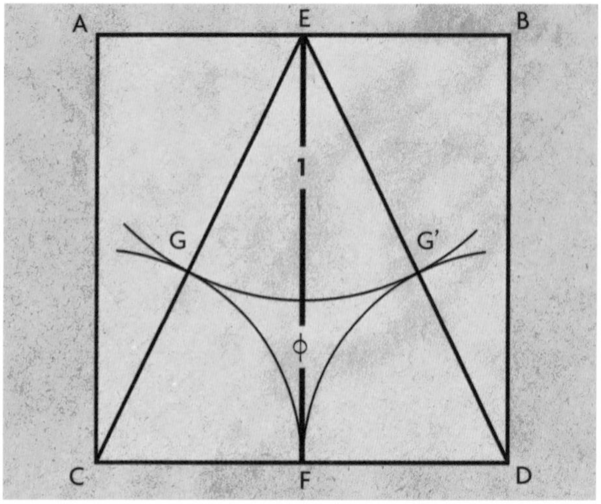

$\Phi = (\sqrt{5} + 1)/2 = 1.618033989\ldots$

$\phi = (\sqrt{5} - 1)/2 = 0.618033989\ldots$

Fig. 150. Dividing a line in the golden section. EF is the line to be divided in the golden section. Make it the vertical axis of a square ABDC. The arcs DF and CF cut lines ED and EC at G' and G. With centre E, draw an arc through G' and G. The point where it cuts EF divides EF in the proportion $1:\phi$.

The golden section number has some peculiar characteristics, confusing and fascinating at the same time. In the first place it is actually two numbers, different but intimately related. They are both written and spoken of as ϕ (phi). According to geometers' lore, this Greek letter was used because it is the initial of Phidias, the architect who built the Parthenon, but an alternative reason is that ϕ has the appropriate numerical value of 500. It is pronounced according to preference either 'fy' as in 'defy' (the English custom) or in the Greek way, 'fee'. The two versions of phi derive from two similar formulas, both featuring the square root of 5. They are:

$$(\sqrt{5} + 1)/2 = 1.618\ldots = \text{greater } \Phi\text{, and}$$
$$(\sqrt{5} - 1)/2 = 0.618\ldots = \text{lesser } \phi$$

This useful distinction between the larger and smaller versions of phi is recommended by Scott Olsen in his book *The Golden Section*. Large phi, he suggests, should be pronounced 'fy' and denoted by the capital letter Φ, with lesser phi spoken as 'fee' and written ϕ.

Examples of the peculiar, punning relationships between 0.618 (ϕ), 1.618 (Φ), and 2.618 (ϕ^2) are:

$1/0.618\ldots$	$= 1.618\ldots$	or in phi symbols	$1/\phi$	$= \Phi$
$1 + 0.618\ldots$	$= 1.618\ldots$	or	$1 + \phi$	$= \Phi$
$1.618\ldots \times 0.618^2\ldots$	$= 0.618\ldots$	or	$\Phi \times \phi^2$	$= \phi$
$1 + 1.618\ldots$	$= 2.618\ldots$	or	$1 + \Phi$	$= \Phi^2$
$1.618\ldots \times 1.618\ldots$	$= 2.618\ldots$	or	$\Phi \times \Phi$	$= \Phi^2$
$1.618\ldots/0.618\ldots$	$= 2.618\ldots$	or	Φ/ϕ	$= \Phi^2$

In all these calculations the phi family numbers have to be taken at their true value rather than as here abbreviated.

The phi ratio is embedded in number itself. If you take any pair of numbers, say 6 and 9, add them together to make 15, then add 9 to 15 making 24, add 15 to 24 and so on, the series develops as 6, 9, 15, 24, 39, 63, 102, 165, 267 . . . The further it goes the nearer it comes to producing true Φ as the ratio between successive terms. The last pair above, 267/165, gives 1.6181818, and the accuracy improves at every step, approaching infinity without ever yielding the perfect phi as a whole-number fraction.

A quicker, more economical way of approaching phi is by the same method but starting with the numbers 0 and 1. Their sum is 1 which, added to the last term, 1, makes 2; then 2 + 1 = 3; 3 + 2 = 5; 5 + 3 = 8, and the series continues, 13, 21, 34, 55, 89, 144, and so on, as far as anyone wishes to take it. The last pair above, 144/89, give phi as virtually 1.618, slightly less than the ideal. The next pair, 233/144, makes it slightly too big at 1.618055, and so it goes on, successive ratios bracketing true phi ever more closely, like a tendril spiralling around a pole.

This progression of numbers was named in the nineteenth century after Fibonacci (Leonardo of Pisa), who came across it in the thirteenth century while calculating the rate at which an enclosed colony of rabbits tends to increase its numbers. The ratio he came up with was close to 1.618. Long before then the golden section proportion was used in the monumental architecture of Egypt and elsewhere in the ancient world. Plato refers to it in the *Republic,* but always guardedly and in few words as if it were an initiate's secret. In his *Timaeus* cosmogony he is similarly reticent about the dodecahedron, the fifth of his geometric solids, whose twelve pentagonal faces are proportioned by the golden section. The secrets of the golden ratio were, perhaps, considered too holy for open discussion.

If that was the case, it is certainly not so today. Since the nineteenth century artists and biologists with philosophical tendencies have become entranced by the golden section and the many different ways in which it determines the forms and patterns of growth throughout nature. There is now a vast literature on the subject. Some researchers have made a cult of phi, seeing its influence in every type of form and motion, to the exclusion of all other systems of proportion. A more rigorous approach has established the science of Phyllotaxis, meaning the arrangement of leaves. It began with the observation that leaves grow round a stem in a certain order, entirely practical in that it ensures the greatest possible amount of light for each shoot, and at the same time conforming to the phi proportion and bringing in the Fibonacci numbers. The same pattern occurs in every manifestation of life. A popular example is the sunflower with the disc of seeds in its head. These grow as two sets of spirals in opposite directions, typically in the ratio 89 : 55 or 55 : 34, both of which are adjacent pairs of Fibonacci numbers. The scales of pine cones, pineapples, artichokes, and all other fruits of that kind are arranged similarly in accordance with phi. Many of nature's spirals, in the growth of ferns for example, display the same tendency. In these studies of life is much pleasure and insight, which is more than can be said for the fruitless battle between the rival dogmatists, religious and scientific, to establish a single, hard-and-fast explanation for the wonders of our existence.

Fig. 151. Pentagonal construction ending in a 30-sided polygon

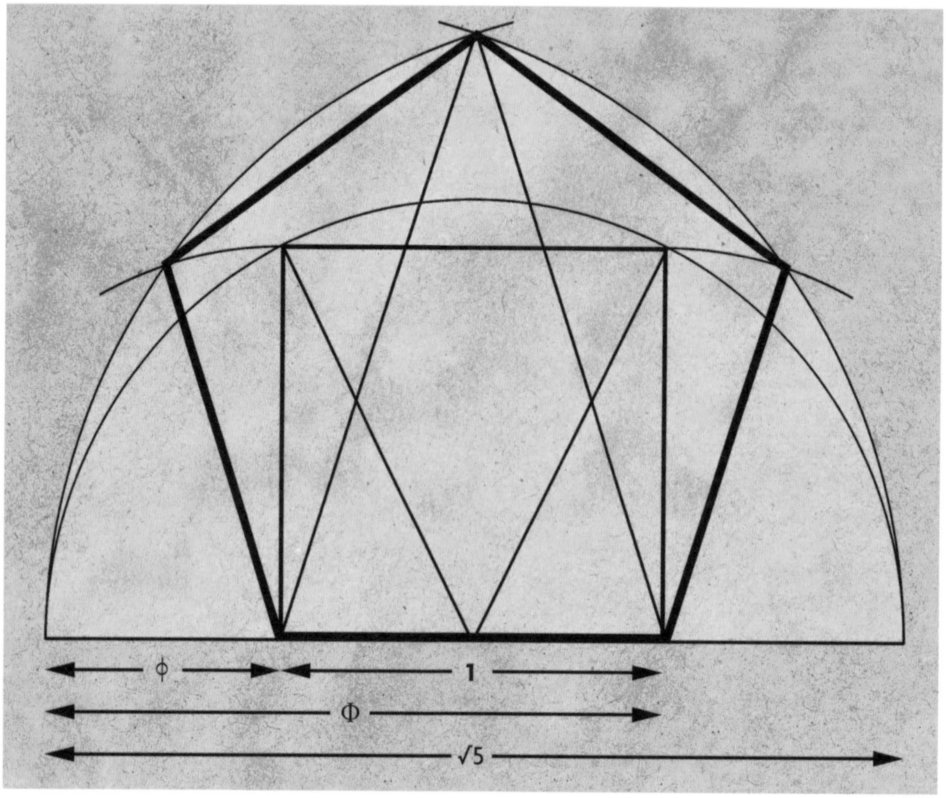

Fig. 152. Constructing pentagons. There are many good ways of constructing a pentagon. Here are two favourites. First, the classical method (starting with a square and an arc from the centre of its base through its upper corners), the second given (below) in Robert Lawlor's *Sacred Geometry*, which divides the circle into 10 parts.

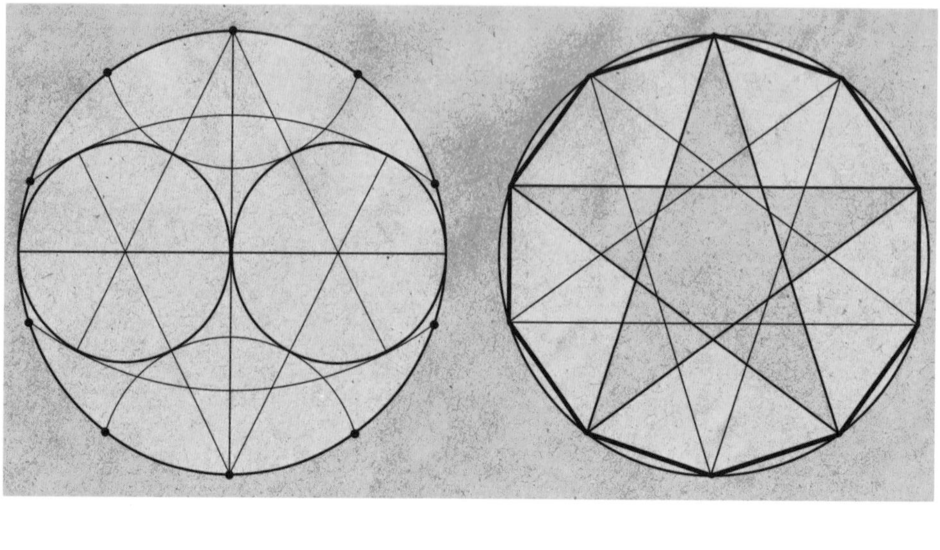

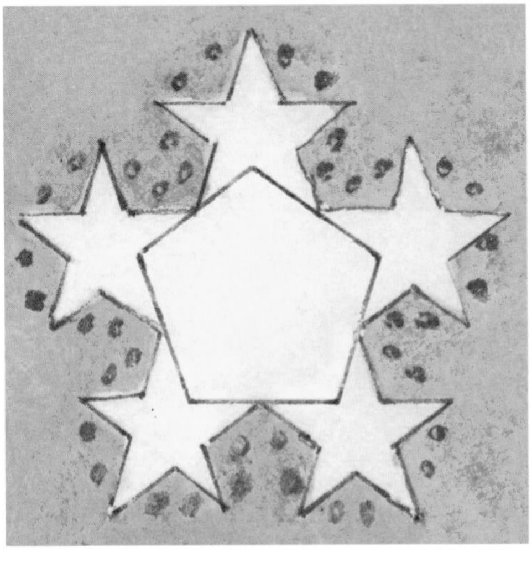

Fig. 153. A striking pentagonal crop formation, found in a field of wheat near Chute Causeway, Wiltshire, in July 2007. The five outer figures (above) are each made up of five pentagrams around a central pentagram (left).

Fig. 154. Developments from a central pentagon. Constructions that start from a central pentagon or pentagram are restricted in their growth. For breeding purposes, a pair of pentagons, i.e., a decagon, should lie at the centre.

Fig. 155. Thorns and rose, developments from a central pentagon

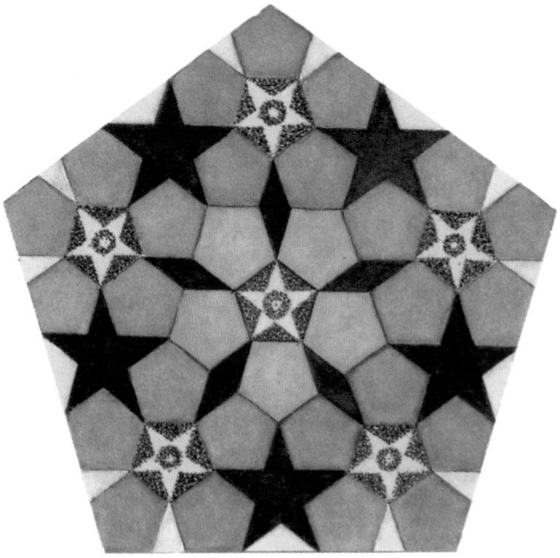

Humanity and the Pentagram

One of the classical exercises in geometry is to construct the ideal, canonical man. As we know from tradition, "man is the measure of all things". We are the sum of creation, possessing all animal traits as well as our own unique humanity, and in our bodily framework are the proportions and measures of the universe. With that understanding, the sculptors of antiquity made statues of gods and heroes, ideally proportioned according to the canon of number by which all human works and activities, from music to statecraft, were carefully regulated.

In the ancient civilisations of Egypt, the East, South America, and wherever societies were founded on the model of the cosmos, standards were set and insisted upon, and innovations were discouraged. In the canon of number could be found all the modes of music and orders of geometry that are true and lawful. Each of these was associated with a certain god or goddess, who thereby accumulated a great many 'correspondences'—her mode of music, dancing, architecture, and, above all, her name in which was expressed her characteristic number. Athena (η Αθηνα) the Greek goddess, for example, has by gematria the number 77, and like all goddesses of wisdom is naturally linked with the number Seven. Her shrines and temples were planned and measured by 7, and her music was the scale of 7 notes rather than the 12-note scale of Apollo. The purpose of this art was magical, to provide the conditions by which each deity could most effectively be invoked.

There were many gods and goddesses, so many types of music and ritual were appropriate at certain times and places. In sculpture also, different orders of number and geometry were used according to the nature of the subject. For representing the canonical man, the standard model was Apollo, the most beautiful among the gods and the most perfectly proportioned. On the human scale his height is 6 feet, so is the stretch of his arms, and his foot is a seventh part of that. His actual dimensions vary according to the particular foot in which they are measured. The Greek kouros, the ideal youth reflecting Apollo, is 6 Greek or 6.048 English feet tall, and his foot measures .864 ft. That is the ideal white male type. Other races have different standards and measures, and female beauty is judged by other criteria, those of Aphrodite rather than Apollo.

All races and both sexes, however, have a natural affinity with the pentagram. Its five points correspond to our extremities, four limbs and a head, and the likeness is emphasized by the proportions of our bodies. These are largely in accordance with the golden section. Much research and measuring has established that in a 6-foot man the average length from the top of his head to his navel is about 27½ inches and from the navel to the ground 44½ inches, a ratio of 55:89 or 1.61818. Another appearance of the golden ratio is between the length of the hand up to the wrist and the forearm. A golden progression of 1, 1.618, 2.618 is exemplified by the three bones in each of our fingers. Our chin and cheekbones provide three points of the pentagon that shapes our faces. The illustrations here of pentagrams dressed up to look like people are certainly fanciful, but they merely exaggerate the truth, that the five-sided figure with its golden ratio proportions is the basic model of the human form.

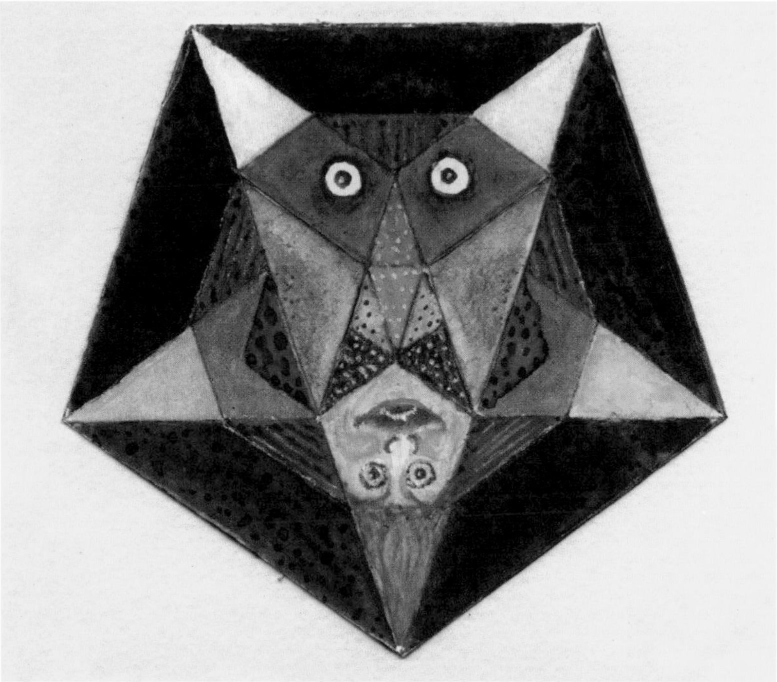

Fig. 156. Superstitious people are wary of the downward-pointing pentacle, seeing it as the image of the horned devil. Turned round, it became another unlikely character.

Fig. 157. A genial host. A welcoming pentagram stands within a 'pentagonal hexagon'.

Fig. 158. Pentagonal acrobats in the spotlight

Fig. 159. Pentagonal house and family. The dimensional difference between the smaller and larger figures is 1:1.618 . . .

Pentagonal Dances

One of the everyday miracles of existence is that ten pentagrams in contact with each other form a perfect ring. It goes with the other basic miracle of geometry, that six circles or spheres touch each other and the central seventh. There is not supposed to be anything supernatural in these happy coincidences. They are facts of geometry and reason. But without them there would be no geometry and no evidence of a creative mind behind the miraculous order of the universe.

One aspect of the universal order that neither of the literal-minded parties, the Darwinian materialists or the religious creationists, even attempts to explain is the humour in it. In the first place, the whole system is based on paradox—on the one hand and on the other—and the only way to accept and reconcile a paradox is through humour. Examples of wit—the highest form of humour—are constantly noticed by cosmologists and occur throughout studies of number and creative geometry. In the structure of number there are many puns and witty juxtapositions. On a more popular level, it is widely accepted by the professors of Fortean studies (mysterious phenomena) that jokes, puns, and playful coincidences are built into the way the world works and the way we experience it. One way of seeing this is to follow Patrick Harpur in *Daimonic Reality,* remembering that Hermes, famous for his tricks and humour, is one of the twelve gods and is bound to have his say in how the world is run.

Pentagrams with their five extremities are not only shaped like the human frame, they share many of our natural habits, especially in their couplings and dancing. One of the most delightful studies in geometry is the various ways in which pentagrams dance. The simplest sort of dance, known to everyone everywhere, is joining hands and singing and dancing in a ring. The singing of pentagrams is for speculative musicologists to investigate—presumably it is based on the pentagonal scale. Their modes of dancing, however, can be discovered and illustrated through geometry. The positions they assume at the beginning of their dance determine how it will proceed—that is, the type of pattern they will form in the course of geometric development.

A group of five pentagrams will dance prettily with a hand on their neighbour's shoulder (figure 162), and ten pentagons will fit around them. Another fifteen decagons can be placed outside the ten, but these are separated by gaps and the pattern goes no further. For a full-blown pentagonal dance five couples are needed, making a ring of ten. Either they stand as widely separated as possible, touching fingertips, or hands and feet are placed together, or they support each other in close contact. Their most intimate coupling is when each pair overlies each other (figure 166), but then they are not exactly dancing.

Fig. 160. In the most widely spaced ring of ten dancing pentagons the figures touch fingertips. The six-sided shapes that separate the dancers above and below are 'pentagonal hexagons'.

Fig. 161. Two identical sets of ten pentagrams form closely packed rings. Their different ways of holding each other determine whether the figure they make, inside and out, is a pentagon or a decagon. Students of pentagonal proportions may calculate the relative sizes of these two shapes. Since the red background in both pictures is made up of rhombuses and half-rhombuses, it is easy to reckon that the area around the central pentagon (10 stars + 25 rhombuses + 5 halves) is larger than the area around the decagon (10 stars + 20 rhombuses + 10 halves) by 11 to 10. But when the central areas are included, which figure is larger overall?

Fig. 162. Five pentagrams dance in a ring with arms on each other's shoulders. Ten pentagons pack in around them and fifteen others outside them complete the development.

Fig. 163. The natural tendency of pentagons to dance is illustrated by these five shapely legs that emerge from the construction of a decagon.

Sex and the Pentagram: Meeting, Mating, and Breeding

The pentagon, as already pointed out, is unproductive on its own and needs to find a partner of its own kind before it can breed. Breeding in the geometrical sense means reproducing itself in such a way that its offspring can do the same, allowing further pentagonal generations to develop. Triangles, hexagons, and rectangles do it simply but lifelessly, in the way that crystals grow. But as an emblem of life, the pentagonal figure breeds organically. And they are also like us in having various ways of dancing, ten in a ring.

Figure 155 on page 177 shows what happens when a pentagon tries to reproduce on its own. The central pentagon will support five others on its five sides, and around them can be placed a ring of five pentagrams, but other shapes are then needed to further the development. If you start with the five-pointed star in the middle (figure 154 on page 176), five pentagons will lodge in its angles, but when another five are added, gaps appear and again it is a dead end.

There are two different forms of pentagonal marriage, resulting in two different forms of reproduction. The first union is between two pentagrams, intertwining within a ten-sided frame. Around it stand ten pentagons in a ring, and upon them ride ten pentagrams with touching fingertips. The next generation of pentagons, twenty of them, fit round the pentagram ring, and then form their own rings round the ten sides of ten decagons. The pattern is illustrated in the sequence of drawings beginning on page 253. It is the foundation plan of Plato's geometrical Atlantis.

The second kind of marriage between pentagons or pentagrams has rarely been noticed or written about. It came to light during research into the pattern that overlies the old city of Jerusalem, where this form of pentagonal reconciliation is a significant feature. In this form of marriage the two pentagrams overlie each other, head to groin, creating a regular-sided but differently angled hexagon. Paired together in that six-sided shape, the pentagrams multiply themselves hexagon-style, though with added subtleties.

Fig. 164. Intertwined pentacles and their ten 10-pointed offspring

Fig. 165. The ten decagons produced by the breeding pair of pentacles in the previous picture have become ten points around them. The ten divisions that proceed from each point merge with the parent couple to create bird-like shapes—or a curly mop of hair.

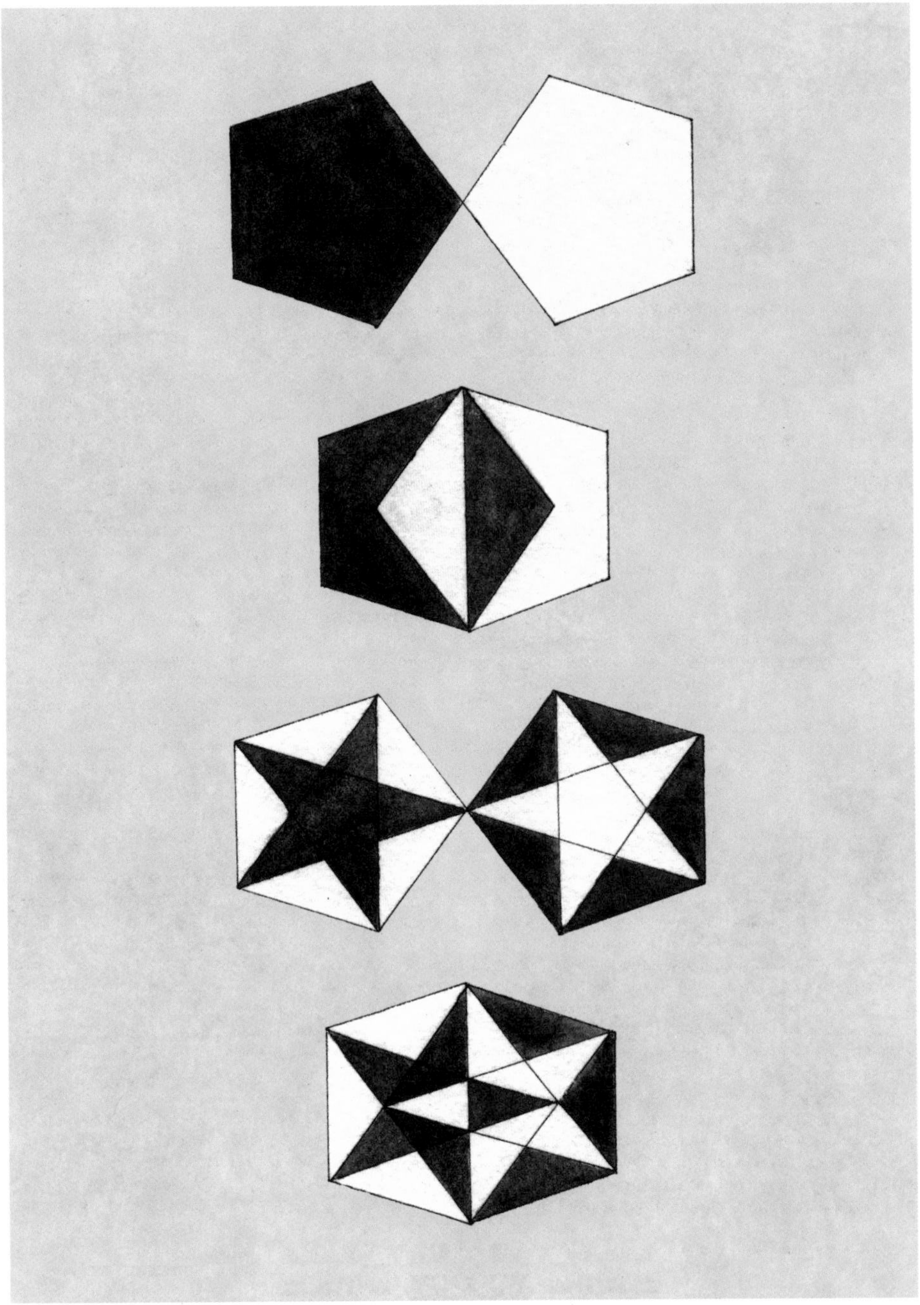

Fig. 166. The second way in which pentagons and pentacles mate. Two pentagons, black and white or male and female, stand point to point and then slip over each other to make an equal-sided 'pentagonal hexagon'. The two pentacles do the same. Pentagons on their own will not pack together to make a continuous pattern, but when two of them are married the hexagonal figure they make can be multiplied endlessly.

Fig. 167. Ten-sided tablecloth with married pentagons

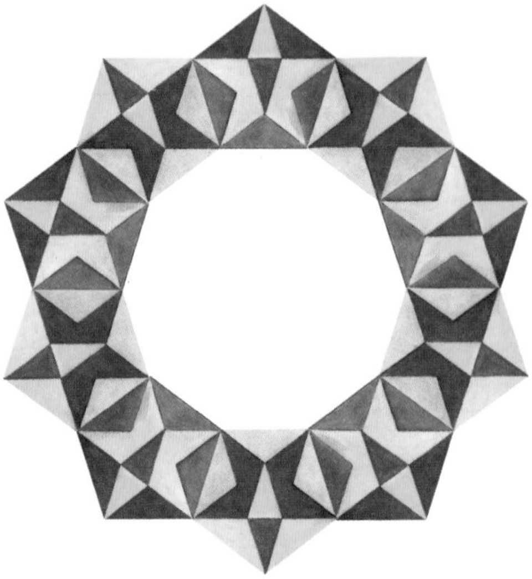

Fig. 168. Ten single figures in a ring

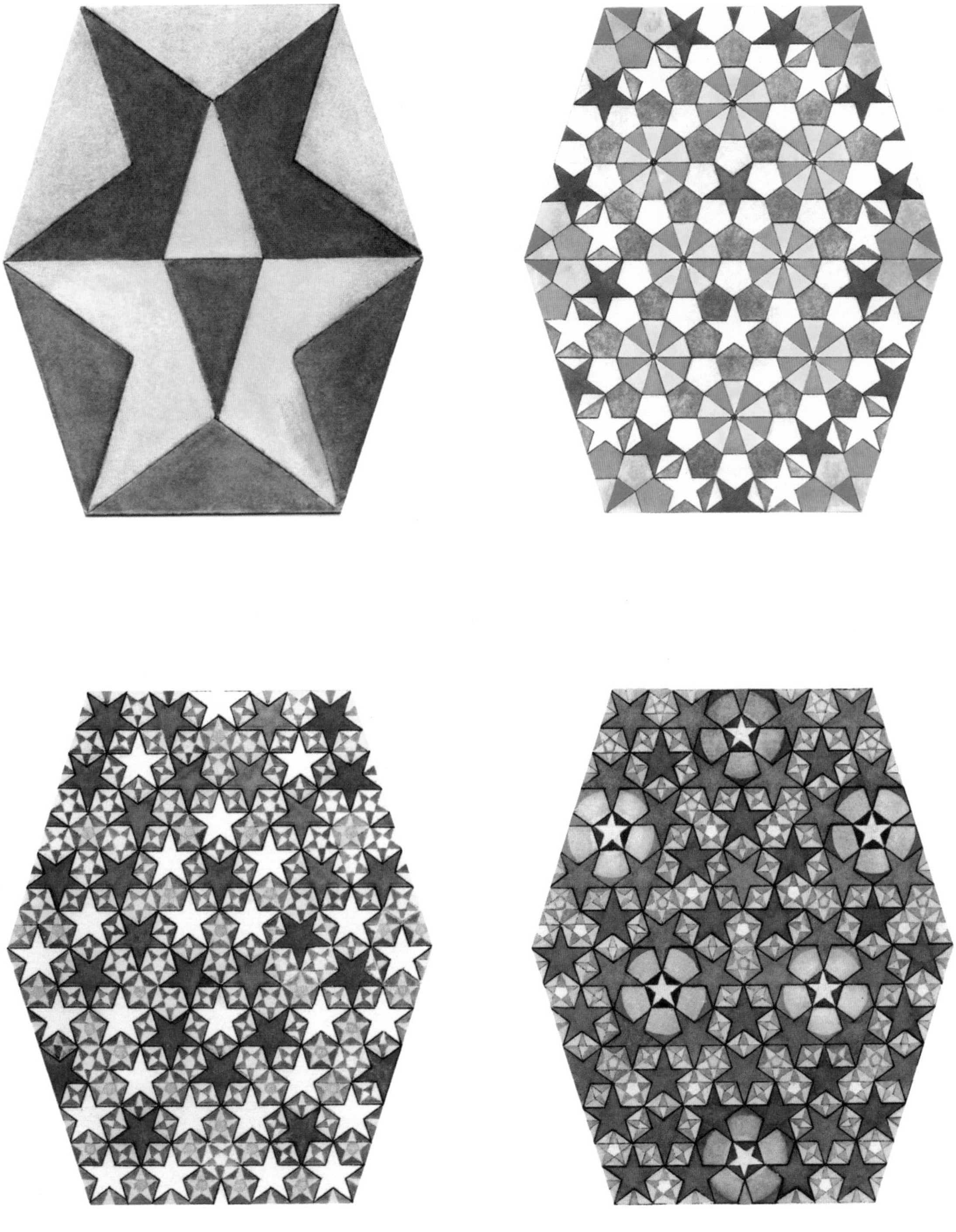

Fig. 169. The pentagonal married couple produce the 6-sided shape referred to as the pentagonal hexagon.

Figs. 170, 171, 172, 173. The patterns generated by the pentagonal hexagon are extended further by tessellation.

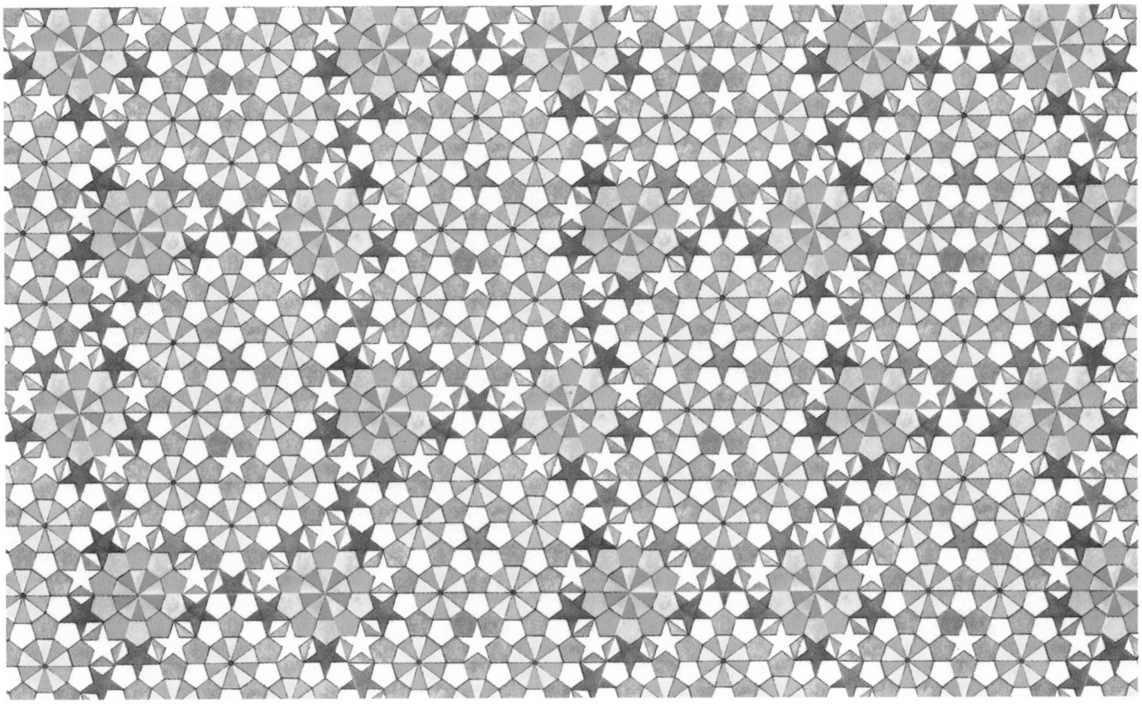

Figs. 171 and 172.

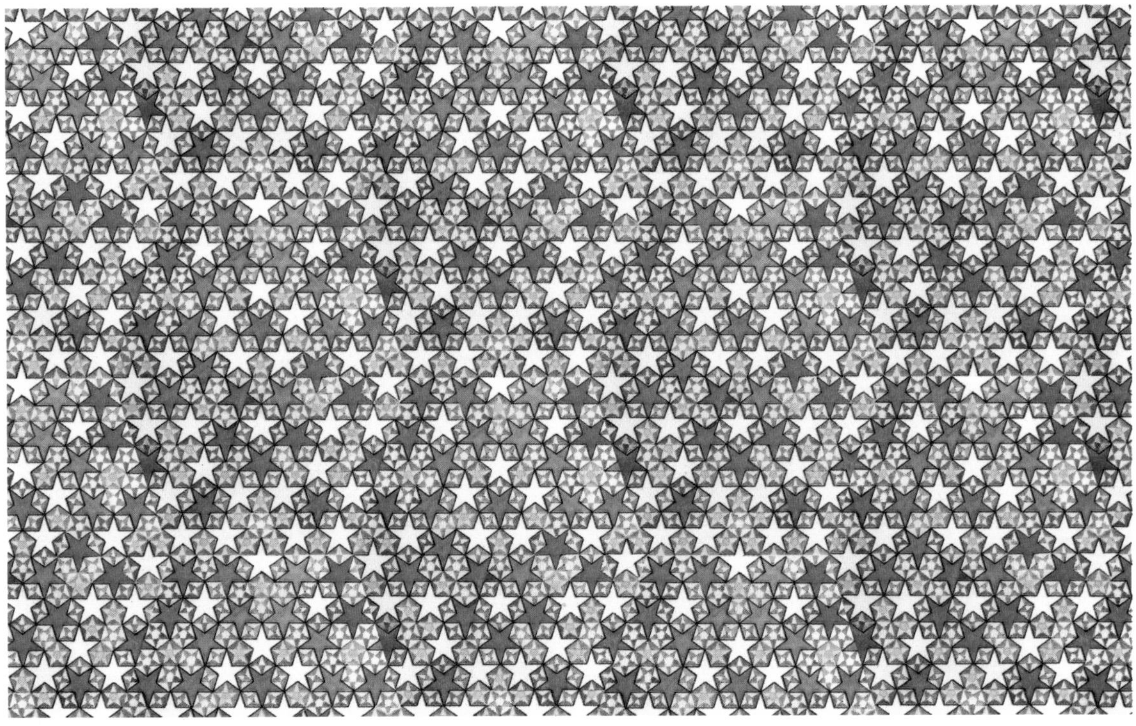

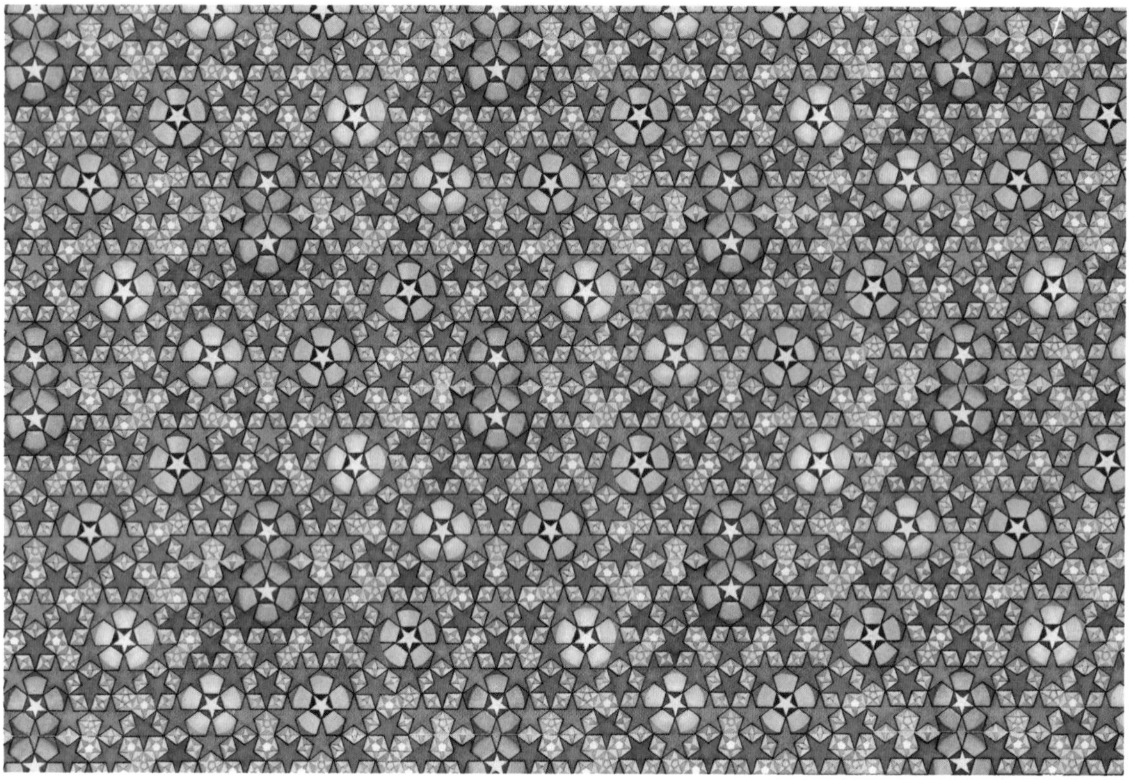

Fig. 173.

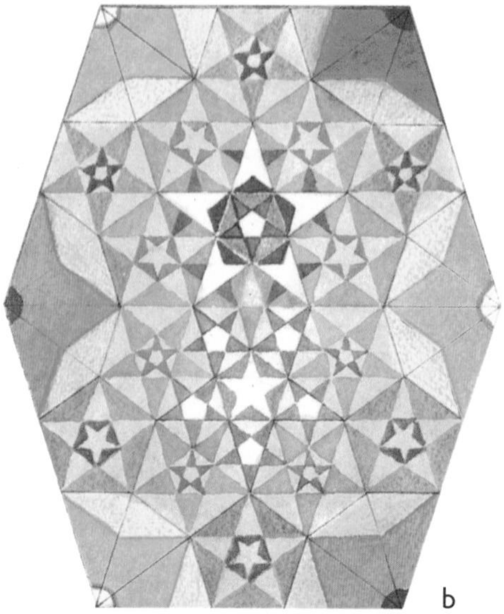

Fig. 174. Two further pentagonal hexagons

Fig. 175. Tessellation of figure 174a

Fig. 176. Tessellation of figure 174b

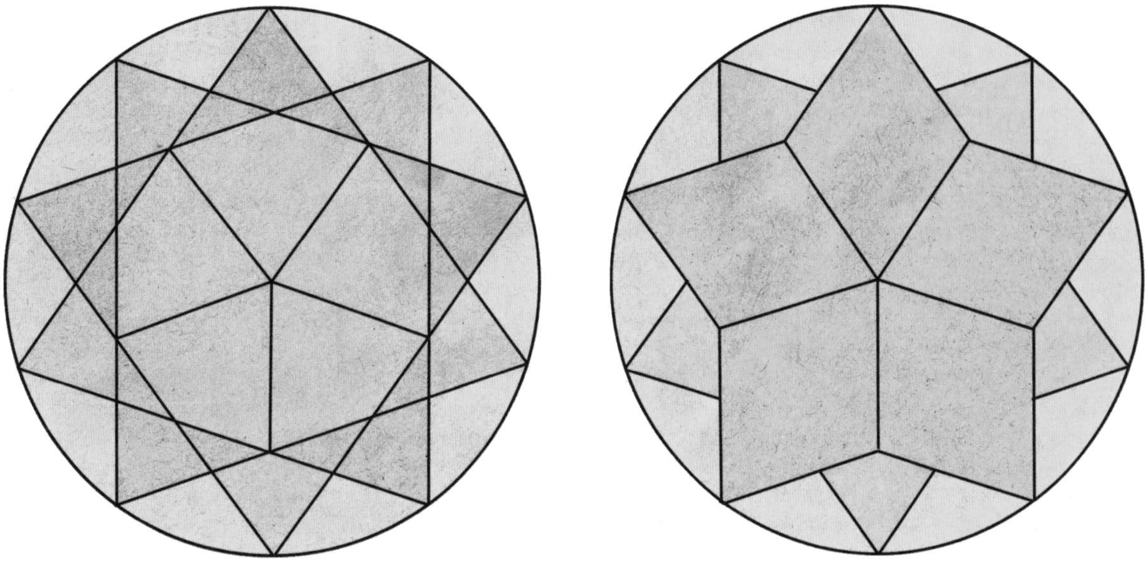

Fig. 177. The pentagonal rhombus. Besides the regular pentagram with five straight limbs forming angles of 36°, there is another five-pointed figure known to geometers and often used by designers. The angle at its points is 72° and it is made up of five pentagonal rhombuses. These are the apex angles of a decagram; the two pentagrams that comprise it have apex angles of 72°.

Fig. 178. Five pentagonal rhombs, each divided into quarters, fit together to make 72° stars or, rearranged, a pentagon with central pentagram.

Fig. 179. The pentagonal rhombus (top) forms the greater part (gold) of a pentagon. The other piece of the pentagon shaped like a paper boat and coloured blue, forms one of the ten divisions of the blue and white decagon below it, giving a spiral effect. The pentagonal rhombus fill the space between two pentagrams and fits their angles.

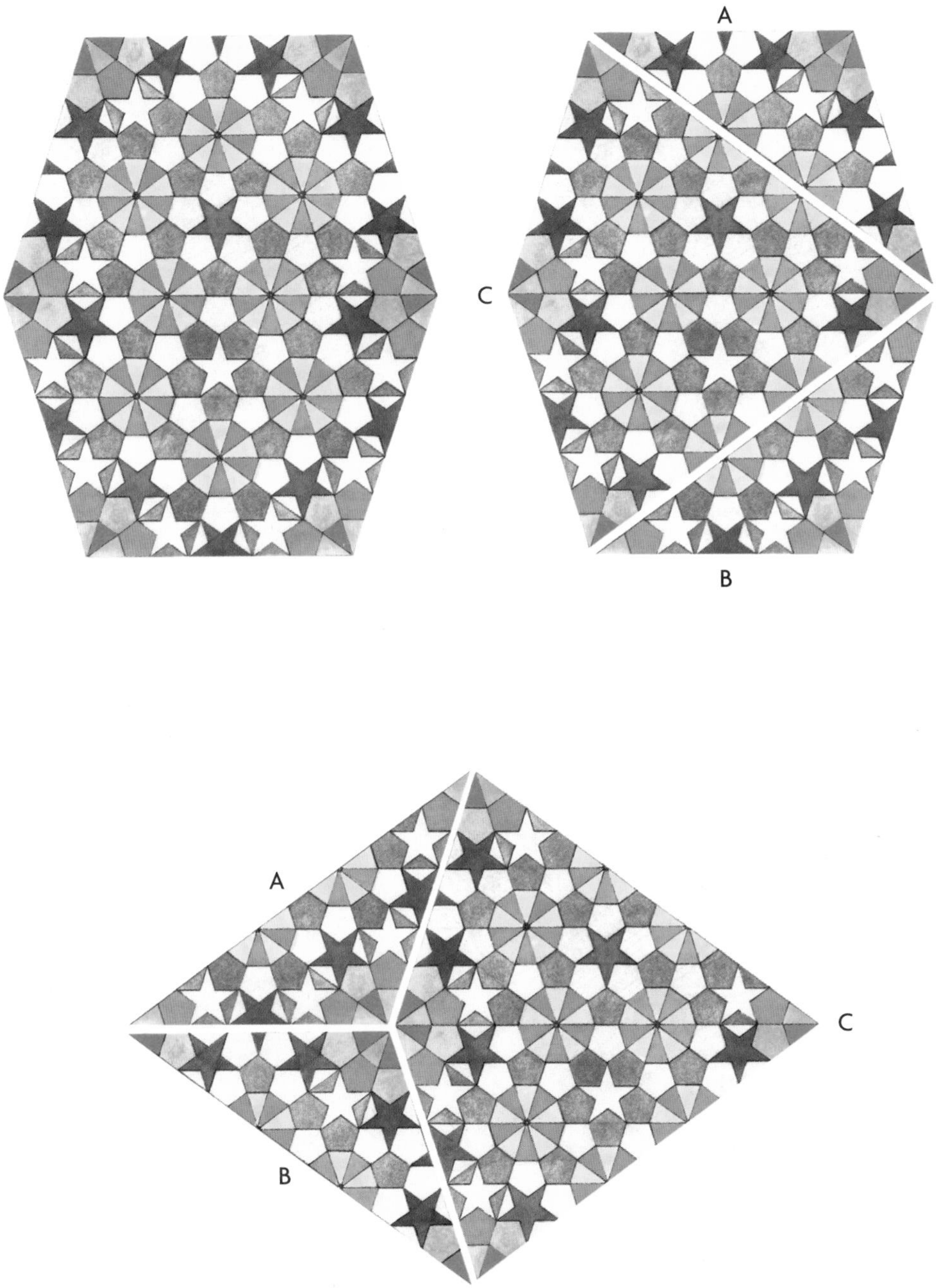

Fig. 180. The pentagonal hexagon behind the tessellated patterns on the previous pages can be cut up and rearranged to produce the pentagonal rhombus.

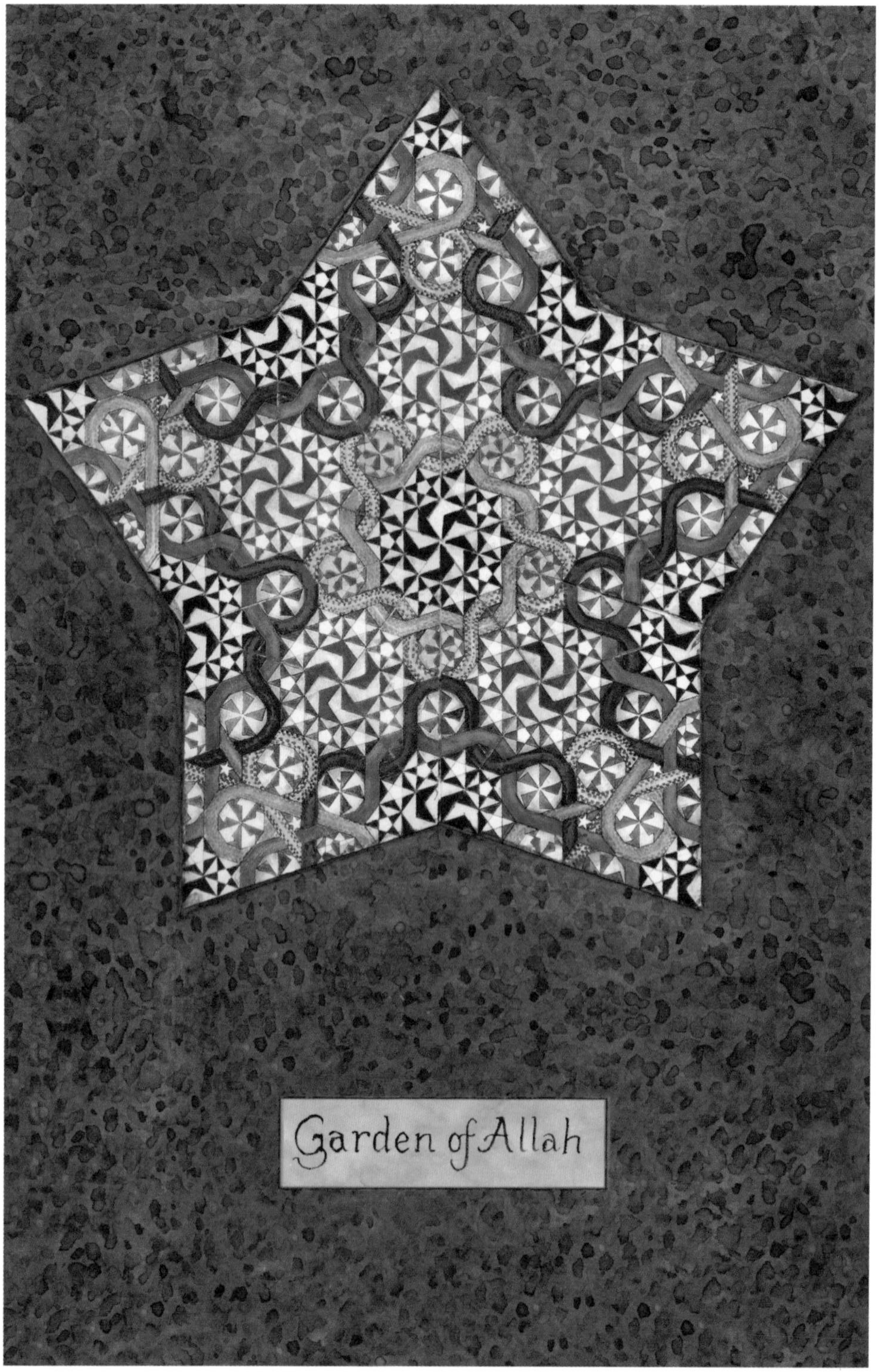

Fig. 181. The Garden of Allah, source of all living things, is reflected in geometrical gardens of paradise on earth.

Fig. 182. The Persian Garden of Cyrus in the fifth century BC is a legendary example. These patterns are made of five pentagonal rhombuses derived from the pentagonal hexagons previously illustrated.

Pentagonal Marriages with Other Shapes

Pentagons are natural breeders and they will also couple with other shapes, most easily with a hexagon. This marriage between the geometries of Five and Six is symbolically satisfying because it combines the pentagonal patterns of organic growth with the crystalline pattern exhibited in the hexagon.

The shapes representing Five and Six belong to different orders, but through techniques of synthetic geometry they can be brought together in one construction to depict the actuality of life and matter in unison.

Fig. 183. Hexagonal shapes emerging from a central pentagon

Fig. 184. From regular pentagrams in the central area some crafty geometry results in the appearance of 15 hexagrams in a ring around the perimeter.

Fig. 185. The overall pentagonal shape is adapted to contain 25 hexagons (disguised as cubes).

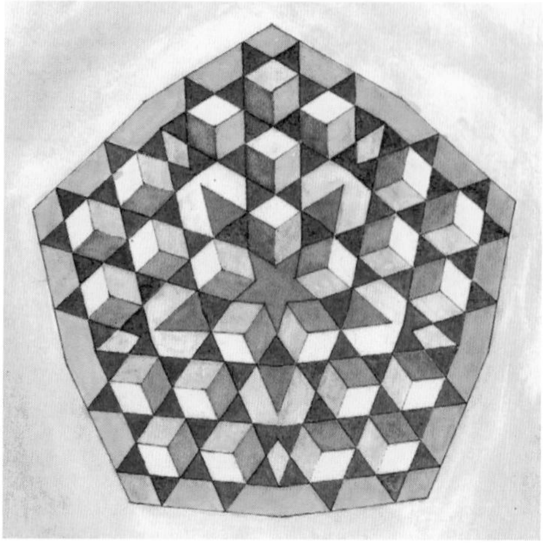

Fig. 186. From a perfectly regular centre the hexagonal geometry transforms itself gracefully to accommodate the pentagons and stars at the six corners of the figure.

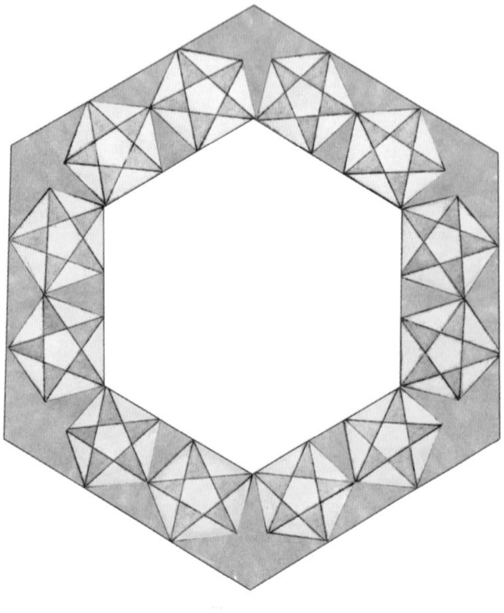

Fig. 187. One way towards combining the geometries of two different numbers within a circle is to divide the circumference by the product of those numbers. Thus in unifying Five and Six the circle is divided by 30. This leads to the construction above. It is shaped by the numbers Six and Twelve which determine its divisions, but the 25 stars within it are all (apart from the central hexagon) pentagonal.

An interesting feature of this diagram, reproduced left, is the ring of 12 dancing pentacles (rather than the usual 10), bounded by hexagons.

Fig. 188. Fives and Fours. Another geometric marriage—in which the pentagon is united with the square, symbol of earth—is illustrated by a circle divided into 20 parts. At the centre, five squares stand on the sides of a pentagon. Around them the ring of ten pentagons (violet) is formed by two large pentagrams (with central red stripes) which also shape the ten pentagrams in the outer ring. The other ten spaces in the twenty-sided outer ring are filled by squares.

Five and Seven

Five and Seven are represented by such different orders of geometry that there is no obvious way of reconciling them. Dividing a circle into 5 × 7 = 35 equal parts is not geometrically possible. Perhaps it is unnecessary, because the combined symbolisms of Five (life) and Seven (holiness and the world soul) convey the idea that life is sacred, and that doctrine is built into the geometer's creation myth from the beginning.

Fig. 189. A contrivance for linking Seven with Five and Ten. The central decagon is surrounded by pentagonal elements, accommodating the ring of seven pentacles.

Fig. 190. Five of the figures above are placed together (with overlapping stars) around a central red pentagon. This marriage of Five and Seven (producing 35) is depicted in the finished pentagon edged by 35 stars and with 35 other dark stars inside it.

A seven-sided figure is impossible to draw
With perfect mathematical precision,
And if you try to do it you are absolutely sure
To find your effort treated with derision.
Yet mystical philosophers will readily declare
That nothing in this world is really true.
So here you see a heptagon from triangle and square.
For any human purpose it will do.

Fig. 191 (opposite). An adequate depiction

Part 4
THE WORLD SOUL

The Mysterious and Holy Seven

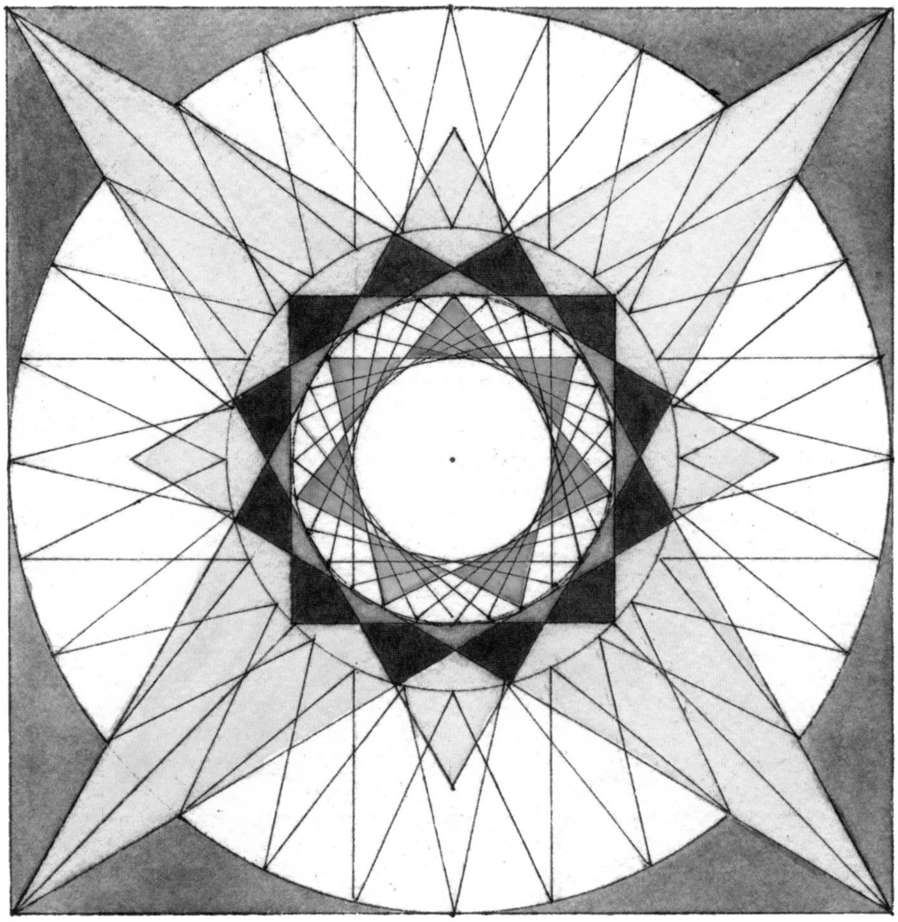

14 • The Holy Seven

Symbol of the World Soul

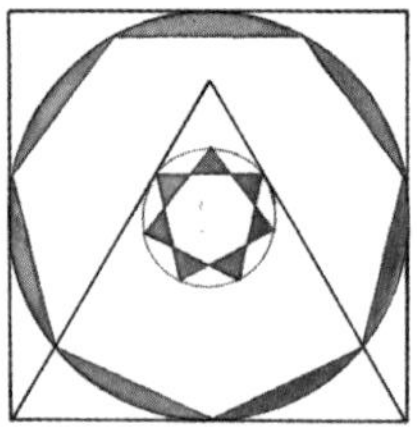

Seven and the Mysteries

With the number Seven the geometer's creation story enters another dimension, going beyond the physical universe and earthly life into the world of divinity. Seven is the number of the world soul. It is not therefore reckoned as a created number, because soul existed before creation, and its corresponding number is given the same priority. It is the divine spirit that appears at the very beginning of the Bible story, in Genesis 1, where:

> the world was without form, and void; and darkness was upon the face of the deep. And the Spirit of God moved over the face of the waters.

That was the state of things before the Creator began his geometry and before he made images of One, Two, Three, etc. Seven was there already, and the Creator honoured it by perfecting his work in seven days, the last of which he made holy. Seven is not often manifest in nature—though certain special plants have seven-fold leaves—but in sacred or symbolic geography the ideal landscape includes seven hills, springs, streams, and other features. In cosmology Seven is taken to be the number of the universal axis, the conceptual pole on which everything revolves while the axis itself remains fixed and unchanging. That makes it a symbol of divine law, which never varies. With 7 as the measure of a circle's axis or radius, its circumference is a whole number, 22 or 44. In the cosmological diagram the radius is 5040 or 7!. Those numbers occupy the pole position in the Decad, balancing the numbers on each side of 7, for $1 \times 2 \times 3 \times 4 \times 5 \times 6 \times 7 = 5040$ and $7 \times 8 \times 9 \times 10 = 5040$.

As a number of eternity, never generated and not subject to dissolution,

Seven is the natural symbol of the eternal feminine principle, typified by Athena, the goddess of wisdom, who was never born but sprang, fully armed, from the head of her father, Zeus. Athena is a constant virgin, and Seven is called the virgin number, the arithmetical reason being that it is the only number in the Decad that was not born (meaning it is not the product of any two other numbers) and does not breed (as, e.g., 2 and 4 'breed' 8 and 2×5 produces 10).

The heptagon, the figure that illustrates Seven, has the characteristics of a virgin, who cannot be made or laid down. It has been proved impossible to construct a perfect heptagon with ruler and compass. There are several techniques in geometry by which it can be done, well enough to satisfy everyone but the pedant, and the results, as here illustrated, are of great beauty and interest. But Seven is ever the virgin, ever wrapped in mystery and never submitting to the mastery of reason.

The feminine nature of Seven is apparent in its relationship with the cycles of the moon and women. Four weeks of seven days are the four phases of the moon in its twenty-eight-day month, the seventh day is the holy Sabbath, and in Jewish ritual every seventh year is Sabbatical, while every seven times seven years is the Jubilee. The great Jewish feasts last seven days, and between two of them are seven weeks. In contrast to the septenary lunar calendar, Twelve is the dominant number in solar time-keeping. This opposition between Seven and Twelve, and their reconciliation in the most perfect of all numerical marriages, is shortly to be illustrated.

Another feminine aspect of Seven is its connection with dreams, prophecies, and the mantic arts. In archaic Greece, before the rise of the Apollonian priesthood, oracles were telluric and necromantic, communicating with the spirits of earth and the underworld and largely operated by women. Wisdom herself is a virgin goddess—Isis, Sophia, or St Catherine in early Christianity. Socrates in the *Symposium* claims to have learnt his wisdom from Diotima, a lady who also instructed him in love. Yet Seven itself is not partial towards either sex, being an emblem of wisdom and exerting its influence wherever virtue and philosophy are cultivated. The tradition of seven oracular priestesses, virgins, sisters, or wise women is paralleled by the seven sages of Greece, the seven roshis of Buddhism, and the 'seven wise masters' whose legend is that they taught the seven liberal arts to the son of a Roman emperor. In the Gnostic imagery of Revelation, there are seven spirits of God and seven angels guard his throne. It is placed within the central, seventh ring of heaven and approached through the seven stages or 'veils' of initiation. These correspond to the natural path to initiation, through the conventional seven ages of a complete lifetime.

In the simplest, most natural stage of the human cycle, the stage of tribal migration or nomadism that precedes civilization and the twelve-part rationalisation of the zodiac, the guiding social principles are those symbolized by Seven. The pattern of life reflects the wanderings of the seven stars or planets, time is measured by the seven lights of the Great Bear and seasons by the seven-fold cycle of the moon, while music is pitched to the seven-note scale of the rustic pipe.

Everything that can be called sacred and eternal is appropriately numbered in sevens. In the system of correspondences, developed in the Mystery schools of pagan and early Christian times, the seven wanderers of the heavens—Sun, Moon, Mars, Venus, Mercury, Jupiter, and Saturn—were each found partners among other septenary groups—the seven metals, colours of the rainbow, musical notes, sounds, tastes, moods or humours, and so on, including the seven vowels of the classical Greek and Hebrew alphabets. Many of these affinities seem contrived and arbitrary, and often they vary according to the view of whoever practises the system. But its categorisations were never meant to be scientific in the literal sense. Tables of correspondences were for use in religious and magical rituals, for the invocation of specific powers and influences. Those who worked with them adapted them as they found most effective.

This table of correspondences (opposite), could be extended further to include other seven-fold categories. But enough is enough. The affinities suggested here have their own fascination and may be of use to magicians, decorators, and dealers in glamour.

The numerical and musical composition of the world soul is calculated in the *Republic,* but Plato's clues to it are too ambiguous to be followed with any certainty. It is made up of the same canonical numbers, mostly duodecimal, that occur throughout all codes of traditional science, cosmology, chronology, music, measurement, physics, and symbolic geometry. As a scale of music, the world soul stretches into the fifth octave, the extreme range, perhaps, of the human voice. It winds around the universe and its axis, connecting all creation with its divine source. From its name, the Universal Soul or Soul of All, comes the number that illustrates the mystical doctrine of the Trinity, where the Holy Spirit or world soul is combined with two other sacred principles as Three in One.

The Soul of All, η ψυχη παντων $= 2997 = 111 \times 3 \times 3 \times 3$

This same number was discovered by Frederick Bligh Bond and Dr T. S. Lea in 1917 and published in their list of holy phrases which produce by gematria numbers that are multiples of 37. The number 2997 is equal to 37×81, and Bond and Lea discovered in it another epithet of the world soul:

2997 = σωτηρια του κοσμου, Salvation of the World

TABLE OF CORRESPONDENCES

Heavenly body	Day	Note	Colour	Metal	Jewel	Greek vowel	Sound
Moon	Monday	A	white	silver	pearl	alpha	short a
Mercury	Wednesday	G	indigo	quicksilver	amethyst	eta	long e
Venus	Friday	F	green	copper	emerald	epsilon	short e
Sun	Sunday	E	yellow	gold	topaz	iota	short i
Mars	Tuesday	D	red	iron	ruby	omicron	o
Jupiter	Thursday	C	blue	tin	sapphire	upsilon	y
Saturn	Saturday	B	black	lead	diamond	omega	long o

Seven, Nine, and the Septenary Number

Nine is a mysterious number, an emblem of esoteric science and the Mysteries. It is the triple three of Trismegistos, thrice-greatest Hermes, the psychopomp or mystic initiator. Followers of Gurdjieff use the enneagram, the nine-pointed figure, as a source and illustration of the master's philosophy. They are jealous in guarding its secrets, possibly because they really know nothing that you cannot discover for yourself. Many claim to have constructed a perfect enneagon, but no such construction has been proved and geometers say it is an impossibility.

Nine is called repetitive because the digits of all its multiples can be reduced to nine: twice nine is 18 and $1 + 8 = 9$; $3 \times 9 = 27$ and $2 + 7 = 9$ and so on. Any number whose digits reduce to 9 must be divisible by 9.

There is a strange affinity between the numbers Nine and Seven. Not only are they both emblems of mystery, with mysterious constructions, but they are both intimately related to the same curious number, the 'septenary number' 142857. That is the number that recurs when any number that is not a multiple of 7 is divided by 7, e.g., $1/7 = .142857142847\ldots$, the six-digit sequence endlessly recurring. Here are the six versions of the septenary number, each beginning at a different place in the sequence, and how they arise.

$$
\begin{aligned}
1 \text{ million} \div 7 &= 142857\ldots = 11 \times 13 \times 999 \times 1\\
2 \text{ million} \div 7 &= 285714\ldots = 11 \times 13 \times 999 \times 2\\
3 \text{ million} \div 7 &= 428571\ldots = 11 \times 13 \times 999 \times 3\\
4 \text{ million} \div 7 &= 571428\ldots = 11 \times 13 \times 999 \times 4\\
5 \text{ million} \div 7 &= 714285\ldots = 11 \times 13 \times 999 \times 5\\
6 \text{ million} \div 7 &= 857142\ldots = 11 \times 13 \times 999 \times 6
\end{aligned}
$$

Every version of the septenary number is a multiple of 999, and wherever you begin the sequence, its first three digits added to the next three produce 999.

$$142 + 857 = 999$$
$$428 + 571 = 999$$
$$285 + 714 = 999$$

Another diversion is to add the six versions of the septenary number together in pairs.

$$\begin{array}{r} 142857 \\ +\ \underline{857142} \\ 999999 \end{array} \qquad \begin{array}{r} 428571 \\ +\ \underline{571428} \\ 999999 \end{array} \qquad \begin{array}{r} 285714 \\ +\ \underline{714285} \\ 999999 \end{array}$$

Then again you can arrange the factors of 142857 in interesting patterns, such as:

$$\begin{aligned} 142857 &= 11 \times 111 \times 117 \\ &= 13 \times 33 \times 333 \\ &= 11 \times 111 \times 13 \times 333 \end{aligned}$$

Moreover, the square of 142857 . . . , multiplied by 7, equals 142857 . . .

This septenary number is mercurial, full of tricks and puns, while at the same time pointing to an arcane code that links the mysteries of Seven with those of Nine. It provides a clue to the construction of the enneagon. This nine-sided figure is made up of three equilateral triangles, but whereas anyone can divide a circle into three, six, or twelve equal parts, the construction of three triangles with their points equally spaced round a circle is an enigma. Geometric tradition says that the first step is to write the numbers 1 to 9 around a circle, with 9 in the 12 o'clock position, and locate points 3, 6, and 9 by inscribing a triangle. These are the three numbers that do not occur in the septenary sequence. To complete the figure symmetrically, the other six points are joined in the septenary order, 1, 4, 2, 8, 5, 7. This figure (see figure 193 on page 218) is not properly a construction. One way of drawing the enneagon with ruler and compass, though not quite perfectly, is shown below in figure 192.

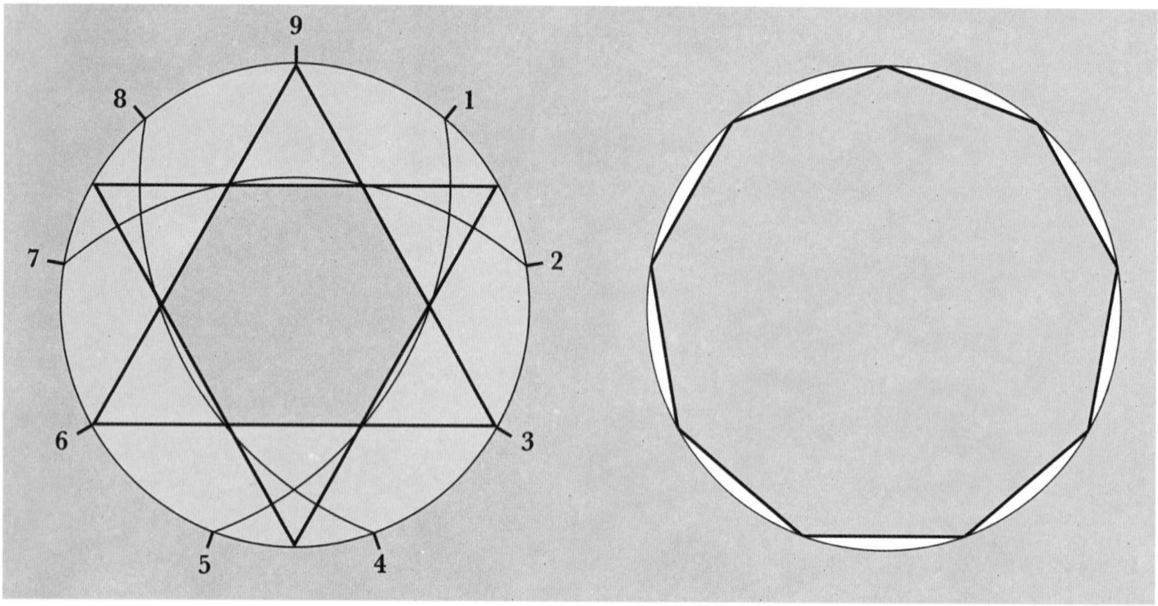

Fig. 192. Dividing a circle into 9 parts. Draw the circle. Inscribe in it a triangle and number its points 3, 6, 9, with 9 in the 12 o' clock position. Inscribe the reciprocal triangle to create a 6-pointed star with a hexagon at its centre. Do not number the points of this second triangle. From each point of the second, unnumbered triangle draw arcs to pass through the furthest pair of points of the central hexagon. Where these arcs meet the circle are the 6 remaining points of the enneagon.

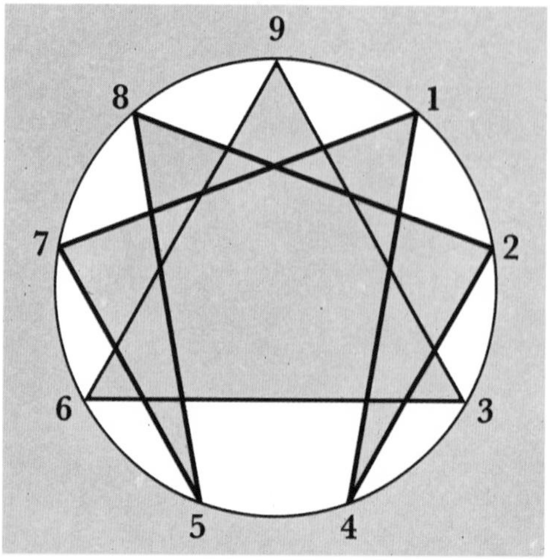

Fig. 193. The septenary pattern in the enneagon. The 9, 3, 6 triangle is drawn, and the 6 remaining points, joined in the sequence of the septenary number, 1, 4, 2, 8, 5, 7, complete the symmetrical figure.

Twelve and Seven: The Supreme Numerical Marriage

The two great opposites in nature—partners through necessity and carefully woven together by the Great Geometer—are body and soul, symbolized respectively by Twelve and Seven. The geometry of Twelve is beautifully proportioned, Apollo-like, a work of symmetry and reason, whereas Seven is indefinable and wrapt in mystery.

In cosmologically ordered societies, in the traditional world plan they imitate, and in geometry itself, Seven and Twelve are bound together in a truly wonderful manner, completing through their union the image of Creation that is the object of the geometer's quest. The construction by which this sacred marriage is illustrated was evidently known in ancient times, for it is an essential element in the cosmological diagram on which ancient institutions were founded.

Twelve and Seven, being abstract number symbols, are not sexualised, but in the lower world they are attached to qualities regarded as male or female. The rational, orderly Twelve plays the conventional part of the man to the female Seven, which stands for imagination and the soul of nature. In early classical societies these two opposites were ingeniously combined. A council of twelve elders decided the affairs of state, but every decision they took was referred to the state oracle, typically conducted by seven sibyls. If the oracle women foresaw trouble through any of the elders' decisions, they could veto it. In this way the interests of Twelve and Seven were happily balanced, following the old principle, man proposes, woman decides. But this is more a tendency than a hard-and-fast rule. As in Plato's *Republic,* women could be on the ruling council and male prophets might serve the oracle.

In all cosmographies and cosmological myths, Twelve and Seven are equally prominent. Cities have 7 gates, are built on 7 hills, and are founded on 7 springs. In St John's visions of heaven and hell, depicted in Revelation, are 7 churches, 7 golden candlesticks, 7 angels, 7 spirits of God, 7 kings, crowns, mountains, thunders, and plagues, a Beast with 7 horns, and a 7-headed dragon. In the divinely ordered city of heavenly Jerusalem are 12 gates guarded by 12 angels,

12 cornerstones, 12 kinds of fruit and gemstones, and the names of the 12 tribes of Israel together with those of the 12 Apostles.

It is impossible to interpret all this imagery, but an overall impression is that St John's Seven is applied to the primordial, elemental world, and his Twelve characterizes the perfect, universal order in the heavenly city. The model by which he expressed this was, as shown earlier, the sublunary centre of the traditional world plan. The main feature in that diagram, after the combination of square and circle, is the marriage of Twelve and Seven. Its geometry is developed in the following pages.

Fig. 194. Dividing a Circle into Seven

You can never do it exactly, but two close approximations to the septenary division of a circle have long been known. Both are simple and beautiful; the accuracy of the first is better than 1 in 1000.

Method 1 (top left to bottom left)

a. The circle is enclosed in a square, and on the base of the square an equilateral triangle is drawn. Lines from the centre of the base to the intersection points of circle and triangle form two sides of a heptagon.

b. The reciprocal triangle on the opposite side of the square allows the circle to be divided into 14 parts. See how neatly the sides of the triangle hold the inner 14-pointed figure.

c. Two triangles added on the other two sides of the square procure the 28-part division of the circle. This is the basic figure behind the complete cosmological diagram of the Heavenly City.

Method 2 (top right to bottom right)

d. Another way of dividing a circle into 7 virtually equal parts is to inscribe an equilateral triangle within the circle and draw an arc from one of its points to bisect two of its sides. Where the arc meets the circle are the two 7-division points.

a. Seven divisions

b. Fourteen divisions

c. Twenty-eight divisions

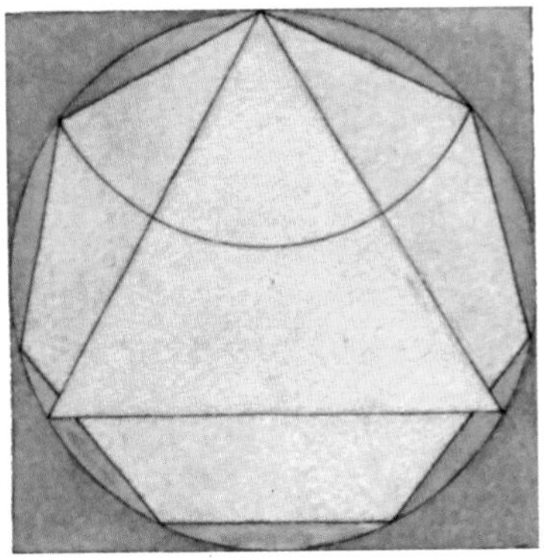

d. Seven divisions

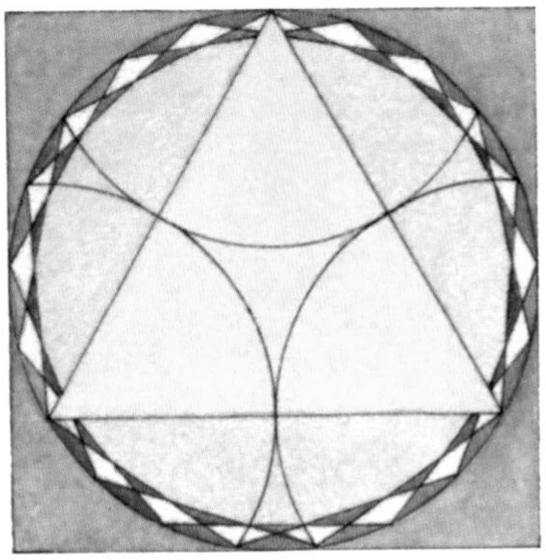

e. Twenty-one divisions

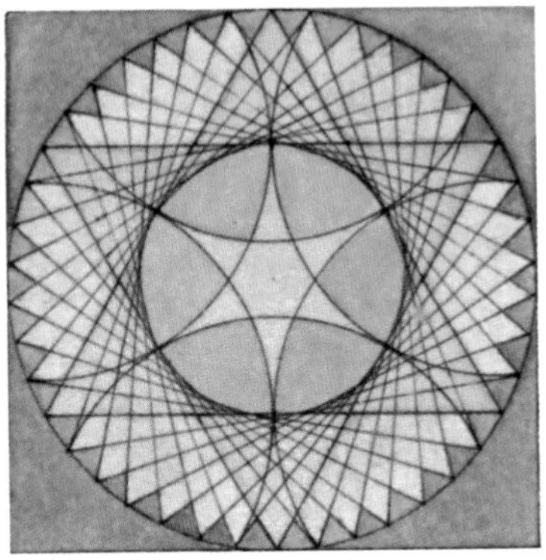

f. Forty-two divisions

e. Two further arcs from the other two points of the triangle divide the circle into 21 parts.

f. A second reciprocal triangle is added to produce a hexagon within the circle and divide the circumference into 42 points.

Fig. 195. The 42 divisions of the circle, shown on the previous page, are doubled through this construction to 84 or 7 x 12. Twelve arcs form the 12 points around the centre, and the 84 divisions accommodate the 7 'petals'.

Fig. 196. The central 12-pointed figure is created by arcs, while straight lines define the 84 divisions and the 7-pointed star.

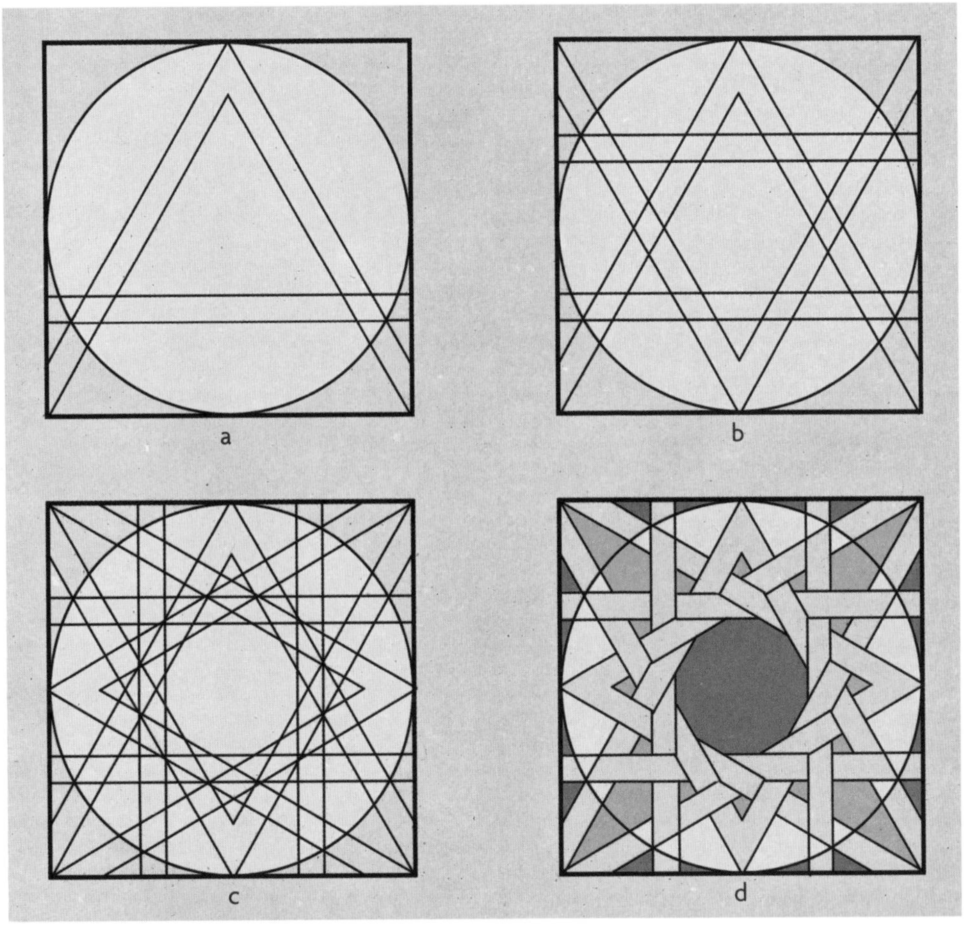

Fig. 197. Twelve and Seven, symbolic opposites, standing respectively for rational order and transcendental imagination, have a natural inclination towards each other. The depiction of their sacred marriage is one of the principal attainments of cosmological geometry. It begins with two constructions (figure 194 on page 221) where two different triangles are used to divide a circle into 7 parts. One of the two triangles is inscribed within the circle, the other stands on the base of the square containing it. When these triangles are drawn to overlie each other, and their sides are extended to the borders of the square, the result is a magnificent display of duodecimal geometry, capable of many different expressions.

The drawings that were originally meant to achieve a 7-fold division have developed spontaneously into a 12-fold figure with a dodecagon at its centre.

a. The two triangles are placed together and their sides extended to the square.

b. The reciprocal triangle is added on the top side of the square.

c and d. The triangles drawn on the other two sides complete the diagram.

Figs. 198 (this page) and **199 (opposite).** Developed from the previous diagrams showing the geometry of Seven, these patterns, both made up of 12 spokes or cardboard strips, are totally duodecimal.

Fig. 200. The duodecimal pattern is incomplete because the 12 strips that comprise it have not yet run their course. It is finished when each of the strips has crossed each of the others, except for the one parallel to it. The result is a 12-pointed, interlaced figure produced in traditional dances with swords or wands.

Fig. 201. The lonely princess. Her window is barred by the duodecimal pattern.

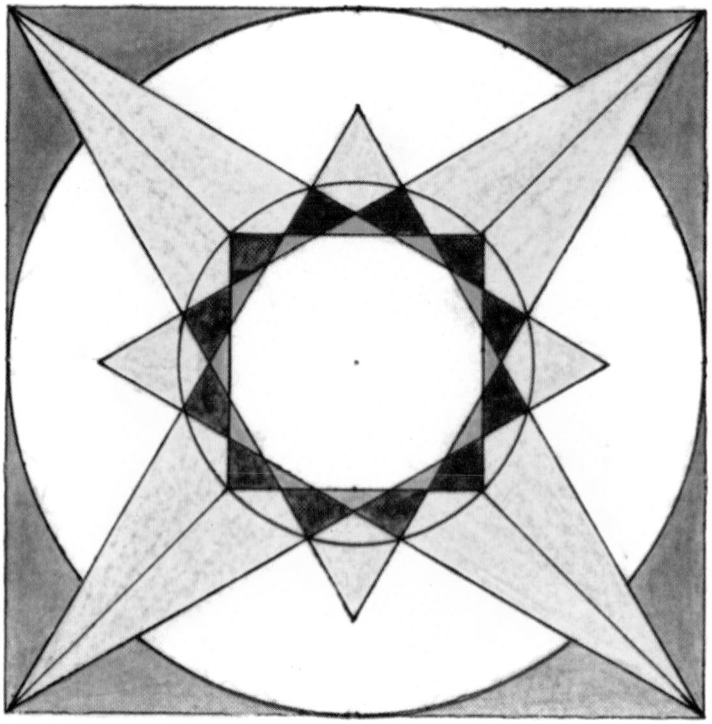

Fig. 202. Constructing the Heavenly City. The first stage in the geometer's depiction of the ideal cosmology is dividing a circle into 28 parts. That, as previously shown, is done with a high degree of accuracy by drawing four triangles within a square, each one based on one of its four sides. This produces the inner dodecagon. The four arcs of the outer circle passing through the yellow areas each cover a twenty-eighth part of the circumference.

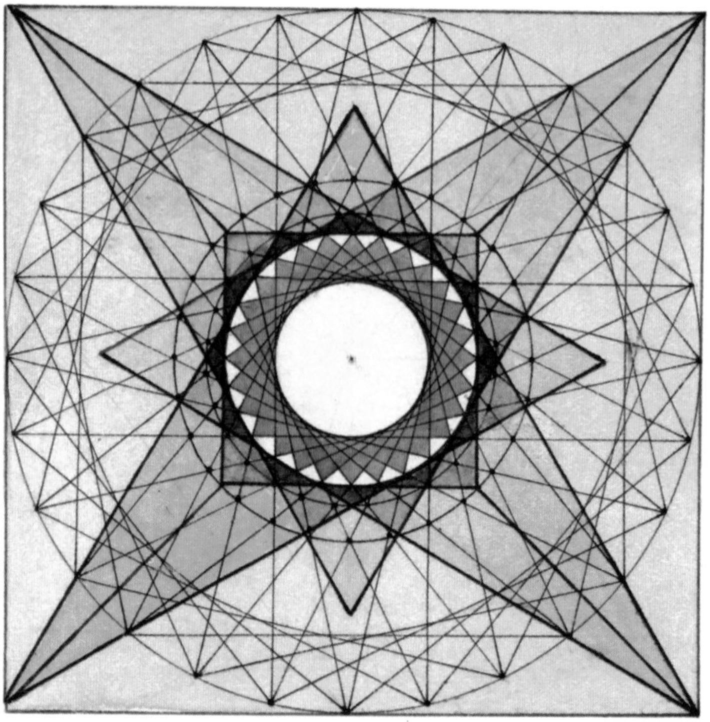

Fig. 203. The outer circle is divided geometrically into 28 parts. Eight of the division marks are given by the intersections of the circle and the four limbs; the other twenty can be located with the compass. The 28 points are joined together in regular order. This creates the 28-pointed ring (pink) around the centre.

Fig. 204. The construction for dividing a circle into 28 parts leads to this pattern (top). The white ring around the centre is occupied (below), by the twelve corners of the three squares produced by extending the lines from the corners of the square.

Fig. 205. The 28-pointed figure locates the positions of the 12 moon circles that stand around the circle of the earth and form the squared circle.

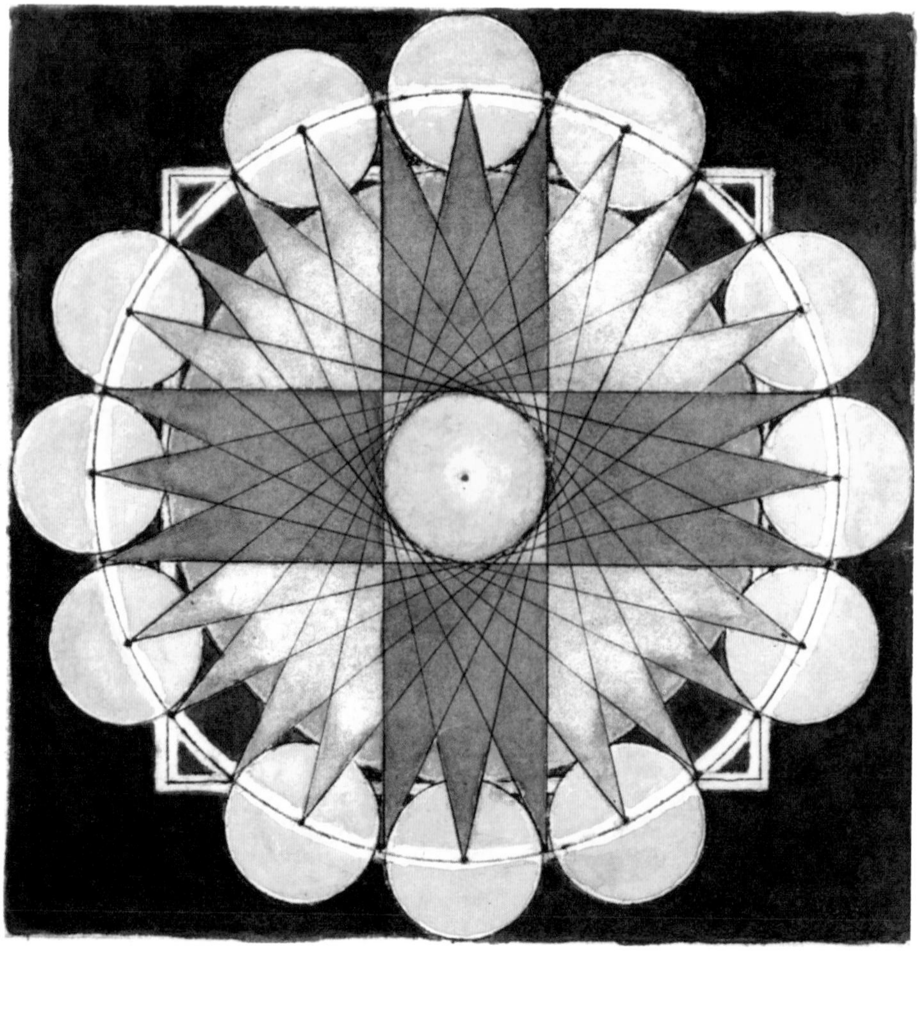

Fig. 206. A jewelled cross set around with twelve pearls in a symbol of the heavenly paradise and a mark of dedication to its restoration upon earth

Fig. 207. Seven and Twelve united and the Heavenly City revealed

15 • Geometry and Love

Approaching the Climax

The geometer's creation myth is an accompaniment to the traditional process of initiation which leads through the arts and sciences towards the ultimate high state of love and understanding. Above the clamour of the rival world-explainers, the literal-minded creationists, and the dogmatic evolutionists, it strikes a note that resonates in the mind, because it is the note of truth. Our story of how the world came into being is not made up from random beliefs and opinions, but exists ready-made in the numbers, shapes, and harmonies that are the essence of nature herself. It can properly be called universal, for the truths on which it is based are ever and everywhere the same.

Universal though it may be, the geometer's myth does not pretend to offer a universal cult or belief system. Everyone has their favourite ways and prejudices, and as long as there are different nations, cultures, and individuals, so it will always be. It is said that "God likes to be praised in different voices". There are many ways of investigating the universe other than through abstract number and geometry, and many people enjoy satisfactory careers without even hearing about traditional cosmology. Those who enter this subject often do so as a last resort, having failed to discover firm ground in the pragmatic sciences or religious dogmas. That, we are told, is how it should be.

Plato in *Ion* rebuked the self-righteous young musician who boasted that he was only interested in the 'best' lyrics, asking him, "How can you recognize the best when you do not know the worst?" He advised his pupils to study everything and take an interest in life generally. In the traditional allegories of a human life span, such as *Pilgrim's Progress,* the traveller descends into dark and dismal places before approaching the distant light of his goal. This suggests that the philosopher's cosmology is acquired, if at all, through personal experience and after many

Fig. 208. The Garden of Epicurus where this most amiable of philosophers taught young women, his favourite pupils, to trust their senses and enjoy life's beauties and pleasures.

disappointments. Those who become aware of its existence do not necessarily give up the faiths they were brought up in. Every religion has its core of initiated mystics, whose common perception is that all expressions of belief, as well as every human soul, have their due place in the divine order. This is true tolerance, not the sort than comes from fear and laziness, but tolerance that is produced by love.

The level of love is the highest of the four stages in the classical process of self-development. The first is the level of ignorance, when you do not even know that there is anything worth knowing; then comes the level of opinion (as in the inconclusive arguments from different viewpoints that constitute media debates); and the third stage, knowledge, is attained by study. The fourth stage, that of nous, or divine understanding, is called the level of love. It could be achieved through initiation, and there is a strange, mystical account by Socrates, quoted in Plato's *Symposium,* of the process by which he entered the state of love. His guide was Diotima, a wise woman who initiated him in love at the same time as she taught him philosophy. She showed him how to cultivate love, first by extending it beyond the body of the loved one until you can love more widely, even universally, seeing the beauty inherent in everything and everyone. Then, said Socrates, comes the moment of climax, when you meet Love itself. That moment, he declared, is worth everything. The example of his life thereafter gives insight into the state of mind of someone who has had the experience of Love itself. Renouncing all ambitions, careless of fame and fortune, he spoke quietly to a few young admirers in the marketplace in Athens. He only spoke the truth, as established by reason, without glamour or deception. When men of rank and authority came to seek his praise and approval, he proved to them through their own admissions that they were ignorant and misguided. Among friends he taught the doctrine of rebirth, reasoning that the soul is the only real and lasting part of an individual and should therefore be given more attention than one's physical appetites. And the nourishment the soul needs are the eternal virtues of justice, truth, and love. So relentlessly honest was Socrates, so incapable of lies and flattery, that he was put on trial for rejecting the conventional values of society, sentenced to death, and executed.

In that way, as if following the script of an eternal drama, Socrates fulfilled his own prophecy, quoted in the *Republic* 361d, that if ever there were such a thing as a perfectly honest man, he would be mocked and crucified. A few hundred years later Jesus followed the same script. Neither of those two men really wanted to be martyrs, but they were caught up in the drama and played their parts to the end. There was nothing else they could do because, having achieved the level of love and understanding, they could never reenter the world of lies and compromises, as their persecutors demanded.

The first attribute of the level of love, it seems, is recognition of soul, in the universe itself and in every creature. A person who has risen to that level sees his fellow beings in their souls, with no regard for their pretensions or self-images. A problem with that, as Socrates found, is that people of importance or self-importance, if not treated with the deference they think due to them, may take offence and become enemies. There are other obvious drawbacks to a life of love and truthfulness, so it is not surprising that few even aspire to that level. Yet, according to those who have gained it, it is the only real and worthwhile way of living. In that case, how do you get there?

The sages who have written about this say that the first step in the path to understanding is taken by whoever wants to take it, who feels the need or is somehow impelled to do so. Sometimes the impetus occurs spontaneously, through a near-death experience perhaps, or in shamanic societies by attracting spirits and weird happenings such as involuntary levitation. Otherwise the first step is taken by someone who has heard about initiation and the state of love and determines to acquire them, by dedicating all senses to perceiving the goodness in human souls rather than their flaws. That perception, further developed, brings into sight another world, the earthly paradise, an image that from early childhood our minds and senses have been trained to obliterate. It is that multicoloured world as described by certain poets and, most vividly, by St John in his vision of the Heavenly City on earth. It's the same as the more familiar world of despair and suicide, but those who have seen the earth as paradise insist that this, its ideal aspect, is far more true and real than the miserable image that materialism and the modern mind project upon it.

The high vision that mystics call reality has also been called the 'primordial' vision, meaning that it has been a property of human nature since the beginning. It is said to be one component of the Holy Grail, the symbol in Celtic mysticism of personal enlightenment and the restoration of divine order. The other component of the Grail is the 'primordial tradition'. That is where geometry comes in, together with number and cosmology. The primordial tradition is based on number, and the constitution of number is the 'first paradigm', the most faithful reflection of pure reason and the mind of the Creator. In whatever times and places this tradition has prevailed, the numerical sciences have been given priority, particularly in the training of administrators. For by these sciences, number, music, and geometry, minds are attuned to reason and proportion, producing justice and wise rulers. That is as good as it gets, by modern reckoning. But there is something even better. The ideal in any constitution, social and political or individual and mental, comes about through the sacred marriage of complementary opposites, as for example the primordial vision and the primordial tradition. Similar marriages are a feature of symbolic geometry, as exhibited throughout this book—the marriage of square and circle, the uniting of numbers Twelve and Seven, the mating dances of pentagrams. All of these can be called acts of love, and their occurrence among and between the archetypal figures of geometry suggests that 'the power of love' is as good a name for the force that produced and maintains the harmony of the universe as any of the terms invented by modern physics.

Fig. 209. Pythagoras said that a lover is "one who is the other I, such as are 220 and 284". For details of the 'amicable' numbers, 220 and 284, and their sum 504, see page 61.

Fig. 210. Mitochondrial DNA strand, or true lovers' knot

Fig. 211. Triangular construction in a crop circle. Justice is represented by the equal areas of dark and light.

Fig. 212 (opposite). This overhead view of Atlantis may look from another perspective like the seaside headquarters of an international corporation, and in a way that is what it was. Atlantis became the capital of a vast empire that came to grief. This is the ground plan as Plato specified it. The green rectangle of 20 by 30 squares is formed by water channels with a wide canal round its borders. The south side of the canal runs parallel to the sea, and its two ends meet at the city of Atlantis (the small, white circle near the centre of the sea coast). Beyond the plain are mountains, well populated and with all kinds of animals, plants, and minerals.

Part 5

ATLANTIS

A Geometrical Diversion

16 • A Geometer's Nightmare

Plato's Pentagonal Allegory

Atlantis: The Historical Record

The most extraordinary geometric structure that anyone has ever dreamt up must surely be Plato's Atlantis. As developed in the following pages, it is a monstrous edifice in pentagonal geometry, a mode that is quite unsuited for city planning. But in Atlantis everything that could go wrong did go wrong, and eventually it fell, catastrophically.

There are two aspects to Plato's account of Atlantis, historical and allegorical. The first step is to separate and sort them out, beginning here with the historical side of Atlantis and moving on to the more certain and interesting part—the meaning behind Plato's elaborate scheme of Atlantean geometry.

Nothing that Plato wrote has attracted so much popular attention as his story of the lost city, capital of an island continent that suddenly disappeared beneath the waves. It is a fantastic story with the vivid unreality of a dream. Yet in the two books that he wrote late in life describing Atlantis, *Timaeus* and *Critias,* Plato insisted on the basic truth behind it—that there really was a vast island in the Atlantic, just beyond the straits of Gibraltar, bigger than Libya and Asia Minor put together. Its eastern shore lay opposite the Spanish region of Gadira (Cadiz) and it extended westwards towards the "opposite continent", which can only mean America. Access to that continent was then possible through a chain of islands that linked it to the western end of Atlantis.

The destruction of Atlantis, according to Plato, took place 9000 years before his time—about 11,500 years ago for us—so sceptics have good reason to reject the episode as true history. There was, however, one medium by which a record of such great antiquity might have survived up to the late centuries BC. That medium was ancient Egypt. In his *Laws* Plato states that, by strictly upholding the canon of law they had received from their divine founders, the Egyptians maintained their high standards of culture for "literally ten thousand years". In their temples the priestly authorities kept records of past events that all other nations had long forgotten.

That, we are told in the *Timaeus,* is how the memory of Atlantis was preserved. In around 600 BC the learned Solon, one of the seven sages of ancient Greece, heard its history from a priest in Egypt. In old age Solon repeated it to a young friend who passed it on to his descendants, and in that way it reached his great-grandson, Critias, one of the brilliant, noble youths who surrounded the master Socrates. As Plato tells the story, Socrates, having spoken to a small group of his disciples about the ideal constitution of ancient Athens, invited them each to discourse on some related subject. Timaeus recited his famous treatise on the numerical composition of the world, and Critias gave the history of Atlantis.

The reason the Egyptian priest brought up the subject of Atlantis while conversing with Solon was to demonstrate the unique antiquity of the Egyptian records. "You Greeks are like children", he said. "You have no historical memory; you cannot even remember the most glorious thing you ever did—when you stood alone against the mighty Atlantean empire, defeating its army and setting free the Mediterranean nations it had enslaved." Soon after that victory, said the priest, there was an almighty cataclysm. Atlantis went under, taking with it the army of Greek heroes (who, presumably, were carrying the war to the enemy's heartland).

Up to this point the story is not implausible. The earth is an unstable creature, subject to sudden shifts in mood and appearance. It is traditionally supposed that over great periods of time areas of land and sea change places. Also, if you look at a chart of the north Atlantic, it is easy to locate the site of Atlantis, just where Plato said it was. To the west of Spain and Portugal, the islands of Azores rise up far into the Atlantic, with shallow waters all around them, and with former river beds extending far out to sea as evidence of larger areas of land under water. From the Azores westwards, a chain of rocks and shoals does indeed resemble a former island chain leading to the wide, shallow banks off Newfoundland. A geological upheaval, eleven or twelve thousand years ago, from the great Atlantic rift that crosses the area could quite possibly have put Atlantis under water.

The first modern writer to revive Atlantis was Ignatius Donnelly, the adventurous, imaginative United States congressman, whose book, *Atlantis: The Antediluvian World,* was published in 1882. It caused a sensation. Mr William Gladstone, the British prime minister, was so impressed by the manifold proofs of Atlantis that Donnelly had assembled that he wanted to send the British navy into the Atlantic to conduct researches. No doubt they would have settled the matter one way or the other, but, sad to say, Gladstone's proposal was vetoed by the Treasury. Ever since then, books about Atlantis have gushed forth, sometimes with channelled messages from long-departed islanders, nearly always with Atlantis displaced from where Plato specifically located it.

All over the world are drowned lands and underwater cities, and their dis-

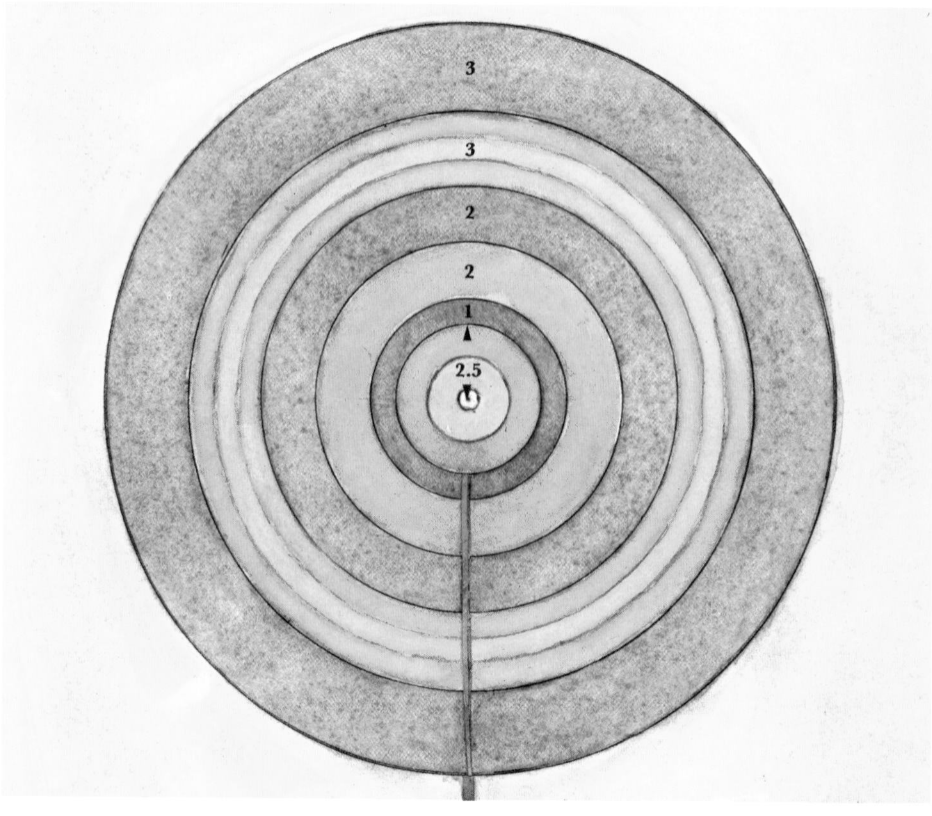

Fig. 213. Rings of water and land in Atlantis city, measured in stadia

coverers like to call them Atlantis. But the only Atlantis that has a right to the name lay just beyond the Pillars of Hercules, forming a partial land bridge to America.

Atlantis: Its Foundation and Growth

Whatever you may think about Atlantis from the historical or geographical point of view, Plato's strange description of its constitutional structure can hardly be called history. It is another of his geometrical allegories. One of his techniques was to take some popular belief or weird happening—the near-death experience of the soldier in the *Republic,* for example—and adapt its framework to accommodate his esoteric teachings. He was interested in the old Atlantis legend and made it useful for his purpose, reshaping it as the story of a nation that was flawed from the beginning, with an imperfect foundation and constitution. Over many generations the Atlanteans prospered, grew rich through trade, and developed a great empire. But finally their imperfections caught up with them. They became greedy and decadent and overreached themselves in foreign adventures. Their defeat by the poor but vigorous Greeks was followed by divine retribution. Zeus called a council of the twelve gods to decide how to punish Atlantis, and amid storms and tempests the great island was obliterated from history.

In Plato's version of the apocalyptic cycle, Atlantis plays the same part as Babylon in Revelation. In this tradition the corrupt, luxurious city, heading for its fall, alternates with the divinely founded, perfectly ordered constitution that Plato projected upon archaic Athens and St John upon the ideal Jerusalem. For the ground plan of his ideal Athens, Plato adopted the traditional, cosmological diagram with its radius of 5040 and its 5040 independent citizens. Its outline as the best possible state pattern—the pattern of the heavens reproduced on earth—is shown on page 250. The pattern on which Atlantis was founded is a sort of parody of the ideal. It is an ingenious scheme of geometry, and the city it produced was magnificent—far richer and more populous than virtuous Athens.

But there was something wrong with Atlantis, a basic flaw in its foundation pattern, that prevented it from working properly and led eventually to its downfall. Instead of the universal Twelve, the Atlanteans adopted Ten as the basis of their state geometry—anticipating the modern fashion for metrics and decimals. The results of that, and the errors and ambiguities that ensued from it, are illustrated in the following analysis of Atlantean geometry.

The history of Atlantis begins with its foundation. At the beginning of the world the twelve gods divided the earth between them, each ruling one of its twelve sections and its traditional twelve nations. Poseidon, god of the ocean, was naturally allotted the sea-girt realm of Atlantis. There he found a mortal woman, Cleito, and married her, and she bore him "five pairs of twins", all boys. When they grew up they inherited the island between them, each with his own province, and thereafter Atlantis was ruled as a confederacy of ten kingdoms, subject to the same laws and customs.

With many curious details Plato dwells upon the splendours of Atlantis, its gardens, fountains, and statues, the coloured stones in its towers and walls and the precious metals that covered its public buildings, temples, and palaces. It is a glorious picture, and no doubt every feature of it has symbolic meaning. But here we are mainly concerned with the ground plan of Atlantis whose dimensions Plato carefully provides. The units in which he gives them are the foot and the stadion of 600 feet.

The city of Atlantis was situated near the middle of the south coast of the island (the reason it was not precisely in the middle will be seen later). On its landward side it was surrounded by a large, fertile plain, enclosed by mountains which ran down to the sea on either side. In these mountains lived a great many country people and animals of all kinds. At the centre of the city was a low hill, Cleito's ancestral home, where she and Poseidon bred their ten sons. The god isolated it by surrounding the hill with five concentric rings, three of water and two of land, equidistant from each other. Later generations of Atlanteans improved the amenities through a vast programme of engineering works.

They regulated the three rings of water, giving them precise dimensions (figure 213 on page 242). The innermost, surrounding the island hill, was 1 stadion wide, the next 2 stadia, and the outermost 3 stadia. Between them were two rings of land, the inner 2 and the outer 3 stadia wide. The diameter of the central island was 5 stadia. All the rings were lined with stone walls covered in various metals. It is difficult to see how the Atlanteans could have adapted the original rings, which were equidistant from each other, so as to give them these proportions without exchanging areas of land and water to no apparent purpose. But they had an overall plan and they stuck to it. Their next labour was to dig a canal, 300 feet wide and 50 stadia in length, from the outermost ring of water to the sea. A narrower extension of the canal was cut inwards through the rings of land up to the ring of water around the central island.

The next thing the Atlanteans did was typical of their awkward habits. The land within the rings of water rose naturally towards the central hill, so the canal through the rings of land had to be cut deep. Over it and across the rings of land they built a road to the island hill, with bridges that made the canal into a tunnel. The bridges were "about" 100 feet wide, probably the same as the canal below them. It is not easy to imagine this arrangement; it is an engineer's nightmare. But it evidently worked well enough, for the city became a bustling port with merchant ships and triremes of all nations crowding its rings of water.

Atlantis was furnished with every delight and luxury, especially the island hill. At its centre, surrounded by a wall of gold, was the holy of holies, the former marriage bed of Poseidon and Cleito where the five pairs of twins were conceived. Enclosing it was the temple of Poseidon, 1 stadion long and 300 feet wide, adorned with gold, silver, ivory (there were elephants in Atlantis), and 'orichalc', a metal peculiar to Atlantis that "gleamed like fire". Statues of the original ten kings with their ten wives stood around it, and the whole was surrounded by the wall of the acropolis, clad in orichalc, and by the outer wall of the island which was covered with tin.

Finally, the whole city and its surroundings were contained within a great wall, beginning at the seaward end of the canal, 50 stadia from the outer ring of water, and continuing at the same distance to make a circle round the city.

Houses were clustered inside the wall and probably, along with their gardens, filled the space between the wall and the outer ring of water. Calculating the area of this space produces a remarkable result. To find this area you deduct the area of the inner city within the rings from that of the whole city within the great wall (with $\pi \times r^2$ as the area of a circle, r = radius and $\pi = 22/7$). The answer turns out to be 4,356,000,000 square feet, and 43560 square feet is one acre, the acre we still use today. That means that the whole area of Atlantis city beyond its outer ring of water is 100,000 acres. Plato does not say how many people there were in Atlantis, but there were certainly many more than the 60,000 families of free citizens who formed the land-owning class. If there had been 100,000 families in the walled city outside the water rings, they would have had an acre of house and garden each.

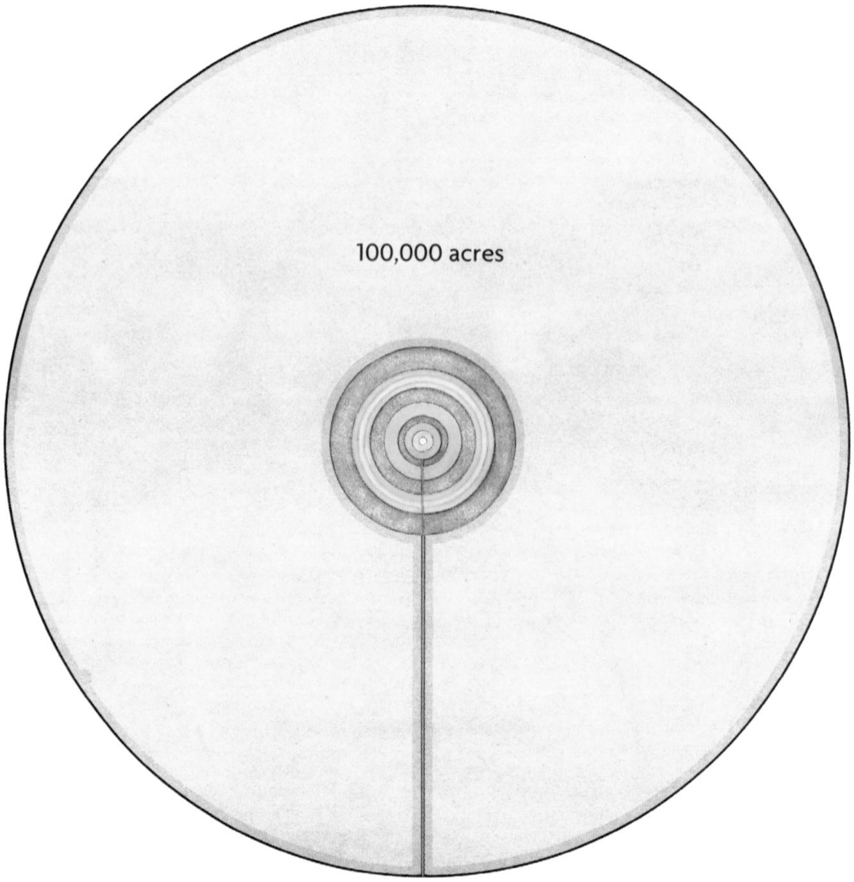

Fig. 214. Rings of water and land in Atlantis city, measured in stadia

Squaring the Circle, Atlantis Style

Every city planned symbolically by geomancers or augers had one indispensable feature, a squared circle. This in the cosmological diagram is represented by the circle of radius 5040 and the square of side 7920, both figures having perimeters of 31680. In the Atlantis plan the squared circle is not immediately evident. It only comes to light when the city is placed in its position on the plain. When this is done the squared circle appears, virtually the same as that of the cosmological diagram but, like everything in Atlantis, slightly wrong.

Like the city itself, the plain on which Atlantis was founded was given regular geometric form by an early generation of Atlanteans. They dug a great ditch all round it, 1 stadion wide, to form a rectangular canal, 3000 stadia from east to west and 2000 stadia from north to south. From the northern side they made smaller cross canals, 100 feet wide, spaced at intervals of 100 stadia, running straight across the plain to its southern sides, and they did the same between the eastern and western sides, thus creating a block of 20 × 30 or 600 island squares. These, says Plato, were each divided into 100 allotments, each of 100 square stadia, and divided among the 60,000 free citizens of Atlantis, each with his family and a large number of retainers from the surrounding mountains.

A geometric problem to this work is how to divide a square area into 100 equal allotments (assuming that each citizen wants equal access to a waterway). And its planners have made an obvious blunder. They have not allowed for the area taken up by the waterways. Nor have they taken into account the area occupied by the city. This gap between the specifications and their possible fulfilment would have frustrated the Atlantean surveyors and been the cause of endless quibbling boundary disputes—the most common cause of friction between neighbours.

The plan of Atlantis, figure 212 on page 239, shows where the city stood in relation to its plain. It was, says Plato, "near the middle of the plain and about fifty stadia inland". That means it was near the middle of the southern side of the plain, at the end of the 50-stadia-long canal from the sea. It could not have been precisely halfway along the plain, because it would then have stood over one of the north-south waterways (31 in all including the arms of the wide canal at each end) that divided the southern side of the plain into thirty parts.

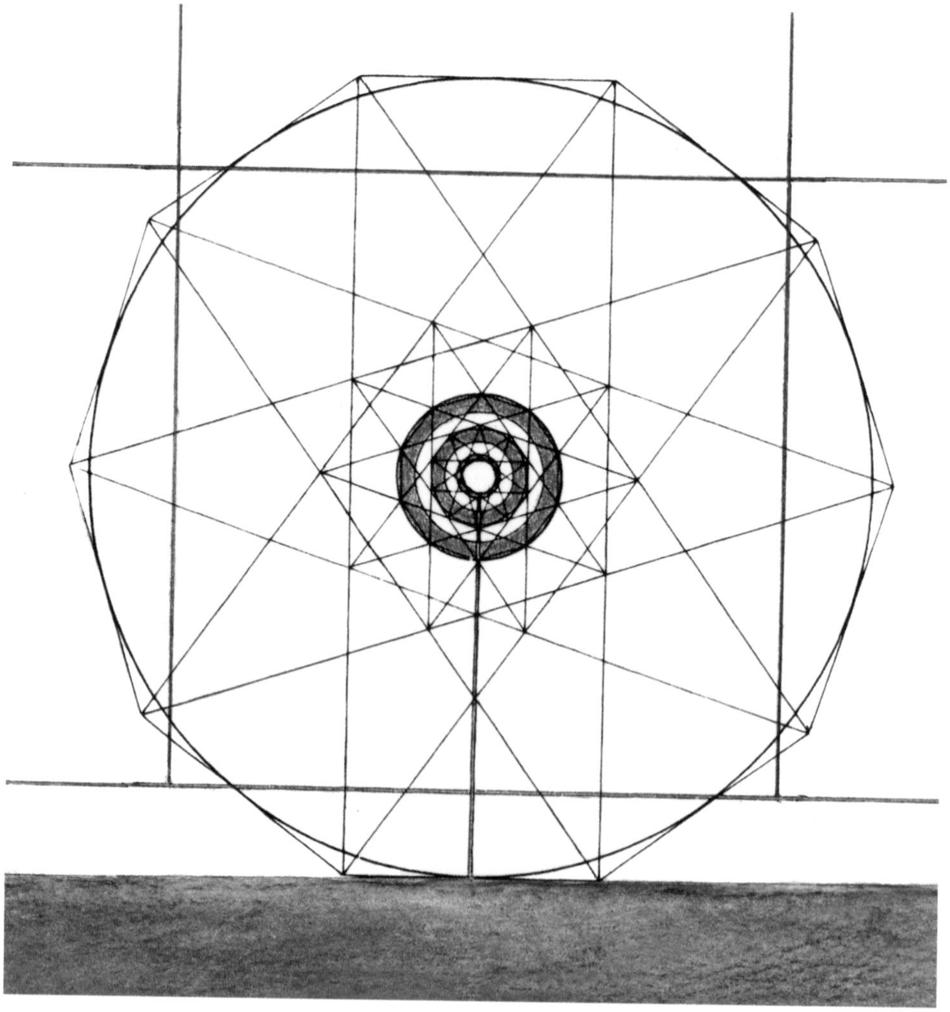

Fig. 215. The inadequate squared circle: A scheme of ten-faceted, decagonal geometry links all the parts of the Atlantis plan from the central, ringed area to the wall around the whole city. Overlaying the circle of the outer wall is the square of blue lines, one of the 600 squares separated by water channels that make up the Atlantean plain. The side of the square is 100 stadia long, making its perimeter 400 stadia. The diameter of the circular wall is 127, so its circumference is 399 1/7—slightly too short for a perfect squared circle.

It therefore had to be placed to one side of the halfway point, on and overlapping one of the square islands. This island—or, rather, the square of water channels around it—is the missing square in the Atlantean squared circle. The side of this square, as given, is 100 stadia, so the measure round its four sides is 400. The diameter of the circular wall around Atlantis, also given, is 100 stadia plus the diameter of the ringed inner city, 27 stadia. Its total diameter is therefore 127 stadia, so the circumference of the wall ($127 \times 22/7$) is not quite 400 but $399^{1}/_{7}$ stadia. Another near-miss by the Atlanteans. How beautifully and wittily Plato makes his point—that the defective foundation pattern of Atlantis meant that everything there was flawed.

At the root of Atlantis and its problems is that its founder, Poseidon, married a mortal woman, and eventually, says Plato, "the mortal element prevailed". Yet the foundation plan of Atlantis was very near the ideal that it tried to imitate, the cosmological or Heavenly City diagram on which Plato's ancient Athens was based. On the following page the two versions of the squared circle, the Atlantean and the traditional ideal, are compared and analysed together. The comparison is purely in number and proportion; scale is not involved. Atlantis is measured in feet and stadia, the Heavenly City in feet and miles, but these units serve merely to bring out the required numbers.

Plato must have worked hard on his Atlantean constitution, making it near enough to the ideal to be worth studying, but full of errors and inaccuracies. No doubt it was useful for the mode of instruction that he attributes to Socrates, leading his pupils through the world of false opinions towards the state of understanding he called 'nous'. This tradition of learning was not invented by Plato, Socrates, or Pythagoras before them, but was apparently reconstructed by them and others of their time from relics of the ancient science, preserved most effectively by the Egyptian priests. Now it is lost—so completely that its very existence is no longer recognized. It is not, however, beyond recall. Being rooted in human nature—as Socrates insisted—and certainly inherent in number, geometry, and cosmology, it is there for anyone at any time who sees good reason to bring it again into light.

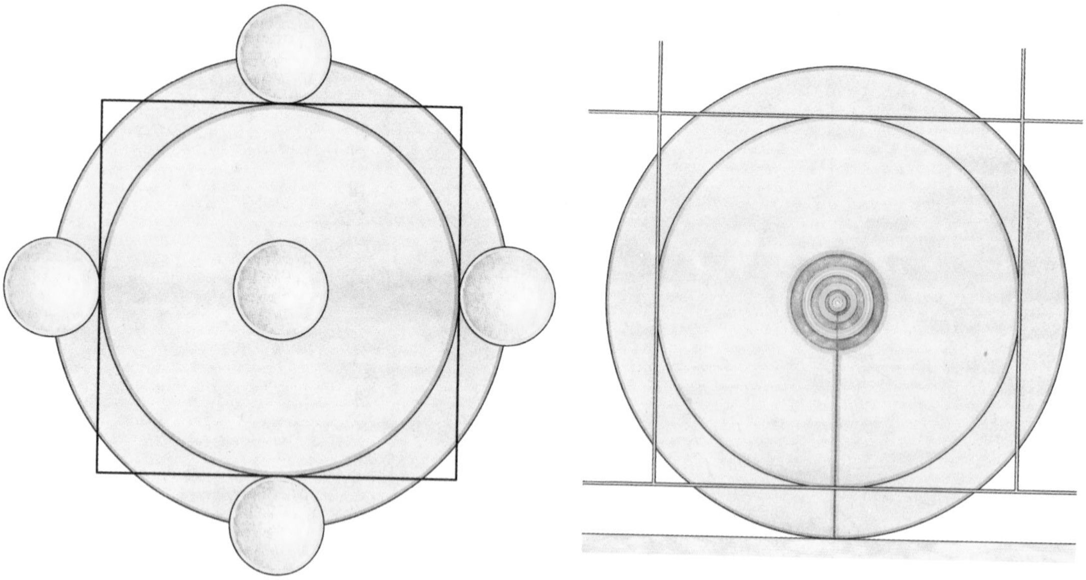

Atlantis and Plato's Ideal City Compared

Fig. 216. The squared circles of Plato's ideal city and Atlantis compared. In each case the difference between the radii of the two outer concentric circles is equal to the radius of the inner circle. Yet the Atlantean squared circle is slightly defective.

Ideal city		**Atlantis**	
inner city, radius	= 1080 ft.	inner city, radius	= 13½ stadia
circle within square, radius	= 3960 ft.	circle within square, radius	= 50 stadia
square, perimeter	= 31680 ft.	square, perimeter	= 400 stadia
outer circle, radius	= 5040 ft.	outer circle, radius	= 63½ stadia
circumference	= 31680 ft.	circumference	= 399 1/7 stadia

Atlantis: The Pentagonal Edifice

An earlier essay on Atlantis, in *The Dimensions of Paradise,* showed the outline of the pentagonal or ten-part scheme of geometry that links together the various parts of the Atlantis plan. Since then, further study has filled out the diagram and disclosed the geometry that determined in every detail the form and dimensions of the ringed city. This geometry is so elaborate and cumbersome that no sane person would attempt to complete it by hand. Perhaps Plato set it as an exercise to punish his lazy or over-confident students. One can go so far with drawing the Atlantis plan (see page 255), but after that it is job for the computer. The following computer-made images of Atlantis, the ringed city in all its pentagonal glory, were executed by Allan Brown.

At the centre of Atlantis is the island with radius of 2½ stadia, focused upon the shrine where Cleito gave birth to her five pairs of twins. It is surrounded by a golden wall. Then there is the temple of Poseidon, the statues of the first ten kings with their wives, the wall of the acropolis, and all kinds of adornments—a gigantic statue of Poseidon with his hundred water nymphs riding on dolphins, springs and hot baths, groves, gardens, houses, and palaces. Behind these details the main features of the plan can be located from Plato's description. The central shrine, birthplace of the ten sons, is obviously ten-sided, the twins being represented by a decagon-star as shown on page 253. Poseidon's temple, 300 by 600 feet, encloses it; the statues of the ten kings and their wives, represented by ten decagons, stand in a ring around the temple, and this whole sacred area, the acropolis, is protected by a wall. Outside it is the ring wall around the island, and then comes the first of the three water rings, 1 stadion in width. Everything here is geometric, made up of pentagons, with rings of pentagrams or five-pointed stars to represents the main three walls of the island, and with decagons for the ten king-and-queen statues and the central shrine.

The picture on page 255, illustrating the natural development of the pentagonal pattern around a central decagon, is also the plan of the central island of Atlantis. Once you see how the pentagon pattern expands in successive bands, one stadion or 600 feet apart, it is then possible to depict the entire city with its rings of land and water. The first thing you notice is that the rings and walls, which in the central area of the diagram begin with a true circle, become more and more like decagons. By the end of the process the circles that are meant to follow the lines of the walls almost lose touch with them and only pass through the pairs of stars at the corners. These pairs, where they stand at the bridges over the canal, can be taken to represent the pairs of guard towers that Plato situated there. One has to pity the Atlanteans. Everything they did was artfully planned and started off so well, but soon began to go wrong and ended in failure. They could not divide their lands properly; they could not get their squared circle right, and the circular rings they planned for their inner city turned into decagons. The pentagon is a beautiful shape and the patterns it produces are among the loveliest in geometry, but it is not suitable for construction work or for the ground plan of a centralized state. The planners of Atlantis, like the Pythagoreans, venerated the pentagon, but they did not understand its nature. It is an organic figure, related to humanity, and the patterns it produces are shaped by the ring dances that pentagrams perform in their different ways (see Pentagonal Dances, page 182). The first ring of ten forms a circle hand to hand and foot to foot, but as the number of dancers grows, always in increments of twenty, they have to adapt their groupings, until their decimal nature takes over entirely and their ring becomes a decagon.

Atlantis: The Basic Geometry

The ground plan of Atlantis starts with a ten-sided decagon in the middle and develops outwards in successive rings of pentagons and pentagram stars. The only other shapes are, first, the rhombus that fills the gaps between the pentagons in their rings and, second, the decagon. Each decagon has ten pentagons around it, accomodating the tendency of the pentagon to form rings and spirals. This construction is well known to students of pentagonal geometry, for only in this way, by alternating rings of stars with rings of pentagons encircling decagons, is a centralized, theoretically endless pentagonal development possible.

Fig. 217. Constructing Atlantis. Stage A. At the hub is the shrine within the temple of Poseidon where Cleito gave birth to her five pairs of male twins, the future kings of Atlantis. This is represented geometrically by a decagon with five pairs of horns.

Fig. 218. Stage B. Pentagons around the central decagon

Fig. 219. Stage C. Around the central decagon develops the inner part of the pentagonal growth pattern on which the city of Atlantis was founded. The ring of stars represents the wall round the central shrine. Within the circle of the wall is the temple of Poseidon (highlighted), 1 stadion long and half as wide. Its curved ends may be the reason why Plato said there was something barbaric about it.

Fig. 220. Stage D. The pentagonal development up to the second ring of stars which forms the wall around the acropolis. The ten decagons in a ring, symbolizing the statues of the first ten kings of Atlantis together with their queens, have been drawn in different ways to illustrate some of the many geometric possibilities.

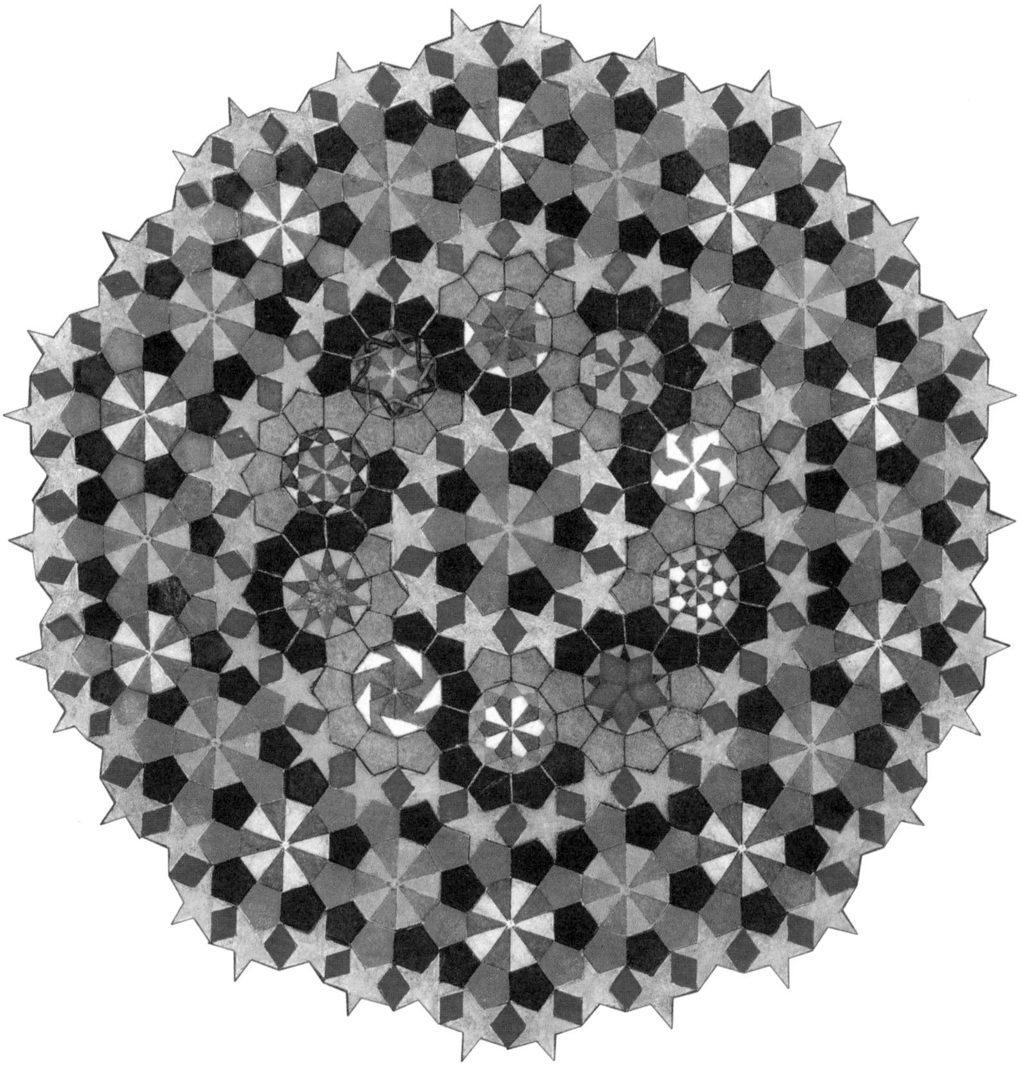

Fig. 221. Stage E. This pattern shows the central island bordered by the third wall made up of 50 stars (they increase at each stage by 20). The distance between each successive wall is 1 stadion, the diameter of the inner ring-wall is 1 stadion, so the radius of the island is as Plato gives it, 2½ stadia. The above image, showing the pentagonal development of Atlantis up to the rim of the central island, was drawn and coloured by hand, but that is about as far as one can take it. It is hard to believe that anyone, even a pupil at Plato's Academy, has ever constructed the entire plan of Atlantis manually. The principle behind the development is simple, but the labour of completing it is vast and mechanical. That makes it a job for the computer. The pictures that follow are computer designs by Allan Brown. They are the first depictions of Atlantis city and its pentagonal geometry that have ever been seen.

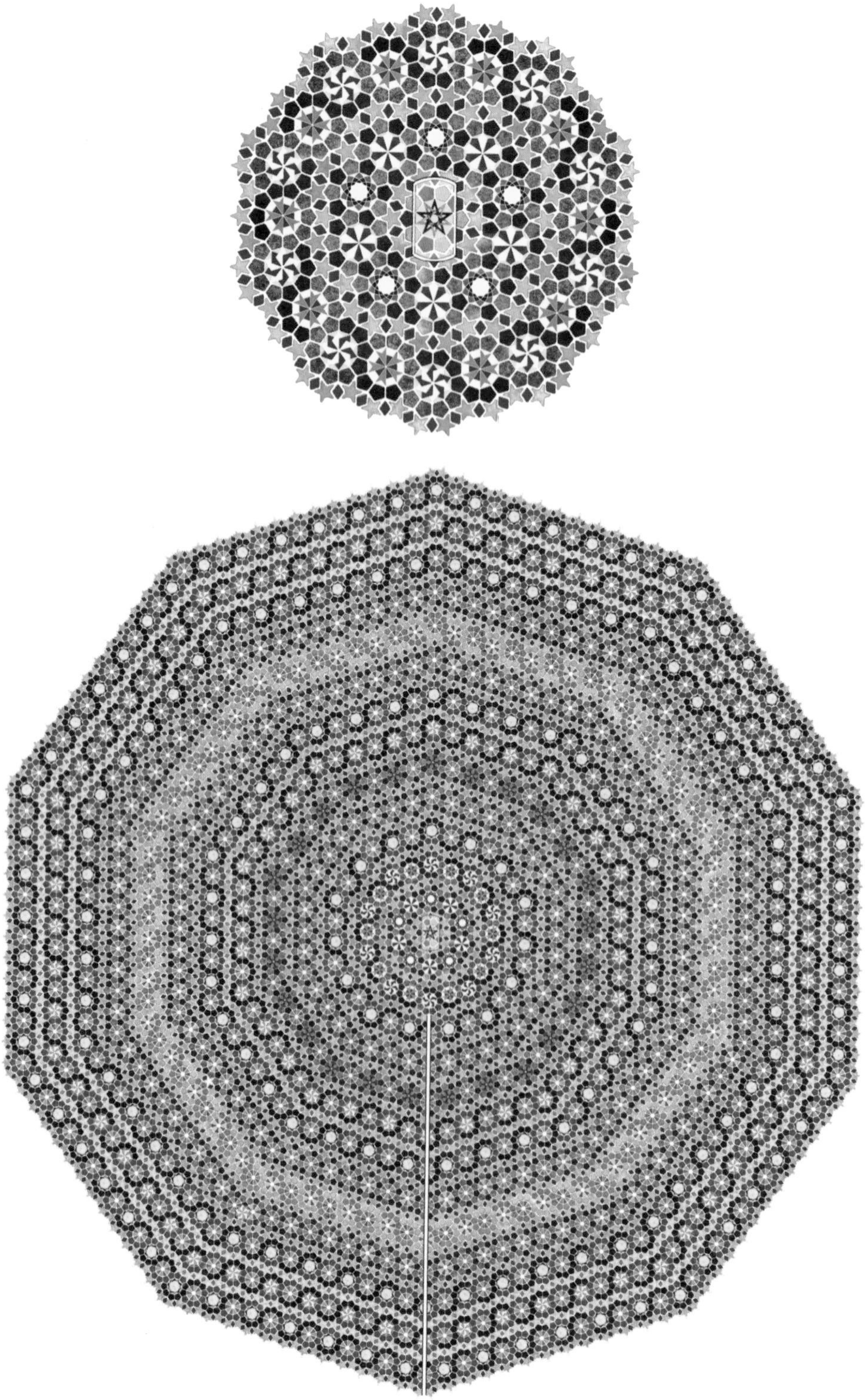

Fig. 222. Stage F. The full pentagonal geometry of the central island (top) and the whole city

Fig. 223. The pentagonal, ten-sided geometry of Atlantis city was difficult to reconcile with its land and water rings. The geometric solution is to draw the rings through the pairs of pentagons (Plato's "guard-houses") that stand at the corners of the successive decagons.

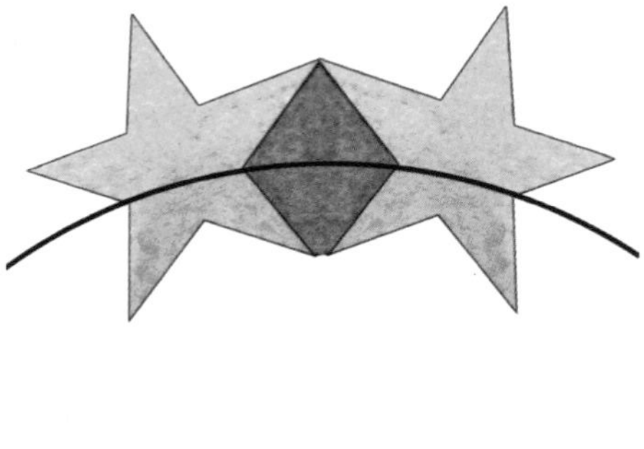

Fig. 224. The rings of Atlantis pass through the pairs of pentagrams that 'guard' the corners of the decagons.

Atlantis and the Golden Section

Plato is careful to provide enough measurements in his Atlantis plan to make it geometrically coherent, and in his description of the city and its foundation he clearly hints that its geometry is pentagonal and ten-sided. With knowledge of his basic plan, further information on Atlantean arithmetic is supplied, such as its units of measure and the numbers used in its pentagonal ratios.

The geometric structure of Atlantis is a compilation of four related shapes, the pentagon, the pentagram, the decagon, and the pentagonal diamond that fills the gaps between the dancing stars. There are only two measurements in the diagram, and they are in the proportion of the golden section, 1 to 1.618 . . . The first appears in the sides of the pentagons, and the second measures the radii of the decagons and the lengths of the diamonds between the pentagrams' limbs. One stadion or 600 feet is the distance between the centres of each pair of decagons in line from the centre of the diagram. This length is made up of five intervals, two of them 1 unit long and three of 1.618. This ratio can be represented by any two successive numbers in the Fibonacci series, but the most suitable pair for the Atlanteans was 21 and 34. These are the numbers that sum up the Decad on which Atlantis was founded, for:

$$21 = 1 + 2 + 3 + 4 + 5 + 6, \text{ and}$$
$$34 = 7 + 8 + 9 + 10$$

With 21 units as the shorter and 34 as the greater length in the Atlantis plan, the length of the stadion is 144 and the radius of the central island is 360 units. This sounds like another Atlantean blunder, for 360 is naturally the circumference of a circle rather than its radius.

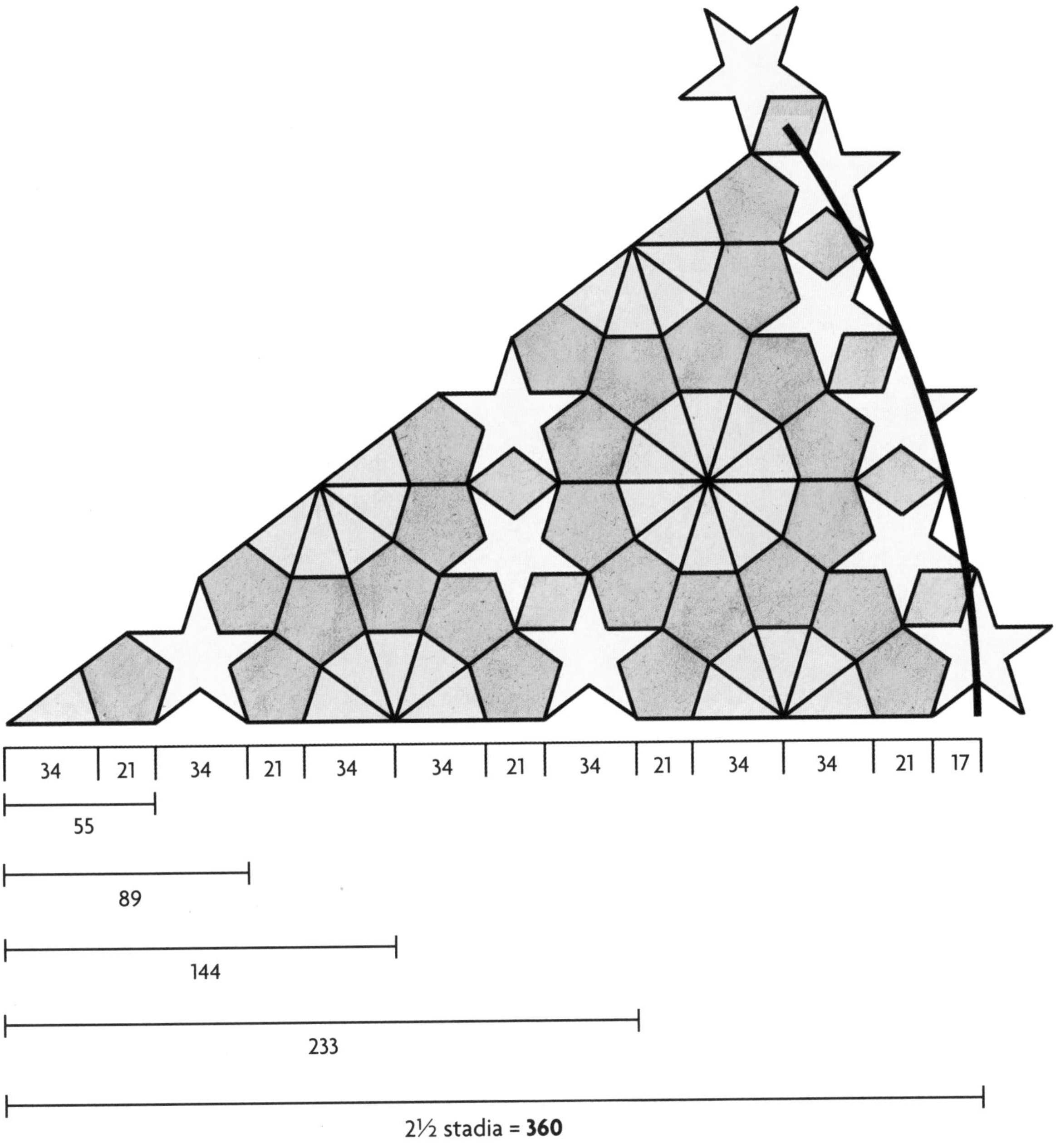

Fig. 225. A section of the Atlantis plan, showing the radius of the central island from its midpoint (left) to the centre of the surrounding wall. Its given length is 2½ stadia which is 360 Atlantis units. The two distances that make up this length are of 21 and 34 units. As seen above, the Fibonacci series, 21, 34, 55, 89, 144 . . . is built into the pentagonal geometry.

The Meaning of Atlantis

The interesting question of what Plato meant by his elaborate account of Atlantis is preceded by a brief summary of its composition.

At the heart of Atlantis is the sacred shrine where Poseidon and Cleito generated the first ten kings. It is enclosed by a golden wall, the innermost of the eight concentric walls of the ringed city. These in the diagram are represented by the successive rings of linked pentagram stars. The inner ring, surrounding the shrine, is made up of ten stars. Its diameter is 1 stadion or 144 Atlantis measures. Poseidon's temple, 144 long and 72 wide in the Atlantis measures, stands over the shrine and contains the central decagon of the pattern. Plato, although giving its length and width, does not say that the temple is rectangular but that there is "something barbaric" about it. It seems that the temple's two ends were rounded in conformance with the circle of the shrine.

Outside and around the temple is the ring of ten statues portraying the ten kings, the original five pairs of twins, together with their wives. They are aptly represented in the diagram by ten decagons. Beyond the circle of statues is the wall of the acropolis, already showing signs of reverting from a circle to a decagon, and then the wall of the island itself. Then come the three rings of water and two of land, all in accordance with the pentagonal ground plan.

What Plato meant by all this—and why he spent so much effort and ingenuity in laying out a constitution that could never work—is not so evident. One possibility is that, through his elaborate exercise in pentagonal geometry, he was satirizing the Pythagoreans who swore by the Tetractys and the number Ten and took the pentagon as their emblem. Pythagoras, whose name yields the 'foundation number' 864, was a semi-mythic character whose followers established his cult and worshipped him as a light-bearer. Like all such movements, with secret rites and radical aims, the Pythagoreans were often looked upon suspiciously by their neighbours, and in the century before Plato their institutions were suppressed throughout Greece. Plato never openly mentioned them but, like his master Socrates, he would not have favoured their cultishness. Nor would he have liked their idolization of Five, Ten, and the golden section, with the humanistic values inherent in that order of proportion. Ten and the pentagon are the rulers of life on earth, but in the philosophy of number Twelve is supreme. The Pythagoreans were high idealists, but Plato's criticism of them seems to be that, in promoting political and social reforms on a practical level, they were diverging from the true ideal, the sanctification of the world through divine justice symbolized by the number Twelve.

The more obvious reason for Plato's Atlantis geometry was to make a contrast between the failed constitution and the pattern of state that he advocated. Everything the Atlanteans did was contrary to the precepts he laid down, especially in his *Laws*. For one thing, their city was near the sea, and Plato's view was that seaports attract ruffians and troublemakers. Then there were too many of them, many times more than Plato's ideal 5040 citizens. The Atlanteans became great merchants, importing foreign luxuries and doing well for themselves individually, while neglecting virtue. Then they conquered an empire and sank further into degradation, and finally, all of a sudden, they came to grief.

It is a great story, and it is a salutary lesson to any nation, group, or individual that is inclined towards greed and tyranny. But its essential, most earnest lesson is on the level of number and geometry. Atlantean number was decimal, reckoned in units of ten, and its geometry was the same. The decagon and pentagon, as already pointed out, produce the most beautiful and interesting patterns, but the pentagonal, golden section system of proportion is too elaborate for construction purposes. In the 'pattern of the heavens', the cosmological diagram from which Plato derived his ideal constitution, the dominant framework number is Twelve. Atlantis was a type of Utopia, a man-made system, good-looking enough from our human point of view, but mistakenly founded upon the number Ten. That was the "mortal element" in the Atlantis constitution and the main reason why it did not work.

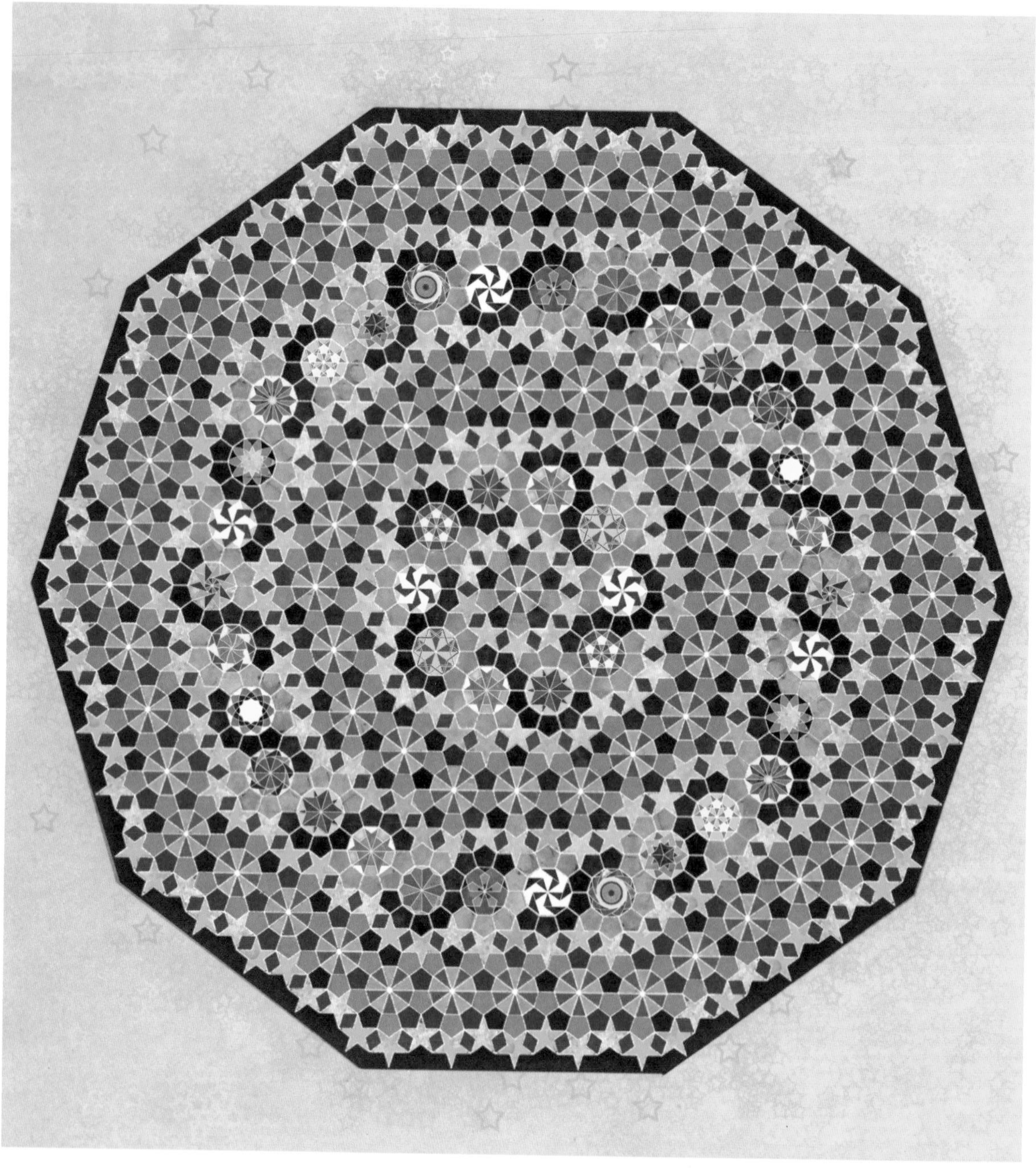

Fig. 226. Downtown Atlantis: the geometry of its centre. Successive rings of stars (pink) frame the centralised pentagon pattern. In the geometrical story of Atlantis the inner ring borders the sacred shrine, the second the acropolis, the third the central island, and the fourth the inner ring of water. The outer ring of stars encloses half the inner ring of land.

Fig. 227. Atlantis, the growth of its pentagonal constitution, and (upside down) its fall

About the Author

John Michell (1933–2009)

John Michell, pictured in Michigan in 1990, while visiting with scholar David Fideler

A pioneer researcher and specialist in the field of ancient, traditional science, John Michell is the author of more than 40 books that have profoundly influenced modern thinking. Michell's legacy began when his interest in UFOs inspired the 1967 book *The Flying Saucer Vision,* which then led to his breakout work *The View Over Atlantis* in 1969. It was this book, which connects sacred sites, number and proportion, UFOs, and forgotten knowledge of ancient traditions and myths, that placed John Michell at the center of the British counterculture and New Age movement.

Those two books, along with their sequel *The City of Revelation* (1971), provided a context for the alternative views that were germinating at the time and brought new, underground ideas into the mainstream.

John Frederick Michell was born in London on February 9, 1933, and grew up in the Hampshire and Berkshire countryside, where he enjoyed collecting moths. This earthy proclivity was a hint at Michell's later preferences—though an academic who graduated from Eton and Trinity College in Cambridge, Michell preferred a bohemian lifestyle to an academic one. After college, he served the Royal Navy as a Russian interpreter and translator before pursuing an unsuccessful career in real estate. Giving up on the property business, he immersed himself in the underground movement and worked for counterculture publications. He had wide-ranging interests, founding a magazine on crop circles and becoming a leader in the fight against the metric system in Britain and the United States. True to form, he favored measurements like pounds and feet because they came from traditional cultures.

In the late 1950s Michell relocated to London, and it was then that UFOs first caught his imagination. He noticed that "it was quite obvious that people were having experiences that weren't allowed for within the context of our education. There was a split between the view of the world we'd been taught and accepted unquestioningly and the world of actual experience."

The popularity of Michell's books brought a surge of interest in Britain's own sacred sites: Glastonbury and Stonehenge. The Glastonbury Festival in 1971 featured a stage built to emulate the pyramid of Cheops as specified by Michell's calculations of its sacred geometry and hosted performers such as David Bowie and Traffic. Michell also guided the Rolling Stones on a UFO expedition at Stonehenge.

In his later work, Michell wrote extensively about the metaphysical and spiritual qualities of the universe—those universal truths that are codified in nature and continually rediscovered, from ancient times to today. He explored the sacred numbers and geometry found in nature and in spiritual mysteries, such as Fibonacci spirals and the golden angle and the divine city of the New Jerusalem.

According to Michell, "Wherever you look, in archaeology and ancient history or in the modern records of parapsychology and strange phenomena, you find evidence to contradict every theory and 'certainty' of official science. The real world is quite different from the way our teachers describe it, and it is a great deal more interesting."

Michell was a member of the Lindisfarne Association and a teacher at its School of Sacred Architecture. He lectured at the Kairos Foundation, an "educational charity specifically founded to promote the recovery of traditional values in the Arts and Sciences," and also lectured at The Prince's School of Traditional Arts.

In addition to his published books, he was the author of numerous humorous short treatises and articles in publications as diverse as the *International Times*, *The Temenos Academy Review*, and *The Spectator*. Since 1997, he wrote a column of humor, philosophy, and social commentary in Britain's *The Oldie magazine*, an anthology of which was published in 2005 as *Confessions of a Radical Traditionalist*.

John Michell died April 24, 2009, at the age of 76 as this final work, *How the World Is Made,* was nearing its final production stages. A complete list of his published books is listed below.

Works by John Michell

1967 *The Flying Saucer Vision: the Holy Grail Restored*

1969 *The View Over Atlantis*

1972 *City of Revelation: On the Proportions and Symbolic Numbers of the Cosmic Temple*

1974 *The Flying Saucer Vision: The Holy Grail Restored*

1974 *The Old Stones of Land's End*

1975 *The Earth Spirit: Its Ways, Shrines, and Mysteries*

1977 *Phenomena: A Book of Wonders,* with Robert J. M. Rickard

1979 *Natural Likeness: Faces and Figures in Nature*

1979 *Inventorum Natura,* with Plinius Secundus C.

1981 *Ancient Metrology: The Dimensions of Stonehenge and of the Whole World as Therein Symbolized*

1982 *Living Wonders: Mysteries and Curiosities of the Animal World,* with Robert J. M. Rickard

1982 *Megalithomania: Artists, Antiquarians & Archaeologists at the Old Stone Monuments*

1983 *The New View Over Atlantis*

1984 *Eccentric Lives and Peculiar Notions*

1985 *Stonehenge: Its Druids, Custodians, Festival and Future*

1988 *Geosophy: An Overview of Earth Mysteries,* with Paul Devereux, John Steele, John Michell, Nigel Pennick, Martin Brennan, Harry Oldfield, and more (a Mystic Fire Video)

1986 *Feng-Shui: The Science of Sacred Landscape in Old China,* with Ernest J. Eitel.

1989 *The Traveller's Key to Sacred England*

1989 *Secrets of the Stones: New Revelations of Astro-Archaeology and the Mystical Sciences of Antiquity*

1989 *Earth Spirit: Its Ways, Shrines and Mysteries*

1991 *Twelve Tribe Nations and the Science of Enchanting the Landscape,* with Christine Rhone

1994 *At the Center of the World: Polar Symbolism Discovered in Celtic, Norse and Other Ritualized Landscapes*

1996 *Who Wrote Shakespeare?*

1997 *New Light on the Ancient Mystery of Glastonbury*

2000 *Unexplained Phenomena: Mysteries and Curiosities of Science, Folklore and Superstition,* with Robert J. M. Rickard

2000 *The Temple at Jerusalem: A Relevation*

2001 *The Dimensions of Paradise: The Proportions and Symbolic Numbers of Ancient Cosmology*

2001 *A Little History of Astro-Archaeology*

2003 *The Traveler's Guide to Sacred England: A Guide to the Legends, Lore and Landscapes of England's Sacred Places*

2003 *Prehistoric Sacred Sites of Cornwall*

2003 *Crooked Soley: A Crop Circle Revelation,* with Allan Brown

2005 *Esoterická Anglie: pr'vodce po posvátn'ch místech, legendách a pov'stech,* with Miloslav Korbelík

2005 *Confessions of a Radical Traditionalist*

2006 *Prehistoric Sacred Sites of Cornwall*

2006 *Euphonics: A Poet's Dictionary of Sounds*

2006 *The Lost Science of Measuring the Earth: Discovering the Sacred Geometry of the Ancients,* with Robin Heath

2007 *The Star Temple of Avalon,* with Nicholas Mann, Philippa Glasson, and Robin Heath

2008 *The Dimensions of Paradise: Sacred Geometry, Ancient Science, and the Heavenly Order on Earth*

2008 *New Light on the Ancient Mystery of Glastonbury*

2008 *Twelve-Tribe Nations: Sacred Number and the Golden Age*

2009 *The Sacred Center: The Ancient Art of Locating Sanctuaries*

2009 *How the World Is Made: The Story of Creation according to Sacred Geometry*

Index

Numbers in *italics* indicate figures or figure legends.

Abraxas, 72, 83
Allen, Jon, xi–xii
Alexander, Steve, 60
America, 240, 243
Amphyctionic league, 152–53
Aphrodite, 179
Apollo, 152, 178–79, 213, 219
Arthur, King, 151, 152
At the Centre of the World, 153, 267
Athena, 81, 178, 213
Athens, *63,* 81, 234, 241, 243
Atlantis, 154, 186, 238–263
Azores, 241

Babylon, 64, 80, 105, 152, 154, 243
Beast, number of, 72–80
Big Bang theory, 4–6
Bond, F. Bligh, 215
Buddhism, 214

Cadiz, 240
Charlemagne, 151
Chartres cathedral, *160*
Cleito, 244–45, 251, *253,* 260
coincidences, 2, 5, 182
cosmological diagram, 12, *29, 42,* 60, 152–55, 220
cosmology, 3–5
Critchlow, Keith, v, 162
  Order in Space, 150
  Islamic Patterns, 150
Cosmati, the, *114–115*
Critias, 81, 240, 241
Crooked Soley, a Crop Circle Revelation, 59–61, 268
crop circles,
  Alton Barnes, *143*
  Avebury, 89
  Chute Causeway, *175*
  Crooked Soley, 59–61
  Silbury Hill, 122–23
  Wiltshire, 38, 57, 59, *89, 122, 143, 161*
  Woodborough Hill, *38*
Cyrus, garden of, 201

Darwin, Charles, 166, 182
David, King, 108
de Bry, Johann, 50
Delphi, 153
Dimensions of Paradise, 69, 78, 251, 267, 268
Diotima, 213, 234
DNA, 59, *59, 237*
dodecahedron, 102–4, *104,* 150, *162,* 172
Donnelly, Ignatius, 242
  Atlantis, the Antediluvian World, 242
Durr, Hans-Peter, xiii

earth spirit, 76
Egypt, 20, 39–43, 66, 82, 172, 178
Eight, *27, 33,* 124–49
Einstein, Albert, 39
Eleven, 13, 86

En Soph, 8
Epicurus, *233*

Fibonacci (Leonardo of Pisa), *36,* 38, 172
  numbers, 21, 67–68, 172–73, 258–59
fish symbolism, 90–98, *94, 95, 96*
Five, 86, 166–210
Four, *27,* 86, 109–18

Galileo Galilei, xiv, 6, 74
gematria, 60–61, 72–83, 98, 178, 215
Genesis, 13–15, 119, 166, 212
geomancy, 22
geometry, uses of, 62
Gibbs, Christopher, v, xi
Gilgamesh, 152
Gladstone, William, 242
Glastonbury, 151, *162*
Gnostics, 43, 72, 78
golden section (phi), 168–77, 258–59
Golgotha, 108
Great Bear, 214
Greek alphabet and numbers, 72
Gurdjieff, George I., 216

Harpur, Merrily, v, 4
Harpur, Patrick, 57
  Daimonic Reality, 182
Heath, Robin, *The Measure of Albion,* 106
Heavenly City plan, xii, xiv, 6, 16, *18, 30–34,* 65–70, *70,* 73, 80, 98, *163,* 220, *228,* 228–31, 249
Hephaistos, 81
Heraclitus, 74
Hermes, 57, 167, 182, 216
Hindu chronology, 74, 82
Hipparchus, 74
Hiram of Tyre, 44–45, *45*

Holy Grail, 6, 153, 236
Holy Spirit, 74, 76, 79, 124, 215

Iceland, 154
initiation, 62
Intelligent Design, 5
Ireland, 151, 154
Irenaeus, 72
Israel, 12 tribes of, 64, 151, *162,* 220
Isis, 213
Italy, *114*

Jerusalem, The New, xii, *34,* 64–66, 80, 82, 108, 219
Jesus, 64, 72, 73, 81, 97–101, *108,* 112–13, 151, 166, 235
Jewish calendar, 74, 213
Jung, Carl G., 57

Kali Yuga, 74
Kepler, Johann, 102, 150

Lawlor, Robert, *Sacred Geometry,* 174
Lea, Rev. T. Simcox, 215
Lundy Island, 106–7

Madagascar, 154
magic squares, 77
Magnesia, 69
Maier, Michael, *Atalanta Fugiens,* 50
Marriages between
  circle and square, 22–32, 42, 45–50, 247–50
  Eight and Twelve, 126, *148–49*
  Five and Seven, 208–9
  Five and Six, 202–6
  Four and Five, 207
  Seven and Twelve, *21,* 219–31

Three and Four, 115–16
two circles, 90–92, *91, 92*
two pentagons, 166, *187–96*
two squares, *125, 140*
two triangles, *91,* 119
Mercurius, 57
metric system, 42, 67, 151
miracles of multiplication, 97
Mithras, 72
moon, 21–24, *21, 24,* 27, *30,* 82–83
Moon, Robert J., 151
Moore, Joan, 105
Mysteries, the, 62

New Testament, 72, 79, 81
Newfoundland, 242
Nine, 216–18
numbers
amicable, 61, *236*
evenly even, 124
perfect, 119
super-abundant, 150
triangular, 77–78, *78*

Odin, 74, 151
Olsen, Scott, *The Golden Section,* 171
One, 8, 16, 87
oracles, 213, 219
Orpheus, 152–53
Ouaknin, Marc-Alain, *The Mystery of Number,* 39

Parthenon, 171
pentagonal hexagons, *183, 191–196, 199–201*
perpetual choirs, 152
Peruvian octagon, 56, *147*
Phidias, 171
phi (*see* golden section)
philosopher's stone, 6
phyllotaxis, 172
pi, 36–56
conventional, 21, *36,* 37
Fibonacci, *21, 36,* 37–38, 67
in the Pyramid, 39–43
pi pattern, 46, 51–56, *58,* 59
Pilgrim's Progress, 232
Pisces, Age of, 101
Plato
Critias, 81, 240, 241
Ion, 232
Laws, 20, 40, 69, 153, 240, 261
Meno, 110
Phaedrus, 103
Republic, 63, 113, 172, 215, 219, 235, 243
Symposium, 167, 213, 234
Timaeus, 13, 15, 98, 102, 103, 240
Plato's Academy, 43, *63,* 69, 255
Platonic solids, 102–3, 104, 151, 162
polygons, 75
decagon, 166–209, 252–57
dodecagon, 86, 150, *159,* 223, *228*
enneagon, 86, 216, 217, *218,*
heptagon, *75,* 210, 213, 220
hexagon, 91, 116–23
octagon, 124–149
pentagon, 166–209
square, 109–14, 150
triangle, *30,* 102–8, 150
Poseidon, 244–45, 249, 251, 253, 254, 260
Pyramid, the Great, 40–42, 82
Pythagoras, Pythagoreans, 61, 83, 112, 236, 249, 260

ratios, geometric, 10–12
Revelation, Book of, 64, 72, 76, 78, 214, 219, 243

Rigveda, 74
Romulus, 22

St Augustine, *City of God,* 119
St Catherine, 213
St Finian, 151
St John, 57, 64–68, 72, 77, 82, 100, 108, 235, 243
St Joseph of Arimathaea, 151, 162
St Peter, 99, 100
Sanctuary, the, 69–71
septenary number, 216–18, *218*
Seven, 86, 155, 178, 208–9, 212–31,
  hills, springs, etc., 212, 219
  planets, notes, colours, metals, etc., 213–14
  sages, sibyls, angels, etc., 214, 219
Six, 119–23
Socrates, 63, 68, 110, 112–13, *113,* 154, 213, 234–35, 241, 249
Solomon, King, 44, *108,* 151, 166
Solon, 241
Sommerville, Ian, 34
Stewart, Malcolm, 31, *31*
Stølum, Prof. H-H., 39
Stonehenge, 39, 43, *67,* 106–7
sun, diameter of, 82
symbolic and canonical numbers
  1080; 16, *17, 21,* 22, 23, 74–83
  11! (= 39,916,800); 17, *18, 21, 24*
  12! (= 479,001,600); 16, *17, 18, 19*
  1224; 23, 98, *98,* 100, 101
  1296; 58–61
  153; 94–101
  1728; 82, 108
  1746; 17–18, 80–81
  2160; 23, 33, 70, 82, 151
  248,832; 66
  28; 32, 74, 213, 228–30
  3168; 22, *24, 67, 71,* 73
  3960; 20, 22, *23, 24,* 250
  5040; 16, *18, 19,* 20–35, 60–61, 69, 73, 212, 243
  666; 16, *17,* 72, 73, 76–80
  720; 25, *25,* 61, 75, 77, *108*
  7920; 22, *23–24,* 26, *33,* 60, 66, 69, *70–71,* 73, 82, 247
  864; 74, 81–83, *108,*
  888; 72–73

Ten, 86, 166–209, 260–61
Tetractys, 260
Three, 90–108
Timaeus, 13, *15,* 98, 102, 103, 172, 240, 241
Tree of Life, xiv
Triangles
  Isosceles & scalene, *104, 137,* 192–94
  Pythagorean, 30, 105–8
Trismegistos, 216
Twelve, 16, *21, 32,* 66, 84, 86, *116, 148,* 148–63, 219–31, 261
  Tribes, fruits, gemstones, etc., 64–67, 219–20
Two, 88–89

Valhalla, 74
Vesica piscis, 90–92, 97–101

Westminster Abbey, *115*
Wilmoth, Stephen, 150
Wisdom, Book of, 9
world axis, 7–8, 87, 212, 215
world soul, 208, 212–30

Zeus, 213, 243
Zodiac, 14, *33,* 66, 81, 103, 151–52